The Literacy Connection

edited by

Ronald A. Sudol
Alice S. Horning
Oakland University

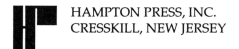

HAMPTON PRESS, INC.
CRESSKILL, NEW JERSEY

Printed in the United States of America

Library of Congress Cataloging-in-Publication Data

The literacy connection / edited by Ronald A. Sudol, Alice S. Horning.
    p.   cm.
    Includes bibliographical references and indexes.
    ISBN 1-57273-216-4. -- ISBN 1-57273-217-2
    1. Literacy--Social aspects--United States. 2. Language arts--Social aspects--United States. 3. Critical pedagogy--United States. I. Sudol, Ronald A., 1943-   . II. Horning, Alice S.
LC151.L482 1999
302.2'244--dc21   98-55712
                                            CIP

Hampton Press, Inc.
23 Broadway
Cresskill, NJ 07626

Contents

Introduction

Public attention to matters of literacy has grown exponentially over the past decade, and although such attention is hardly new, contemporary research and scholarship have helped us comprehend literacy as a socially and culturally active concept. National goals aimed at improving the level of public literacy are laudable as long as the methods devised for achieving them are framed by an understanding of language as entirely bound up in human social existence. Deepening that understanding is an important element of the academic enterprise. At the same time, however, the sites of public efforts aimed at literacy development often and quite properly lie outside schools and colleges.

We invited the contributors to this collection of essays to explore the connections between the academic and social/cultural sites of literacy development—hence, the literacy connection. We begin with a historical review and a psycholinguistic perspective. Next comes a report on a statewide writing assessment designed, in part, to fulfill public demand for improved literacy. This is followed by several essays describing various service learning activities in which some element of community literacy is incorporated into a school curriculum. We conclude with essays describing literacy connections in a women's shelter and in a nursing home. These contributions are more fully summarized at the end of this introduction, but first a survey of definitions is in order.

"Critical literacy" is the term that has come to represent the social and cultural features scholars insist on associating with literacy when it is viewed from the perspective of teaching and learning. To move beyond the conventional definition of literacy, there are many possible starting places. One such place is Miles Myers' 1996 volume, *Changing Our Minds: Negotiating English and Literacy*, which traces the history of American views of literacy from the beginnings of the country around 1660. He argues that we have moved from a notion of literacy centered on being able to sign one's name, to literacy focused on recording, to a literacy of recitations and reports, to a literacy of decoding, defining and analyzing, and finally, most currently, to critical literacy. The latter means going beyond literal comprehension of texts to interpretation and evaluation (Myers, 1996, pp. 20-139).

Using a similar historical focus, Mike Rose, director of writing programs at UCLA, demonstrates that concern about students' abilities to read and write dates back several hundred years in America, at least to Harvard College's early development of writing courses following acknowledgement that incoming students lacked appropriate reading and writing ability (Rose, 1989, p. 5). Rose goes on, after describing his own experience, to define critical literacy as follows:

> Many young people come to the university able to summarize the events in a news story or write a personal response to a play or a movie or give back what a teacher said in a straightforward lecture. But they have considerable trouble with what has come to be called critical literacy: framing an argument or taking someone else's argument apart, systematically inspecting a document, an issue, or an event, synthesizing different points of view, applying a theory to disparate phenomena, and so on. . . . Ours is the first society in history to expect so many of its people to be able to perform these very sophisticated literacy activities. (p. 188)

Rose provides a more specific, task-based definition of critical literacy and demonstrates that it may not be possible or reasonable to expect every member of society to achieve this level of literate ability. Another way of looking at this analysis might be that, as Rose says, the goal of critical literacy may not be achievable in current U.S. schools and colleges. However, it may be one that a majority of Americans can achieve over the course of their lives.

Along with Rose, numerous other scholars give similar definitions of critical literacy: Robert Calfee, a Stanford professor involved in the educational reform program Project READ, defines critical literacy as "the capacity to use language as a tool for thinking and communication" (Calfee, 1994, p. 23). Calfee goes on to give a fuller definition as follows:

> *Critical literacy* includes the capacity for action, but also incorporates a broader sense of understanding and insight, and the ability to communicate with others about "texts" whether these are written or spoken. It is the difference between understanding how to operate the lever in a voting booth versus comprehending the issues needed to decide for whom to vote and why. (Calfee, 1994, p. 27)

Calfee's definition hints at the reason why there is an essentially political dimension to the definition of critical literacy: this level of literacy provides political empowerment.

Literacy education is always necessarily political as Friere and Macedo pointed out years ago (1987) and also social, as found by Scribner and Cole (1981). Literacy teachers choose what and how to teach; both are political and social choices. Patrick Shannon observes that literacy and the teaching of it are both "liberating and dominating" (Shannon, 1992, p. 1) in the following ways:

> Even apparently innocuous decisions about setting goals for programs and lessons, selecting materials, and deciding how to interact with students during lessons are actually negotiations over whose values, interests and beliefs will be validated at school. . . . The consequences of these negotiations can be seen in the ways in which literacy is defined in school programs, in what is read and written at school, in who is and who is not considered literate and in how literacy is taught. (p. 2)

Much has been written about the choices educators make concerning literacy teaching in schools. The important thing for the present argument is that the political and social dimensions be kept in mind as we focus on more descriptive and linguistic definitions of critical literacy *per se*.

One of these more task-based definitions comes from a national survey of adult literacy abilities, *Adult Literacy in America*, published in 1993. According to the survey, critical literacy involves abilities to read and understand prose texts; synthesize and integrate information in documents; and extract, manipulate and draw conclusions from numerical information in texts (Kirsch, Jungeblut, Jenkins, & Kolstad, 1993). In the survey, more than 26,000 adults completed an assortment of literacy tasks, and more than half of the subjects were between the ages of 16 and 39 (Kirsch et al., 1993). The sample was designed to reflect the population of the United States based on the 1990 census and included representative proportions of males and females, racial and ethnic groups, persons with disabilities, prisoners, persons of differing educational and socioeconomic levels and both native and non-native speakers of English (Kirsch et al., 1993). This definition provides a fairly detailed description of the specific abilities involved in critical literacy, which were then turned into tasks to be completed by the subjects in the survey.

It is interesting to note that this definition from contemporary America is not very different from the definition of the practice of literacy among the Vai people of Liberia described by Scribner and Cole (1981). They define literacy as "not simply knowing how to read and write a particular script but applying this knowledge for specific purposes in specific contexts of use" (p. 236). Literacy is thus more than the mechanics of reading and writing. Any full definition must explore the purposes and uses of literacy. Educators, linguists and politicians are all likely to agree on this, even if the exact definition is still in dispute.

One further definition is drawn from linguistic work on literacy. James Paul Gee, a sociolinguist, and hence, a scholar with an awareness of the political as well as linguistic aspects of literacy, defines literacy carefully through his concept of discourse (Gee, 1991). Gee makes a distinction between primary and secondary discourse, identifying primary discourse as oral discourse in a person's native language, developed through internally driven processes of acquisition; that is, primary discourse is not formally taught. By contrast, secondary discourse is that used for dealing with schools, government, the workplace and so forth. Literacy, then, is "control of secondary uses of language (i.e., uses of language in secondary discourse)" (p. 8). Notice that, by Gee's definition, critical literacy develops through both acquisition and learning processes found conventionally in schools. The essays in this collection will discuss the ways in which critical literacy is best understood, developed, and supported not only in traditional and nontraditional kinds of school settings, but in other places, such as nursing homes, homeless shelters, and even in formal testing situations.

The authors of the following essays explore the dynamics of these multiple levels of literacy in a variety of settings and situations. The contemporary debates over literacy do not signify a uniquely contemporary concern. Thus, we begin with Jay L. Gordon's historical survey of critical literacy. Gordon argues that down to its classical roots, critical literacy has been related to the cognitive and psycholinguistic values to which societies and cultures aspire. The kind of critical literacy we value today is essentially the same that enabled the growth of democratic society from its origins in ancient Greece.

Alice Horning explores the development of critical literacy and the characteristics it shares with other psycholinguistic processes such as first and second language acquisition and the development of reading and writing abilities. Her argument reveals that all of these processes share a staged character, all are influenced by people's personality preferences, all involve systematic errors, and all show the importance of psycholinguistic redundancy to the development of critical literacy. Horning claims that we cannot meet the national goal of widespread critical literacy without this fundamental understanding of its character.

Public attention focused by such national goals has led to widespread efforts at assessment and accountability. Ellen Brinkley and Ronald Sudol report on their work designing and supporting a writing assessment framework for the State of Michigan that takes full account of critical literacy as a feature of public education. Making this assessment work required a delicate balance among the interests of numerous public constituencies, including teachers, students, specialists, and taxpayers. Above all, the assessment would need to do more than standardize the criteria for judging written literacy skills; it would also need to support a curriculum based on the broader scope of critical literacy.

The concept of service learning is one way to add texture and depth to notions of literacy. Emily Nye and Morris Young report on the course they taught at the University of Michigan in which undergraduate students studied literacy in a service learning format. The undergraduates tutored children in communities outside the academically charged atmosphere of Ann Arbor, and through journal writing, discussion, and theorizing, they grappled with the many dimensions of literacy learning that emerged from the interpersonal character of the service learning experiences.

Lu Huntley-Johnson and Elizabeth Ervin consider the impact of critical literacy in preparing college students to teach English through a program they developed, enabling preservice and veteran teachers to meet and share ideas through a project called "Sharing Worlds: Preservice Teachers Meet Veteran Teachers." They redesigned a course called "Writing for Teachers" to allow veteran teachers to discuss their classroom practices and theoretical understanding of literacy with students in the process of becoming teachers. To achieve widespread literacy, they believe that preservice teachers can benefit greatly from exposure to practicing teachers as well as discussions of theory and reflections on teaching and learning writing.

The critical literacy situation described by Dan Frazier goes beyond encouraging the self-awareness of undergraduates and the preparation of preservice teachers. The service learning course at Springfield College encourages students to explore the dominant power relations that exist in a community and to reframe problems in order to critique underlying cultural assumptions. The aim of these processes—

understanding and evaluation—is to create the kinds of collective understanding that enables social transformation.

Mary Salibrici has developed an approach to the growth of critical literacy among college writers through their collaboration and mentorship of high school students. The college students meet with the high school class, provide mentoring to those students as they work on their own class assignments, and then report on the experience through case studies and reflective writing. Her findings suggest that college students become critically literate through their deep engagement in their own and their high school partners' writing development.

Anita Helle's chapter shows how such critical literacy can be extended to graduate education in English. In an outreach program supported by the State of Oregon, students seeking Master's degrees in English engage in community literature and folklore projects. Helle argues in support of such an approach to graduate education in English as a valid substitute for traditional programs intended to prepare teachers in public schools and community colleges.

Rosemary Winslow expands the view of critical literacy into the setting of a shelter for homeless women in Washington, DC. There she found that women can develop key critical literacy skills that lead to social and political empowerment as well as a sense of community through their participation in a poetry-writing group. Her work with five women who were writing group members for about five months shows how literature can help create community and how the resulting literacy capability changed these women's lives and views of themselves.

Elizabeth Oates Schuster takes critical literacy into yet another setting, a nursing home. Working with residents in a writing group, Schuster found that key concepts of critical literacy such as preserving autonomy, participating in a social group, and creating a discourse community all contribute to literacy activities among nursing home residents. As participant-observer in a writing group over the course of a 3-year study, Schuster found that writing not only had a transformative impact on the residents and those around them, but that critical literacy's influence with regard to autonomy and empowerment extended beyond schools to other institutions in our society.

REFERENCES

Calfee, R. (1994.) Critical literacy: Reading and writing for a new millennium. In N. J. Ellsworth, C. N. Hedley, & A. N. Baratta (Eds.), *Literacy: A redefinition* (pp. 19-38). Hillsdale, NJ: Erlbaum.

Freire, P., & Macedo, D. (1987). *Literacy: Reading the word and the world*. South Hadley, MA: Bergin and Garvey.

Gee, J. P. (1991). What is literacy? In C. Mitchell & K. Weiler (Eds.), *Rewriting literacy: Culture and the discourse of the other* (pp. 3-12). New York: Bergin & Garvey.

Kirsch, I. S., Jungeblut, A., Jenkins, L., & Kolstad, A. (1993). *Adult literacy in America: A first look at the results of the National Adult Literacy Survey*. Washington, DC: Government Printing Office.

Myers, M. (1996). *Changing our minds: Negotiating English and literacy*. Urbana, IL: National Council of Teachers of English.

Rose, M. (1989). *Lives on the boundary*. New York: Free Press.

Scribner, S., & Cole, M. (1981). *The psychology of literacy*. Cambridge, MA: Harvard University Press.

Shannon, P. (1992). Introduction: Why become political? In P. Shannon (Ed.), *Becoming political: Readings and writings in the politics of literacy education* (pp. 1-11). Portsmouth, NH: Heinemann.

About the Contributors

Ellen Brinkley is an associate professor of English and director of the Third Coast Writing Project at Western Michigan University. A former high school teacher and president of the Michigan Council of Teachers of English, she is the primary author of the *Michigan Proficiency Examination Framework for Writing* and chaired the group that designed Michigan's statewide writing assessment. She has published a number of articles and made presentations concerning writing assessment and is co-founder of Michigan for Public Education, a citizens' group advocating educational equality and excellence.

Elizabeth Ervin is an assistant professor of English at the University of North Carolina at Wilmington, where she edits *North Carolina English Teacher* and teaches undergraduate and graduate courses in composition, English education, and literature that depicts school life. Her scholarship currently focuses on service learning and the ways in which public discourses shape relations between academics and nonacademics in her local community. She has published articles in *Rhetoric Review, Journal of Advanced Composition*, and *Pre/Text*, and has contributed chapters to *The Place of Grammar in Writing Instruction* and *Keywords in Composition Studies*.

Dan Fraizer directs the Writing Center at Springfield College. His work on publishers and textbooks has appeared in *The Writing Instructor* and the forthcoming *Two Year Colleges and the Politics of Writing Instruction*. His interests include critical literacy, basic writing, writing across the curriculum, and popular culture.

Jay Gordon is a doctoral candidate in the Rhetoric program at Carnegie Mellon University. He is currently working on his dissertation, which will be about the history of the relationship between psychology and rhetoric, focusing on theoretical developments in the 20th century. He is also interested in the history of literacy and has published an article on literacy and social history with Daniel Resnick. In addition to these specific areas, Mr. Gordon is generally interested in the connections between history, philosophy, psychology, and rhetoric.

Anita Helle is Assistant Professor of English at Oregon State University, where she coordinates the English Department's Master of Arts in Teaching Program. Her research on gender, literacy, and literature has appeared in *English Leadership Quarterly, Northwest Review, Oregon English, South Atlantic Review,* and the *National Women's Studies Association Journal.*

Alice Horning is a professor of Rhetoric and Linguistics at Oakland University in Rochester, Michigan where she teaches in the writing program and also teaches courses in language acquisition, psycholinguistics, and literacy issues. Her research interests include the psycholinguistics of literacy and language and literacy development. She is currently at work on a book-length study of revising. With Ronald Sudol, she is coeditor of *Understanding Literacy: Personality Preference in Rhetorical and Psycholinguistic Contexts* published by Hampton Press.

Lu Huntley-Johnson taught secondary English for nine years in the North Carolina public schools. She is currently an assistant professor in the Department of English at the University of North Carolina at Wilmington and teaches courses in English education and literature. Her research interests include literacy education, teacher professional development, and classroom-based inquiry. She has published in the *Journal of Reading* and *North Carolina English Teacher.*

Emily Nye is an assistant professor of English at New Mexico Institute of Mining and Technology, where she coordinates the composition program and manages the writing center. In addition to her work with service learning, Nye has also done research on how literacy (writing) can be a tool for healing outside of academia. She has conducted writing workshops with senior citizens, children, and people with AIDS.

Mary Salibrici teaches writing at the Syracuse University Writing Program and while there has been involved in many cross-curricular writing projects. Her interest in more wide-ranging campus outreach with public schools stems from a desire to deepen the literacy experiences of her writing students as well as from her past tenure as an elected member of the Board of Education for the public schools in Syracuse. She is currently a Ph.D. student in the School of Education at Syracuse University.

Ronald A. Sudol is Professor of Rhetoric at Oakland University where he teaches writing, communication, television criticism, and American Studies. He works with the State of Michigan, the Educational Testing Service, and the College Board on writing assessment and curricula. With Alice Horning, he is coeditor of *Understanding Literacy: Personality Preference in Rhetorical and Psycholinguistic Contexts*, published by Hampton Press.

Elizabeth Oates Schuster is an Associate Professor in Gerontology and has been the Director of the Gerontology Program at Eastern Michigan University since 1986. During her career, Dr. Schuster has been involved in senior center program development, conducting needs assessment survey research; development of an adult day care center; facilitation of educational workshops on various topics; and coordination of a social service program for older adults and their families. Research interests and areas of publication include ethical considerations when conducting ethnographic research in nursing home settings, sensitization to aging issues, critical pedagogy, and the transformative function of writing in a nursing home. Dr. Schuster is a member of a number of gerontological professional organizations and advisory boards.

Rosemary Winslow is Associate Professor of English at The Catholic University of America, where she teaches American literature, lyric poetry, stylistics, the teaching of composition, and directs the undergraduate writing program and the program for underprepared first year students. She has published in the areas of style, metrics, American poetry, composition theory and practice, business and technical writing, and writing across the curriculum. At present, she is at work on a study of rhetoric and civil society focusing on the issue of homelessness. In her spare time, she writes poetry and leads a creative writing group at Bethany Center for Women.

Morris Young received his doctorate from the joint Ph.D. program in English and Education at the University of Michigan. He is currently assistant professor of English at Miami University of Ohio. His research interests include Asian American literature, the politics of literacy, and composition theory.

Emergent Critical Literacy: A Historical Perspective on Western Literate Practices

Jay L. Gordon
Carnegie Mellon University

INTRODUCTION

The purpose of this chapter is to explore evidence of critical literacy emerging in a variety of historical contexts. For this brief exploration, I depend on a broad view of "critical literacy" as both an advanced stage in cognitive development and a difficult but useful social skill. I discuss a handful of Western literate practices going back to Greco-Roman society and relate details of these cases to this perspective on critical literacy, which is deliberately open and flexible. My aim is to promote a dialogue between contemporary views of critical literacy and literate practices in different times and places because our current definitions, theories, and critiques tend to be applied best only to our immediate situation.

Defining "critical literacy" for historical study is essential for anyone entering into such a dialogue. This is a complicated problem for two reasons. First, our current definitions of critical literacy are not uniform. The differences seem to depend on the sense of "critical" intended. Definitions using cognitive and developmental concepts (e.g., Calfee, 1994) focus on the relationship between literacy and critical thinking; those using social and political concepts (e.g., Mayo, 1995; McLaren, 1993), focus on the relationship between literacy and the ability to form cultural critiques and achieve sociopolitical emancipation. In between are sociocognitive definitions stressing the child's emerging ability to "read the world" in a general sense (see Jongsma, 1991).

The second difficulty in defining critical literacy for historical study is that because relatively few people in the West could either read or write until the 19th century, and mass literacy was not achieved in many parts of Europe and America until the 20th, it is difficult to talk about "critical literacy" of any kind as a significant feature of the historical landscape of most cultures, at least until relatively recently.

My tentative solution is to define critical literacy as the ability to apply both reading and writing skills to important tasks, decisions, and processes, both public and private. By "emergent" critical literacy, I refer to a moment or interval during which a society finds more and more of its members acquiring critical literacy, for whatever reason. This approach preserves the characterization of critical literacy as a social and cognitive achievement without leading to the conclusion that largely illiterate societies are somehow inherently deficient or low achieving. In stressing that critical literacy applies to important private as well as public tasks, my approach also avoids leading to the conclusion that an illiterate individual in a literate society is necessarily unhappy. As Biggs (1991) argued, the view that literacy always leads directly to a better life is a cultural artifact— not a proven fact—built on what he called "lay theories" of literacy usually promoted by a literate elite.

Observing and discussing instances of emergent critical literacy across a diverse group of societies is important for orienting our own definitions and perspectives. Ideally, we should look at a large number of historical contexts so that we can begin to isolate patterns and draw meaningful comparisons. My aim in this chapter is more modest—it is merely to point to some of the research on the social history of literacy, working with a broad and flexible conceptualization of critical literacy, and to draw some inferences and tentative conclusions. Such a survey is necessarily derivative, but I hope that by collecting these various historical studies in one place the reader will come away with a sense of the diversity and complexity of the history of critical literacy and perhaps further pursue some questions.

One caution to be kept in mind throughout this chapter, but especially in the sections considering Europe after the Middle Ages, is that the relationship between literacy and schooling is complex. As Maynes (1985) notes,

> In early modern Europe, people learned to read and write in a great number of settings; the teaching and learning of these skills was by no means limited to the classroom. . . . Conversely, the agenda for classroom instruction, although it nearly always included at least reading if not writing, was by no means restricted to these skills. The curriculum of many early modern schools, especially those sponsored by church authorities, municipal governments, or charitable endowments, often emphasized religious instruction first and foremost. (pp. 7-8)

In general, we should not assume that schooling alone teaches critical literacy, nor that an individual's ability to produce and/or exploit written materials is evidence of a formal education.

ANCIENT GREECE AND ROME: THE LOGOGRAPHERS

Greco-Roman civilization, particularly from 500 BCE to 100 CE, is conventionally considered the historical foundation of Western society. It is thus not surprising that a good deal of research on the history of literacy has focused on the literate practices of ancient Greeks and Romans, particularly during periods of relative democracy. Typically, historians of literacy studying Greco-Roman civilization (e.g., Goody, 1986; Havelock, 1991; Ong, 1982) have been interested in the development of a phonetic alphabet, the subsequent inscription of a previously oral tradition, and the psychological and social effects of this development. These scholars have tended to view the alphabetization and inscription of oral transactions as a major advance in the technology of literacy, permitting the growth and propagation of Western civilization. The major thrust of their arguments is that written inscriptions extend the human memory beyond its everyday capacities, fostering a variety of advanced modes of thought such as reflection, criticism, analysis, and synthesis. As Havelock (1991) put it, "without modern literacy, which means Greek [alphabetic] literacy, we would not have science, philosophy, written law, or literature" (p. 24). Havelock and others would seem to agree, at least indirectly, that ancient Greece, and particularly Athens circa 500 BCE, was a paradigm case of emergent critical literacy.

Psychologically oriented histories of literacy such as Havelock's are important, but they must be complemented by close accounts of actual literate practices. There are many important practices that can help us understand the role of critical literacy as it emerged in Greco-Roman civilization. Literacy was used for many purposes in ancient Greece; Harris (1989) lists over 40 basic functions of reading and writing, some of which include indicating ownership, maintaining accounts, making contracts, writing letters, making notes of useful information for oneself, making wills, displaying political slogans, casting a vote, recording trial proceedings, recording manumissions, memorializing the dead, recording prayers, circulating prophecies, cursing someone, and transmitting compendia of information such as textbooks.

It is worth noting that none of these uses of literacy includes the forms of ancient literacy with which most of us are familiar—epic poems, plays, and philosophical treatises. Although such canonical forms of literacy are of great significance in Western history, there are other general forms of literate practice—reflected in Harris' list—that are just as important because they represent the actual glue which held Greco-Roman society together. One major form of literate practice that has not received a great deal of attention is the practice of logography, or speech writing. Although we do not have a great deal of evidence of logography, we do have enough to draw some inferences about its role as critical literacy in action.

The *logographos* performed an important function in Athenian society. He tended to be a speechwriter first, a teacher second, and a publishing author third. Those who played all three of these roles exceptionally well have had the most luck in being passed down through the Western canon. Demosthenes, the man who improved his delivery by shouting at the crashing waves with a mouth full of stones, is familiar to most who have ever taken a course in speech communication or ancient history. However, there are several other logographers who deserve mention, in part because they may represent the typical logographer somewhat better than Demosthenes.

Antiphon, for example, is neither very famous nor particularly obscure. His name turns up in some collections of Athenian orators, often along with that of Lysias and other members of the "Canon of Ten." Here I focus on one of his speeches, "On the Murder of Herodes," as an interesting case study in critical literacy. This speech was written for Euxitheus, who had been accused of murdering Herodes, a fellow passenger on a ship's voyage. Although written by Antiphon, this speech would have been recited, probably from memory, by Euxitheus, the defendant. The wording of the speech, while considered reflective of Antiphon's skill, also had to be consistent with what the jury might expect a man of Euxitheus' unique social, financial, and political position to say. When examining the text, then, we can ask ourselves not only "Why did Antiphon say this?", but also "Why did Antiphon put these words in Euxitheus' mouth?"

Given this perspective, it is easier to understand why Antiphon uses numerous intimate references to the jury, including direct pleas for mercy and pity (e.g., "my danger is great and my safety depends on how far you come to the right decision, while my ruin depends on how far you are defrauded of the truth"; "be assured that I deserve pity from you, not punishment"), as well as statements that sound more like what Antiphon wants to say through Euxitheus. For example, in one telling passage, Antiphon—an oligarch, not a democrat—is clearly speaking (via Euxitheus) against what he feels is the prosecution's disregard for hallowed Athenian laws and customs. The main argument is that both Euxitheus' imprisonment and trial are illegal and that the case should be dropped. Early in the defense, Euxitheus/Antiphon says:

> But you [the prosecution], for personal reasons, are trying to deprive me, and me alone, of a privilege accorded to every Greek by framing a law to suit yourself. Yet everyone would agree, I think, that the laws which deal with such cases as this are the finest and most hallowed of all laws. They have the distinction of being the oldest in this country and always remained the same concerning the same matters; and this is the surest sign of laws well made, since time and experience show mankind what is imperfect. Hence you must not use the speech for the prosecution to discover whether your laws are good or bad, but you must use the laws to discover whether or not the speech for the prosecution is giving you a correct and lawful interpretation of the case. . . . The laws on homicide are excellent and no one has ever before dared to change them. (cited in Edwards & Usher, 1985, p. 35)

These kinds of statements point to an important understanding that must have existed between state institutions, citizen males, and the logographers—an understanding that the defense was permitted not only to provide an argument but that this argument could include statements critically evaluating the prosecution in light of established laws, customs, and historical precedent. This seems to be an excellent example of "critical literacy" in action because it permitted the citizen not only to argue his case but to act as the voice of his speechwriter, within the context of a social process that depended on the literacy of all participants to function well. However, we should remember that very few people in Attica were citizens, and thus very few would have had the right to enact this form of critical literacy. "Critical literacy" in ancient Greece, then, was emergent in two ways. Relative to the society itself, critical literacy was spreading slowly across Attica and other urban centers through the proliferation of a variety of literate practices. Because ancient Greece provides one of the earlier examples of critical literacy in the West, however, practices like logography can also be seen as part of the emergence of critical literacy across not just ancient Greece but across the West in general.

MEDIEVAL AND RENAISSANCE EUROPE

As in Classical Greco-Roman civilization, most people in Europe through the Middle Ages and the Renaissance could neither read nor write. But it would be wrong to assume that literacy played no role in people's lives until after the Renaissance. McKitterick (1989) argues, for example, that during the so-called Dark Ages (the period between the fall of Rome and roughly 1000 CE) reading and writing were used throughout the Carolingian kingdom (roughly modern-day France) for legal and administrative purposes. Kelly (1990), whose research is discussed later, argues a similar point in regard to Anglo-Saxon England. During the Italian Renaissance, "communal" or secular town schools, established by parents and local officials to prepare young men for various professions, supplanted Church schools. Luther's literacy campaign, discussed in the next section, could not have succeeded without the presence of at least a semiliterate public. Therefore, although most societies had neither the means nor the mandate to promote critical literacy, we should do as much as possible to isolate instances of emergent critical literacy, as I do in the cases that follow.

Anglo-Saxon England

Goody (1986) notes, "writing has been used in England from the Roman period," and the "under the Anglo-Saxons, writing was employed for charters and for some other legal and administrative purposes, as well as in important literary and religious ways" (pp. 159-160). Kelly (1990), who has researched Anglo-Saxon literacy intensively, draws on historical evidence to paint a picture of Anglo-Saxon society as one just coming into a period of literacy among the nonclerical population. Particularly interesting about the period under discussion is the tension between Latin and English in public discourse. For up until this time, literacy meant primarily Latin literacy among the clergy. But, as Kelly observes,

> In the tenth and eleventh centuries, English had a respected place as an alternative literary and documentary language. Some ecclesiastics composed extensively in the vernacular and many manuscripts written in this period contain vernacular texts, such as sermons, poetry

and translations from Latin. English was a medium of instruction in schools and was regularly used by the draftsmen of leases and agreements and by the royal administration for sealed writs and law codes. (1990, pp. 51-52)

But why did English catch on as it did? The answer seems to be, in part, that by the early Mediaeval period Latin was no longer familiar to most people in Anglo-Saxon society:

The reasons for the early development of the non-Latin vernacular as a vehicle for legal documentation must lie partly in the circumstances of early English history, which included the apparent disappearance of spoken Latin and of all vestiges of the late Roman bureaucracy; Latin was so remote from the secular side of society that greater use had to be made of the vernacular in all areas of administration and social regulation. (Kelly, 1990, p. 57)

In early medieval England, then, we see both the demand for and the prevalence of literacy skills pushing beyond the realm of the Church. England predated most other Western societies in this respect, and Anglo-Saxon society perhaps represents one of the earliest examples of a society undergoing the emergence of critical literacy in a vernacular. Still, we must put our claims about Anglo-Saxon literacy into perspective. Even if we can claim that a fair number of people could read (5% or 10%), fewer could write, and fewer still applied their literacy as extensively or intensively as a typical sixth-grader would today. Moreover, the documents that formed the material of literacy seem to be of a sort that would be produced periodically at most—leases, wills, some business transactions. Nevertheless, these are very important documents and the ability to read as well as produce them would have been essential for anyone wishing to own or transfer property. Thus, we see that even in a society in which the vast majority are illiterate, the utility of literacy is clear; Anglo-Saxon England, in this light, may be viewed as a society for which the relevance and potential of critical literacy outside the Church was just coming into being.

Renaissance Italy

By the 14th century, formal education had become an institution throughout much of Europe. For most of the Middle Ages, however, the Church controlled education. But during the Renaissance period, the Church ceded much of its control to secular institutions, particularly in the area of elementary education. Beginning in the 14th-century, Italy witnessed a proliferation of communal schools, or schools sponsored by city and town governments, such that "almost all Italian cities and towns about which information is available had a mixture of independent, church, and communal schools in varying proportions between 1300 and 1600," with the Church schools declining rapidly after 1300 (Grendler, 1989, p. 71).

The development of the Italian communal school system is particularly interesting because it represented a positive effort by parents and local officials to see that all boys, not just those destined for the clergy, got some form of education, both for the humanistic purpose of improving their minds and souls and for the practical purpose of giving them professional skills. This seems to be an excellent example of the ways in which critical literacy becomes woven into a society's evolving needs and values. But acquiring critical literacy does not always mean being able to exploit it fully. Although some girls and working-class boys could attend Renaissance schools, the role of education in a girls' life was to better enable her to fit with social norms, not to give her the tools of critical literacy. In general, Grendler (1989) argues, the pedagogical attitude of the time was that

> a girl should acquire vernacular reading and writing skills appropriate to her expected role as virtuous and practical spouse and mother. Upper-class girls needed to be able to read and write well, and perhaps to keep accounts, in order to fulfill social expectations and to manage a household. Girls lower on the social ladder needed less learning. Those at the bottom should be able to read prayers or, more accurately, to recite aloud prayers learned by rote. *A girl ought not to acquire Latin learning, because she had no public role to play.* (p. 89; emphasis added)

I emphasized the last line above because it highlights an important problem in defining critical literacy. If we consider critical literacy to be only a cognitive-developmental achievement, then we may miss important contextual differences in the social implications of literacy. In Renaissance Italy, a girl or woman could be highly literate—well read in Cicero, Dante, Petrarch, as well as the Bible, and skilled in writing letters and poetry—without having much chance to hold a profession, own property, or seek public office. In contrast, working-class boys, who were at least as likely to get an education as middle- and upper class women, often pursued careers as artisans and merchants. Moreover, these working-class boys could look forward to a life of relative independence and a chance of owning property and other assets.

LUTHER'S GERMANY

It is fitting to follow the section on medieval and Renaissance literacy with an account of literacy in Germany during the early days of the Reformation. And, as Resnick and Gordon (1999) note,

> no reformer played a more significant role in promoting lay literacy in northern Europe, in Germany in the 16th century and in Sweden through the next century, than Martin Luther, and largely through a home- and church-based pedagogy in which Luther's own *Small Catechism* served as a literacy text.

Luke's Pedagogy, Printing, and Protestantism is a good place to begin to understand the role of Luther's literacy campaign in 16th-century Germany. As a Foucaultian history of the concept of "childhood," Luke's argument focuses attention on the ways in which Luther's pedagogical methods were applied to the "disciplining" of German society in the early to mid-1500s, following the peasant rebellions of the 1520s. As she explains:

> Ideas about the education of the young, initially surfacing in the prescriptive discourse of Luther's pamphlets which urged parents to send their children to school, now reemerged in a discourse that was to serve as an observational template for educational authorities in their surveillance of schools. Visitations were undertaken to accumulate data on schools, teachers, communities, parents and children; this data, in turn, was meant to lead to a complete overhaul of existing educational practices. (pp. 83-84)

Luther's campaign was an early example of a widespread, national campaign to bolster education, not merely by spreading literacy, but by establishing and developing a complex bureaucracy for managing the dissemination of educational directives and materials, all as just one component of a larger, national governing bureaucracy. With this development, we begin to see a major shift in belief about the level of literacy sufficient for serving in various kinds of professional offices. As Luke notes, Luther believed that Germany had a need for an "educated civil service trained in the classical languages, in church and civil law, and history; facility only with German was considered insufficient for church and state government" (p. 85). We also begin to see a shift in attitude about who should learn to read and write. As Luther himself argued,

> Without any doubt, I should not have come to this if I not gone to school and become a writer. Therefore go ahead and send your son to study . . . your son and my son, that is, the children of the common people, will necessarily rule the world, both in the spiritual and worldly estates . . . the born princes and lords cannot do it alone. (quoted in Luke, 1989, p. 86)

With these two shifts—toward both the wider application of literate practices and the spread of literacy education across social classes—we also begin to see an early distinction forming between notions of high and low, advanced and basic, literacy skills. For example, in an early debate over literacy policy, we see parents in Luther's time resisting recommendations that their children pursue book learning beyond the most basic levels. As Luke explains,

> parental resistance to a formal education for their children may have been implicitly supported by the wide dissemination and availability of the vernacular Bible that Luther had claimed all along to hold the key to personal enlightenment. Why, then, send children to school when the most authoritative and important knowledge—the vernacular Bible—lay available in every household? (p. 85)

Luther's literacy campaign was perhaps the first such campaign of its type in the West. It was aimed at raising the literacy level of all people and providing higher education for a good portion of them, and was probably the first major step in the direction of mass literacy in Europe (see Gawthrop & Strauss, 1984, for a study of the relationship between Protestantism and mass literacy). It was also progressive in the sense that it worked in concert with other emerging phenomena such as the increasing prevalence of print and increasingly complex bureaucracies. Few people became literate until Luther's time, even though something like public schooling was widely available in many parts of Europe by the early Renaissance. After the mid-1500s, however, more and more countries instituted some form of public elementary schooling, to the point that by the 19th-century most Western nations had adopted the cause of literacy as a matter of national policy. A full history of literacy in early modern Europe is far beyond the scope of my chapter (for a good introduction, see Houston, 1988. Two particularly useful chapters are "Sources and measures of literacy" and "Profiles of literacy," which together give a clear and detailed picture of emergent literacies across several centuries).

REVOLUTIONARY AND 19TH-CENTURY FRANCE

Revolutionary France: The Cahiers de Doléances

Critical literacy issues should be especially salient during times of great social upheaval. Indeed, a major text of interest to historians of literacy are the collected *cahiers de doléances*, or records of grievances, collected by lawyers and others from towns across France during Spring 1789, on the eve of the Revolution. The *cahiers* are particularly interesting, albeit complicated, examples of critical literacy in action. They reflect the power of writing in expressing grievances to state powers. By collecting grievances in written form, they provide an important record of public dissatisfaction. But because of the way in which they were collected—by literate individuals transcribing the statements of the illiterate—they point to an interesting question about the very nature of critical literacy. If a person can neither read nor write, but he or she has access to someone who can, has this person acquired critical literacy, at least in some sense? In the case of the cahiers, for example, the peasants did not have to be literate to participate in literate practices. Were the French peasants literate or illiterate?

We could answer this question in at least two ways. On the one hand, the illiterate person who depends on others to participate in literate practices cannot be considered literate because he or she cannot always count on having the appropriate social apparatus available for helping him or her through every task requiring critical literacy. The peasants, for example, could not have gotten their grievances recorded and heard were it not for a small group of literate people making a special point of traveling the countryside to build the *cahiers*. (We can be reasonably sure, though, that the peasants were not unduly influenced by those writing up the *cahiers*; see Shapiro & Markoff, 1990). On the other hand, as long as the literate practice suits the aims of its participants as a group, then the precise literacy levels of individuals are not important. In other words, as long as the peasants got their grievances heard and addressed, they were indirectly literate or "co-literate" with the ones who inscribed their grievances.

An alternative approach would be to view the situation in pre-Revolutionary France as one characterized by emergent critical literacy. Although most people in France were illiterate, and few even spoke Parisian French, it would have been clear to all by the end of the 18th century that literacy served useful and important social purposes. Indeed, "the ability to read, write and count was central to many areas of early modern life" (Houston, 1988, p. 116). Still, the social contexts for applying critical literacy were off-limits to most peasants—rendering the personal utility of literacy generally very low, at least until the 19th century.

Nineteenth-century France: The French Literacy Campaign

During the 19th century, one goal of the French government was to ensure ideological unity across France. This broadly nationalistic theme was reflected in a national literacy campaign. Weber (1976) tells the story of this movement to bring French peasants not only into the literate class but also into ideological unity. The campaign began against a background of prejudice against the peasants of the countryside, who were generally viewed as primitive by their Parisian countrymen. It continued until, as Weber explains, "the spread of urban values through the countryside" (p. 22) was more or less complete, a development that unfolded from the early part of the 19th century to roughly the end of World War I.

The stated aim of the campaign was the standardization and homogenization of all forms of communication, from systems of weights and measures to the dialects permissible in the rural classroom. However, although we might assume that the aim of these standardization procedures was to ease the administration of the bureaucracy, the real aim behind the linguistic homogenization of France was indeed ideological. As Weber explains, "Linguistic diversity had been irrelevant to administrative unity. But it became significant when it was perceived as a threat to political—that is, ideological—unity" (p. 72).

In retrospect, the campaign was neither efficient nor entirely successful. From the start, rural peasants were suspicious of outsiders. Modernization may have brought literacy, but it also brought a despised class of bureaucrats (Weber, 1976). Up to the early 20th century, illiteracy was still widespread in France. The reason for resistance to the French literacy campaign seems clear: Neither the French language nor formal schooling nor their combination were especially useful to the majority of people until the last decades of the 19th century, when the opportunity to earn a living in the bureaucracy, as well as the need to record one's accounts and correspondence, became greater than it had been in the early part of the century. This situation is not unique to France's literacy campaign—Cressy (1980), for example, observes a similar situation in early modern England, with a literate elite on one side proclaiming the value of literacy to a largely indifferent majority. According to Cressy,

> it is possible that the writers who proclaimed the advantages of literacy overestimated its value to ordinary men and women. People who were not unduly troubled about salvation, who were content within their horizons of knowledge and experience, and whose daily or seasonal routine required no mastery of print or script, had no pressing need of literacy and could hardly be persuaded to seek it. (pp. 1-2)

From the period just before the Revolution to the beginning of the 19th century, then, France provides an interesting case study in emergent critical literacy. In one sense, France's literacy campaign was just one example of a trend that had been sweeping Europe for at least two centuries. As in Germany and Sweden, the French movement was at least in part the product of an educational reform impulse that drove most of Europe to pursue some sort of literacy campaign during the 17th, 18th, and 19th centuries. Maynes (1985) summarizes the general goals of reform campaigns in the modern epoch as

> the commitment to universal childhood education, the ultimate control of the state over the realm of education, the careful effort to link schooling with both civic preparation and occupational training, and the assumption that schooling is a prerequisite for political and economic adulthood. (p. 179)

Such campaigns seem to reflect a fundamental shift in Western cultural attitudes—for the first time, critical literacy can be seen as a linguistic achievement toward which all people were expected to strive, not just the few fortunate enough to hold a high social position.

The case of France was marked by some unique features as well. The *cahiers* were not collected for the purpose of spreading literacy, but their collection instantiated what now may be viewed as something like a prototypical literacy campaign—after all, the *cahiers* at least demonstrated to the illiterate people in the countryside that literate practices could be powerful tools for social change. In addition, the 19th-century campaign was somewhat different from earlier campaigns in that it was based firmly on nationalistic, ideological motives rather than on a religious commitment to biblical literacy (as Luther's had been). Finally, because the bulk of the campaign was carried out in the latter 19th century, it was accompanied by massive innovations in communication technologies that simply did not exist before the 1800s. This development in the technological landscape created some of the very conditions that permitted the campaign to be successful.

19TH-CENTURY AMERICAN SOUTH

The situation of slaves in the American south during the 19th century provides an interesting glimpse into some of the complexities of critical literacy not yet explored in this chapter. During the 1700s and 1800s, many African slaves in the southern United States learned to read and write. However, the implications of this emergent critical literacy are complex. On the one hand, it represented a threat to slaveowners who feared slave literacy on more than one level—knowing how to read and write gave the slave a chance to learn about the outside world, knowledge that could inspire a desire to escape. Literacy also allowed slaves to perform specific tasks that threatened the slaveowners' authority. A literate slave could, for example, forge an escape pass or manumission notice. Literate slaves could also organize and circulate information among themselves.

On the other hand, there was a strong religious motivation to learn to read and write across all of Western society, to the point that even some slaveowners felt compelled to give their slaves some form of literacy education. The religious mandate for literacy was not a new phenomenon—the Bible had been an important literacy text for centuries. A good account of the social and religious complexity of slave literacy during the decades before the Civil War is given by Cornelius (1991):

> Southern African-Americans' rights to literacy were restricted in the 1820s and 1830s, but as sectional tension accelerated with the Mexican War and the nations' two great popular churches, the Methodists and the Baptists, split over slavery-related issues, "Bibles for Slaves" became an appealing cry. It merged nicely with the benevolent societies' and educational reformers' belief that a reading and writing public was essential for a Christian and democratic nation. To offer "Bibles for Slaves," though, was also divisive. Every gesture which reminded the nation that blacks were humans and threatened slaveowner "property" rights stimulated southern opposition. In the 1850s the South became more defensive than ever about slave rights vs. slaveowner property rights. Ironically, "Bibles for Slaves" also divided antislavery forces. Those who believed a focus on slaves' religious and literary rights would divert efforts from the fight for black freedom contested with others who saw literacy as the first step toward freedom and "Bibles" as an attractive way to gain broader support among whites for a black liberation. (pp. 125-126)

Understanding these kinds of social and political complexities gives us a subtler perspective on slave literacy than one that stresses only that literacy was emancipating for blacks or, as one writer put it, that "the alphabet is an abolitionist" (Dalton, 1992, quoting an 1867 *Harper's Weekly* editorial). Although this viewpoint is compelling in some ways, it does not help us understand the role of literacy among slaves beyond pointing to the fact that slaves produced various sorts of psychologically validating documents. Although literacy *could* be psychologically emancipating, some simple facts can keep us from assuming too much about the allegedly emancipatory power of slavery. Genovese (1976), for example, highlights an important story:

> That slaves did not perform heroically and kill themselves trying to grasp the mysteries of the book means little, for the conditions were appallingly difficult. The story lies with those who managed to do it. The obstacles did not all concern fatigue, limited cultural horizons, a lack of books and paper or of an available tutor. Beyond all these worked another. Mrs. Kremble suggested to the son of a literate plantation slave that he ask his father to teach him to read. He answered "with a look and manner that went to my very heart. 'Missus, what for me learn to read? me have no prospect.'" (p. 816)

Lacking "prospect" in a nation still broadly and deeply oppressive of African Americans even after the Civil War would be a significant psychological foil to any potentially emancipatory effect one might find in keeping a journal or reading the Bible. This argument is echoed in other contemporary scholars' writings on the social problems of schooling in today's African-American community. Ogbu (1988), for example, argues that the "cultural ecology" of late 20th-century American schooling includes a pervasive feeling among African-Americans that they, like the young man in Genovese's account, have "no prospect" and that, in a sense, the acquisition of critical literacy would be of little use.

Nevertheless, it would be misleading to suggest that literacy has not been at all emancipatory for African Americans. Some slaves profited from their literacy by acquiring positions as artisans and mechanics, which could substantially improve their social standing and well-being. We must also look to the consequences of having a class of literate slaves come of age after the Civil War, one of which was that the growing network of social bonds acquired during slavery was formalized and expanded in the form of churches, fraternities, and other benevolent and activist social groups such as the NAACP. Cornelius' (1991) conclusion is particularly apt for the study of critical literacy as it emerged among African Americans toward the beginning of the 20th century:

> The experiences of generations of African-Americans who endured the slave experience sparked the drive for literacy after slavery and perpetuated education as a cherished value and a basis for freedom within the black community. Many black leaders in the ministry, government, and education in the first decades of freedom had learned to read and write as slaves. Others carried with them from

slavery a resentment that literacy had been withheld from them. The belief in the value of literacy and education was instilled deep within the African-American consciousness and took shape during the slave experience as a form of resistance to oppression and maintenance of psychological freedom. (p. 150)

SUMMARY AND CONCLUDING REMARKS

Critical literacy is itself an emergent concept. In this brief survey I have attempted to show that something like "critical literacy" occurs in a variety of cultural and historical contexts. But my aim has not been to assume a rigid definition of critical literacy to test against the historical evidence. Rather, I have assumed that "critical literacy" is a flexible concept, fuzzy around the edges, but always having some relation to cognitive abilities and social skills. By exploiting a historical concept of "emergent critical literacy," we can learn something about the social and psychological roles of critical literacy in times and places for which direct, documentary evidence is relatively sparse. Even from this brief survey of the history of critical literacy we can draw some tentative conclusions.

First, we must consider that the value of critical literacy as a cognitive, psycholinguistic achievement stands in relation to the needs and conditions of the society in question. Until the 19th century, most people in Europe and America lacked access to both the materials of literacy and the kinds of occupations and activities in which literacy was useful. This meant that the vast majority of people in these societies were not permitted the opportunity to achieve critical literacy. But we should not assume that widespread illiteracy indicates a poorly functioning or deficient society; rather, we need a subtle understanding of the historical conditions in which literate practices occur. One way toward this kind of understanding is to look at instances of emergent critical literacy, or moments in a society's history when reading and writing become widespread and play an increasingly important role in people's lives.

Second, critical literacy skills seem to have had a growing repertoire of applications after the fall of Rome. From the early medieval period up to the Renaissance, the most immediate applications were related to the production of ecclesiastical and legal records, as well as documentation of business transactions. The Reformation seems to be a turning point, for this period witnessed the first conscious literacy campaigns in western Europe, fostered by the invention of the printing press. After 1600, more and more people became literate through some form of schooling and, in response to the growing needs for mass communication and bureaucratic control, people began to apply these literacy skills to a much wider variety of situations.

Third, it seems as though the overall benefits of critical literacy have not changed much since classical Greece. When people are permitted to acquire literacy skills, they are more capable of participating in the whole range of a society's literate practices, from mundane activities such as storing information and keeping accounts to the production and propagation of literature, science, philosophy, and history. What has changed is the range of people who are taught to read and write. Since Luther's unprecedented literacy campaign, Western society has been the site of numerous national literacy campaigns, to the point that universal literacy seems to be a fundamental mandate of any democratic society.

REFERENCES

Biggs, D.A. (1991). Literacy and the betterment of individual life. In E.M. Jennings & A.C. Purves (Eds.), *Literate systems and individual lives: Perspectives on literacy and schooling* (pp. 117-135). Albany: SUNY Press.

Calfee, R. (1994). Critical literacy: Reading and writing for a new millenium. In N.J. Ellsworth, C.N. Hedley, & A.N. Baratta (Eds.), *Literacy: A redefinition* (pp. 19-38). Hillsdale, NJ: Erlbaum.

Cornelius, J.D. (1991). *"When I can read my title clear": Literacy and slavery in the antebellum South.* Columbia: University of South Carolina Press.

Cressy, D. (1980). *Literacy and the social order.* New York: Cambridge University Press.

Dalton, K.C. (1992). "The alphabet is an abolitionist": Literacy and African Americans in the emancipation era. *The Massachusetts Review, 32,* 545-580.

Edwards, M., & Usher, S. (Eds. & Trans.). (1985). *Antiphon and Lysias.* Chicago: Bolchazy Carducci.

Gawthrop, R., & Strauss, G. (1984). Protestantism and literacy in early modern Germany. *Past and Present, 104,* 31-55.

Genovese, E.D. (1976). *Roll, Jordan, roll: The world the slaves made.* New York: Vintage Books.

Goody, J. (1986). *The logic of writing and the organization of society: Studies in literacy, family, culture, and the state.* New York: Cambridge University Press.

Grendler, P.F. (1989). *Schooling in Renaissance Italy: Literacy and learning, 1300-1600.* Baltimore: Johns Hopkins University Press.

Harris, W.V. (1989). *Ancient literacy.* Cambridge, MA: Harvard University Press.

Havelock, E. (1991). The oral-literate equation: A formula for the modern mind. In D.R. Olson & N. Torrance (Eds.), *Literacy and orality* (pp. 11-27). New York: Cambridge University Press.

Houston, R.A. (1988). *Literacy in early modern Europe*. New York: Longman.

Jongsma, K.S. (1991). Critical literacy. *The Reading Teacher, 44*, 518-519.

Kelly, S. (1990). Anglo-Saxon lay society and the written word. In R. McKitterick (Ed.), *The uses of literacy in early medieval Europe* (pp. 36-62). New York: Cambridge University Press.

Luke, C. (1989). *Pedagogy, printing, and Protestantism:The discourse on childhood*. Albany: SUNY Press.

Markoff, J. L. (1990). Peasant grievances and peasant insurrection: France in 1789. *Journal of Modern History, 62*, 445-475.

Maynes, M.J. (1985). *Schooling for the people: Comparative local studies of schooling history in France and Germany, 1750-1850*. New York: Holmes and Meier.

Mayo, P. (1995). Critical literacy and emancipatory politics: The work of Paulo Freire. *International Journal of Educational Development, 15*, 363-379.

McKitterick, R. (1989). *The Carolingians and the written word*. New York: Cambridge University Press.

McLaren, P.L. (1993). Critical literacy and postcolonial praxis: A Freirian perspective. *College Literature, 19/20*, 7-27.

Ogbu, J.U. (1988). Literacy and schooling in subordinate cultures: The case of black Americans. In D. Resnick (Ed.), *Literacy in historical perspective* . Washington, DC: Library of Congress.

Ong, W.J. (1982). *Orality and literacy: The technologizing of the word*. New York: Methuen.

Resnick, D.P., & J.L. Gordon. (1999). Literacy in social history. In D.A. Wagner (Ed.), *Literacy: An international handbook*. Boulder, CO: Westview Press.

Shapiro, G., & Markoff, J. (1990). L'authenticité des cahiers. *Bulletin d'Histoire de la Révolution Francaise*, 17-70.

Weber, E. (1976). *Peasants into Frenchmen: The modernization of rural France, 1870-1914*. Stanford, CA: Stanford University Press.

Developing Critical Literacy

Alice S. Horning
Oakland University

There are perhaps a dozen or more definitions of critical literacy currently under discussion in politics, education, and other realms of contemporary society. Conventionally, literacy is usually thought of as the ability to read and write. However, to fully understand critical literacy, the range of definitions must be explored. Different definitions from diverse perspectives are presented in the chapters in this collection. An exploration of the definitions shows that the concept of *critical literacy* in the United States has arisen from a long-standing concern with language abilities. In addition, the varied definitions of critical literacy show that it has a fundamentally political base. A rigorous definition of critical literacy makes clear its relationship to other aspects of language and literacy development and shows that literacy is a central aspect of our humanity that permeates our lives.

The many and varied definitions of critical literacy help to clarify its relationship to other aspects of language development. Appropriately defined, critical literacy connects clearly to first language acquisition, second language acquisition, and to early and maturing reading and writing development. Gee (1991) offers an especially useful definition of literacy drawing from his background in sociolinguistics. The development of literacy, he argues, arises through the processes of acquisition and learning. Following the concepts presented originally by Krashen concerning the relationship of first and second language acquisition, Gee (1991) claims that acquisition is an internal process, not subject to direct teaching by parents, teachers, or others, but driven by internal processes and, in fact, resistant to instruction. Learning, however, is conscious knowledge developed as a result of instruction by a teacher or other person knowledgeable about the material under study.

Gee (1991) uses the acquisition-learning distinction to make several observations about the development of literacy. First, he claims that any discourse is developed chiefly through acquisition and not through learning. Literacy "requires exposure to models in natural, meaningful, and functional settings, and teaching is not liable to be very successful— it may even get in the way" (p. 8). What must be learned is the ability to critique one discourse with another (a secondary discourse), using metaknowledge of both discourses. Critiquing and metaknowledge are best developed by learning. Ultimately, Gee shows that what often goes on in schools looks like learning secondary discourse but is actually the acquisition of literacy through meaningful models before and during school. What students in schools are learning is the ability to critique discourse, if they are taught intelligently and effectively and if what is taught does not exclude or denigrate the students' primary discourse. Critical literacy involves this use of one discourse with another, developed through acquisition and learning.

Gee's analysis provides a base for the rest of this discussion for several reasons. Not only is the development of critical literacy partly a byproduct of acquisition, as Gee and others suggest, but it also is the culmination of a number of other language development processes, similarly driven by acquisition strategies. Moreover, if the development of critical literacy is a byproduct of both acquisition and learning, then it is easy to see why and how this development might reasonably continue over the entire human lifespan. The case studies presented by Morris and Tchudi (1996) demonstrate the ways that people have developed their literacy above and beyond formal school settings. Critical literacy is not exclusively, necessarily, or even best learned in school settings, but hinges on acquisition in meaningful settings: These might well be senior citizen centers, twelve-step programs (Daniell, 1996), nursing homes (Schuster, this volume), or shelters for the homeless (Winslow, this volume). If critical literacy provides the empowerment that those who focus on the political aspect suggest, it must continue to unfold in such settings. Only if it does so can we realize the basic goal of having a truly critically literate society that is the essence of democracy.

The historical, as well as the political and linguistic views, of critical literacy provide a context for the argument that it is the summit of human linguistic ability. While not excluding the definitions discussed in the preceding paragraphs, this chapter focuses most closely on the linguistic and task-based definitions of critical literacy. In these definitions, the relationship of critical literacy to other aspects of human language capability stand out most clearly. For the purposes of this argument, then, *critical literacy* is best defined as *the psycholinguistic processes of getting meaning from print and putting meaning into print, used for the purposes of analysis, synthesis and evaluation; these processes develop through formal schooling and beyond it, at home and at work, in childhood and across the lifespan and are essential to human functioning in a democratic society.*

To achieve the goal of a critically literate population thus defined, a deeper understanding of the nature of critical literacy is needed. Critical literacy is fundamentally a linguistic ability that represents the top step in the development of human language abilities. It is a natural outgrowth of the processes of L1 and L2 acquisition, early literacy, and maturing literacy. These processes share with critical literacy four key features: the development of language and literacy abilities are staged processes, all are influenced by the personality preferences of language users, all are characterized by errors, and all show in learners' error patterns the redundant character of psycholinguistic processing by language users. An awareness of these characteristics explains how and why critical literacy can and should be developed and supported across the lifespan.

STAGES

Linguists have long observed the staged character of children's early language. Language acquisition (L1) refers to the development of a first or native language, and it characteristically proceeds by stages of increasing linguistic complexity. For normal children, language acquisition begins with crying, cooing, and babbling; with sound production at each stage reflecting children's increased control over the vocal tract; and with increasing awareness of the language that will be their native tongue. In the later part of the babbling stage, for instance, children begin to sound like they are talking, chiefly because the babbling is marked by the intonation patterns of the native language. Although no recognizable words are present, children in this stage seem to have a specific message to send.

Once recognizable words are present, the staged character of L1 becomes even more sharply defined. A longitudinal observational study of three children conducted by Brown (1973) in the early 1970s and subsequently replicated by other studies of both cross-sectional and longitudinal design reveals clear stages after children begin saying recognizable words with consistent meaning. Brown's study showed the increasing linguistic complexity and sophistication of language development beyond the first words, into two-word combinations and through the addition of essential grammatical elements such as plurals, verb markers, and so on. Other studies show that children follow a staged pattern of language development in terms of not only grammatical structure and elements in their utterances, but in terms of semantic relationships they perceive among people, objects, and events (Bloom, 1991).

Moving into the school years, Chomsky's (1969) landmark study established in the 1960s that the staged character of language development persists through at least age 10. The stages described by Chomsky for children in early elementary school as well as in the earlier stages of language development have been found consistently in cross-linguistic studies on many different types of languages including sign language, and languages spoken by people with differing family structures and child-rearing practices (Slobin, 1985). There can be little doubt that first language development is a staged process from its beginnings through full linguistic fluency.

Turning to second language acquisition, scholars also think there are staged characteristics to the course of L2 acquisition. Ordinarily, second language acquisition refers to the development of ability to communicate in a second language after L1 acquisition is well under way. For many Americans, exposure to a second language comes only in later elementary or middle school. Most studies of second language acquisition focus on learners who are at or above age 10. L2 researchers use the term *acquisition* to suggest that stages are a feature of L1 that also applies to L2 development. In discussing second language teaching and learning, Krashen, among others, has argued that mastery of L2 is at least in part a process of acquisition by learners (i.e., like L1 development) as well as a byproduct of some conscious learning (Krashen, 1985). As noted earlier, Gee (1991) proposes that the development of critical literacy also comes about through processes of acquisition.

The stages proposed for L2 development are fewer in number than those observed in children's first language development, but like those of L1, they reflect the linguistic complexity of the task that confronts language users. Learners of a second language start with no knowledge of the target language, move into a stage called Interlanguage based on error patterns first observed and so characterized by Selinker (1972, 1992), and ultimately move to fluency in L2. Certain aspects of L1 may persist in L2 learners' production such as an accent or difficulty with prepositions, articles, and the like.

Common error patterns and consistency of types of errors support the view that L2 acquisition occurs in stages. A fluent Japanese-English bilingual of my acquaintance, for instance, every now and then uses an incorrect English preposition or article, even though his English is otherwise flawless. A woman I know who learned Polish as her native language and began English around the age of 8 has occasional difficulty with word order although her English is only slightly accented and otherwise perfectly like that of a native speaker. The persistence of such "fossils" (Selinker's term) only provides more support for the view that L2 acquisition is a staged process. Like L1, the staged aspects of L2 are generally immune to direct teaching, and no amount of drill and practice prior to a ready state in the learner will cause the correct forms to appear.

Another staged development process like first and second language acquisition is the development of emergent literacy. The term *emergent literacy* best describes the processes of acquiring reading and writing skills before the onset of formal instruction at age 5 or 6, at least as the term has been used by Teale and Sulzby (1986, pp. vii-viii). Children's print awareness may begin with recognition of the Golden Arches sign on the freeway or picking their favorite cereal off a store shelf even though they cannot read the name on the box. Although Stanovich (1991) notes that the ability to identify such isolated instances of "environmental print" does not necessarily carry over to full reading ability, he too sees this as an early stage in emergent literacy (p. 24). Byrne's (1991) research shows that although children may start with such whole word identifications, they must move on to alphabetic and phonological principles for reading if they are to learn successfully. Chall (1983) proposed a detailed sequence of stages in reading development consistent with cognitive development theory and much other research on reading. The point here is that the reading side of literacy skill moves through reasonably clear developmental stages.

The other dimension of emergent literacy—early writing, characterized by a few letters and much scribbling—shows the beginnings of awareness of letters and the shape of written forms, including some marks of punctuation as noted earlier. Although Sulzby (1986) is careful to point out that these phases are not necessarily a linear developmental sequence, the development of writing shows patterns that may well constitute a staged sequence with further research. Sulzby also reports on longitudinal data showing that children have some ideas about the distinctions between oral and written language forms as well as the continuities of oral and written forms, as she notes that emergent literacy begins while oral language acquisition is still significantly in progress. At a later stage in the growth of literate ability, children demonstrate clearly that they know what stories are supposed to sound like, from "Once upon a time. . ." to "happily ever after," as the awareness of discourse genres moves forward.

Reading and writing are, like language acquisition, efficient and meaning-driven processes that move quickly beyond early mechanics of sounding out, spelling, and letter and word recognition to generating and getting meaning from printed forms. Children learning to read quickly become sensitive to differences that make a difference in meaning, such as the shapes of "b" and "p" that distinguish "bat" from "pat" and the differences that do not make a difference in meaning, such as the distinction in shape between upper and lower case "B." (The phonological difference between "b" and "p," a difference in the presence or absence of vocal cord vibration or voicing, is a meaningful difference, sensitivity to which appears to be present at birth [Eimas, 1991]). Moreover, recent research makes clear that phonological sensitivity, including children's abilities to rhyme and otherwise notice sound patterns, is an important predictor of success in learning to read (Stanovich, 1991).

Like the related processes of language and literacy development previously described, maturing literacy, too, shows stages in development among college writers and in adults after college. The term *maturing literacy* refers to development of literacy both once formal instruction begins and through the rest of formal instruction and beyond. Maturing literacy is the focus of much college literacy instruction, in courses in literature, research writing, and perhaps historiography. Maturing literacy also can develop in work settings, as language users become sophisticated in their ability to read specialized texts in their field and to write in the discourse of their profession. Basic writers in college attempting to master maturing literacy may be in an early stage of development wherein their control over the requisite word endings and other features of academic English is limited (Horning, 1987; Kutz, 1986). Shaughnessy's (1977) work contains innumerable examples of basic writers' rule-governed writing systems. The writing is clearly not yet well-formed academic discourse but shows an early stage of development in that direction.

Shaughnessy's insights into the nature of basic writers' development, her discussion of error, and her awareness of the need to provide a supportive and meaningful environment for the acquisition of maturing literacy skills has become an unquestioned basis for most current approaches to the development of maturing literacy among beginning college writers. Because many students in the early stages of maturing literacy development (in basic or developmental writing courses, for instance) are not native speakers of English, it is especially important to keep in mind the shared staged character of both spoken and written language acquisition in both L1 and L2.

This observation holds not just for basic writers, beginning the development of maturing literacy abilities, but also for more sophisticated reader/writers who are adept at basic skills. When college students begin to develop research writing abilities, which call for analysis, synthesis and evaluation, they also show a series of stages in their development. In suggesting a redefinition of plagiarism in college writing, for instance, Howard (1985) argues that students' early inappropriate uses of source material should be seen as a necessary developmental stage. Citing an assortment of other scholars, she shows that patchwriting— students' copying and rephrasing of a source, perhaps without citation—is a step on the road to appropriate quotation or paraphrase with complete citation. Seen this way, Howard says, patchwriting becomes a "pedagogical opportunity, not a juridical problem" (p. 788). This view is consistent with the developmental character of maturing literacy and especially with the growth of abilities to analyze, synthesize, and evaluate, which are central to it and to critical literacy.

A similar developmental process in even more advanced students has been carefully described by Sternglass (1988). Sternglass examined introspective accounts of reading and writing by graduate students in English. She makes clear that even these capable readers and writers move through several stages in their development of self-awareness and literacy ability during and after direct instruction concerning reading and writing. Because Sternglass asked her subjects to read and comment on her book some two years after they completed the class, the subjects themselves are able to reflect and comment on their own developmental course as readers and writers.

Yet another example is presented by Berkenkotter, Huckin, and Ackerman (1989) in their study of Nate, a graduate student developing writing skills early in his studies. The study traces Nate's growth as a writer within the discipline of rhetoric and composition studies by examining the opening paragraphs of three papers written over the first three semesters of his graduate program. Berkenkotter et al. see a clear developmental pattern in Nate's writing as he develops his knowledge of the discipline and his understanding of the social science discourse style in which he is expected to write. His work "increasingly shows signs of the adoption of the conventions of social science research reporting, the conventions of his newly adopted community" (p. 8). These examples support the claim that maturing literacy develops over time and through a sequence of stages or levels of ability.

The prevalence of and strong evidence for the staged nature of first and second language acquisition, as well as similar findings in emergent literacy and maturing literacy, offer a base on which critical literacy presents itself as a similarly staged process. The growth of critical literacy across the lifespan is illustrated by the other chapters in this book. The stages of its development, however, should be clear from this review of the characteristics it shares with other aspects of human language ability. Critical literacy development begins before formal school instruction, as children interact with print in their environment and begin to produce written forms—a kind of preschool stage. It continues in school, through processes of acquisition and learning as byproducts of formal instruction and continued interaction with printed language both in and out of school. This stage might be seen as an instructional stage.

Critical literacy development clearly crystallizes at the college level and in graduate education, when maturing literacy develops for many students including those who are well outside the traditional age range for college students (Lynch & Sellers, 1996). With the expansion of the Internet, it is likely that critical literacy will be pushed in new directions as students in school and others traveling the information highway become more sophisticated users of hypertext links and the wealth of material on any topic to be found on the World Wide Web. People may also expand their critical literacy skills in formal or informal programs in career- or work-related settings, a kind of professional development stage. Later in life, there might be a beyond-school or an extra-school stage, in which key skills are further developed and enhanced.

Formal education is not the only place to develop the skills of critical literacy as suggested in earlier research by Scribner and Cole (1981). As the programs and projects in this book make clear—and as new research reveals the growth of key literacy skills among adults outside of school, seniors, and the elderly—critical literacy is a life-long enterprise. Critical literacy is more than being able to read for meaning and more than being able to summarize ideas in written form. According to the definition proposed earlier, it involves synthesis, evaluation, and the ability to draw conclusions from written material and to write about the results of such efforts in formal prose. This writing is perhaps the most complex and sophisticated human task language users are capable of, but it is very closely related, in terms of its development, to the other aspects of language development being described here. Its staged character is important for teachers and learners to understand; the stages surely continue over time and beyond formal schooling. For this reason, it is useful to think of critical literacy as developing before, during, and after school, across the lifespan.

PERSONALITY PREFERENCES

Human language ability, including speaking and understanding a first or second language and literacy capability, is inevitably influenced by the psychology of the human being developing the language skills. The importance of human variation in personality in terms of its role in how people acquire and use language has not received as much attention as it deserves, but it plays a key role in how people approach the language task. There are few direct references to personality preference in first and second language acquisition, although the relationship between personality and language development has been getting more attention (Horning & Sudol, 1997). My personal experience suggests the relevance of preferences in the development of reading ability, although there is no formal evidence to support my observations. On the writing dimension, detailed case studies of writers presented in Jensen and DiTiberio (1989) show the value and relevance of understanding personality preferences in language and critical literacy development.

The notion of personality preference comes from the work of Swiss psychiatrist Carl Jung (1971/1921). Jung's analysis shows that people have preferences along four dimensions that bear on energy sources, preferred ways of taking in information, preferred bases for decision making, and preferred ways of interacting in the world. These preferences are established early in life and help account for choices people make in their lives and in their strategies of language and literacy development. Jung's work was expanded and discussed by Katharine Briggs and Isabel Briggs Myers; their collaboration led to the development of a psychological instrument, the Myers-Briggs Type Indicator (MBTI) to measure personality preferences and the psychological types that reflect those preferences (Myers & McCaulley, 1985).

The preferences Jung described, as expanded by Briggs and Myers, yield four dimensions of personality. The first dimension pertains to how people get energized. Those who get their energy principally from the outer world of people and things are characterized as extraverts (assigned letter E in Type Indicator results), whereas those who draw energy from the inner world of ideas and concepts are introverts (I). A second preference dimension deals with how people take in information. The perceiving process may focus chiefly on information available through the five senses, yielding a sensing (S) preference on the MBTI. Or, the perceiving process may focus more on possibilities and mental opportunities the information represents, yielding an intuitive type (N).

The third dimension of personality in which people show preferences is decision making. Some people prefer to make most of their decisions based on facts, logic, and reason—a preference for thinking (T). Other individuals make decisions based on their feelings and human values, including consideration of how other people might feel or be affected by the decision at hand—a preference for feeling (F). The fourth dimension of personality reflects characteristics Jung described only generally. Myers (1980) extended Jung's observations to this fourth dimension of personality development having to do with preferences for lifestyle. Individuals may prefer a planned, orderly way of life, in terms of their interaction with the outside world, in which case they are said to be judging types (J). Those who have a more flexible, adaptable style of life and prefer a more spontaneous approach are perceiving types (P).

The four dimensions of personality preference play out in various ways in language and literacy development. In first language acquisition, some studies have examined the differences between referential children and expressive children (Nelson, 1981). Referential children are those who seem to focus their attention on concrete items in their world, working in first language acquisition principally, although not exclusively, through learning the names of things. A 2-year-old who takes an adult by the hand and points to many objects, saying "Zat?", is likely to be a referential child, persistently requesting specific object names. A different driving mechanism seems to work for other children who are interested in human connection and focus their attention in language acquisition on learning ways to interact with others. Saying "hi," "bye," and "thank you" are the kinds of social terms that attract the attention of expressive children.

Both kinds of children will learn object names and expressions of social intercourse, but as with all aspects of preference, this aspect has to do with natural inclinations to focus attention in certain ways. In terms of personality preference, referential children are perhaps more likely to prefer introversion and sensing, focused on the here-and-now details of experience, whereas expressive children may have preferences for extraversion and feeling, energized by people and the outer world and making decisions based largely on human impact. Although there is not yet research to support these speculations (despite an instrument to examine type preferences in children, the Murphy-Meisgeier [Murphy, 1992]), the identification of these patterns in children suggests a connection between personality preference and strategies of language acquisition.

In second language acquisition research, a more overt connection between personality type and strategies of L2 acquisition has been made by scholars such as Ehrman and Oxford (Ehrman & Oxford, 1989) and Brown (1994). The work of these scholars suggests that learners who are most willing to take risks and engage in conversation in the target language, even though they lack vocabulary and make errors in grammatical structure, are more likely to be extraverts in terms of personality preference, that is, those energized by people and events in the world. Introverts may be more likely to succeed in more solitary language learning tasks like reading, translation, and writing. Schumann's (1978) proposals suggest that introverted-thinking language learners, as in the one case he discusses, may face greater challenges in attaining communicative competence in their second language unless they develop strategies to allow them to work outside their natural preferences.

In emergent literacy as well, the nature of personality preferences may help to explain children's beginning reading strategies and other aspects of reading development (Myers, 1980). Reading is an inherently intuitive kind of activity (Lawrence, 1993) because readers must predict and see possibilities in text without much reliance on the visual display. Smith's description of the ways in which readers move from the visual display directly to meaning supports an intuitive analysis of reading (1994).

The impact of personality in reading behavior is clear in my two daughters. One child went to first grade in September not knowing how to read and by November could not only provide an oral rendition of *Ten Apples on Top* but was also able to give a substantive summary of the text that indicated she was getting meaning from her oral rendition of print. And yet, this youngster had always been a reluctant reader, partly, I am sure, due to her personality preferences. She has a sensing preference, preferring to take in information from concrete reality, and is not naturally inclined toward the kind of intuitive speculation that reading requires as a generic activity. Her early reading was limited by a general unwillingness to take risks with text.

My other daughter was one of those ready to learn to read long before first grade teaching and so went to kindergarten having plunged into reading. Although specific vocabulary items, letter-sound relationships, and sometimes important aspects of meaning eluded her, she pressed on through book after book of Richard Scarry, *Frog and Toad*, and almost anything else. Missing parts, taking risks with text, and trying books too hard for her were all part of her intuitive drive to read. Approaching the writing side of early literacy, she showed the same disinterest in the facts and details of spelling, using invented spelling with abandon. Her extraverted intuitive preferences seemed clearly to drive her willingness to take risks, guess at unknown words or skip them entirely, and explore the full range of possibilities in the literate world. Because both girls have mastered literacy skills, the differences in their strategies and approaches seem to reflect the differences in their personality types.

Turning to maturing literacy in, for example, the work on a formal research paper using college writing, the tasks involved and students' success in developing the relevant skills may be partly governed by their personality preferences. Sternglass' (1988) portraits of her graduate student subjects reveal the importance of self-awareness and preferences, although she does not address personality type directly. Similarly, Jensen and DiTiberio (1989) provide an extensive description of how different types address writing tasks. For example, each part of the process of preparing an academic research paper calls on different personality preferences, and different types will excel at different parts of a research project as a function of their preferences.

Introverts, for example, will have an easier time formulating a research question on their own, through their natural preference for internal meditation and energizing by solitary reflection. Extraverts may need to talk to one another to arrive at a question. Students who prefer perceiving will be very thorough in their approach to research, whereas those who prefer judging will have no trouble completing their papers by the deadline. Understanding these differences and others described by Jensen and DiTiberio can make a difference in teachers' expectations about how students will perform and free students to develop skills they lack because the skills do not arise from their natural preferences. All types of students can get blocked in the research process and then may find that developing their nonpreferred skills, as Jensen and DiTiberio (1989) suggest, can get them "unstuck."

The work of Jensen and DiTiberio reminds us that writing skills arise, like other aspects of language and literacy development, from students' underlying personality preferences. These preferences, Jung argued, are present at birth, and like the capacity for language itself (Jackendoff, 1994) form the underpinning for language behavior. Critical literacy may be the most sophisticated linguistic task human beings can achieve, but it shares characteristics with first and second language acquisition and early and maturing literacy development, including its staged character, as discussed earlier, as well as the influence of innate personality preferences. From this perspective, in school settings teachers can present not only strategies at which students can excel because they arise from their natural personality preferences, but also strategies students can learn that arise from the nonpreferred end of each dimension. In later life, adults may take up or expand their critical literacy as a tool for following through on Jung's observations about working on nonpreferred aspects of personality in the second half of life. According to Quenk (1993), who has written about the development of these aspects of personality in midlife and later life, Jung "put a heavy emphasis on the developmental tasks associated with the second half of life" (1993), when development of nonpreferred aspects of personality is a major goal. Critical literacy, then, shares with other language development processes the clear influence of personality preferences across its lifespan development.

ERROR

Another feature shared by all aspects of language development culminating in critical literacy is the feature of learner errors. All processes of language development share the phenomenon of error, and error may be the most revealing aspect of all facets of language development. Psycholinguists who have studied L1 and L2 acquisition, scholars in reading and writing development, and those working on maturing literacy share the view that errors have a systematic character that sheds light on learners' awareness of the language system. The consistent research findings across the acquisition of L1, L2, emergent, and maturing literacy support the view that errors reveal how learners develop their language system.

Studies of L1 development show children's rules as they begin to acquire the linguistic system of their native language and those rules as they move in a direction consistent with adult use. Children's errors, again across different languages and different cultures, show their systematic approach to language rules. The parameters of the rules are governed, according to some researchers, by Universal Grammar, but the specific settings of the native language must be established by the learners themselves (Pinker, 1990). The settings are worked out by children through a process of formulating hypotheses and testing them through use and interaction and through the data available from caregivers and others in the children's environment.

An example of this process appears in English-speaking children's development of past tense forms (Pinker, 1990). They begin with a hypothesis that the past tense is formed by adding -ed to the ends of verbs because that is the dominant pattern of regular verbs. Thus, forms like played, walked, studied, and so on all fit this pattern. When children confront the exceptions of irregular verbs, they make errors when they try to impose their general hypothesis of adding -ed. Thus, they first form the past of go as "goed." When they become aware of the different form of the past for go, they may persist in the use of -ed, and the result is "wented." Finally, in the third phase, children master the adult form and use "went." A similar pattern occurs in learning the plural forms, so that young children will create the plural of foot by adding -s, according to the regular rule for forming plurals in English, and produce "foots" followed by "feets" when they become aware of the vowel change form for this irregular. These patterns of errors are common among English-speaking children, and other similar types of errors occur in other languages (Slobin, 1985). The errors reveal the children's systems at various stages in their development.

Second language learners show similar error patterns in the Interlanguage stage of L2 development. In second language learning, the pattern of error is partially influenced by the learners' first language (Broselow, 1988). Broselow gives numerous examples. If the patterns of L2 are like those of L1, there will be "positive transfer" in the learners' hypothesized rules. If the patterns and rules of L2 are different, the result can be "negative transfer" and sometimes errors that "fossilize" (Selinker, 1972) in the learners' version of L2. However, the errors in any case are not the random result of learners' inattention or lack of ability. Instead, the errors reveal a systematic effort by learners to construct in their heads the rule system of L2.

In emergent literacy, young readers' and writers' errors again reveal their awareness of the system of written language. Early writings show children's awareness of paragraph breaks, capitalization, and marks of punctuation. Often the uses of these elements are unconventional in nature, but reveal children's sense of the rules that govern their use. A similar observation accurately reflects children's development in spelling. Chomsky's (1970) study shows that although English speakers' invented spelling may deviate greatly from standard spelling, it has a systematic character that is consistent with the underlying phonology of English. Treiman's (1993) study supports this view with an analysis of children's spelling in terms of the phonological system. And at a much later level of literacy development, Shaughnessy's (1977) study of error in the spelling patterns of basic writers reveals similar consistencies.

The systematic character of errors by learners in early reading may be the key insight offered by Kenneth and Yetta Goodman's work in miscue analysis. The Goodmans' use of the term *miscue* arose in part because they wanted to remove all traces of stigma from readers' systematic deviations from the written text. Their studies show that if a young reader says "woods" when the word "forest" appears in a text, it is clear and important to recognize the reader's awareness and preservation of meaning. The Goodmans' work shows the many systematic features of beginning readers' errors, as they may preserve letter-sound relationships in text, or grammatical structure, or may hold on to all of these and, most importantly, preserve meaning (Goodman, 1993; Goodman & Burke, 1972).

In the development of maturing literacy among adult learners, their errors are similarly systematic in nature and reveal underlying hypotheses readers and writers have about the character of written language. The inexperienced basic writers described by Shaughnessy (1977) show only the beginnings of awareness of the shape of written forms.

Thus, their paragraphing, capitalization, and punctuation show many inconsistencies with standard usage. However, they are not random errors but, like the errors of those engaged in L1 and L2 development and the errors of emergent literacy, are systematic in character. Errors, for instance, in subject-verb agreement show a systematic pattern that may reflect a basic writer's native language or a speaker's transfer of nonstandard oral forms into writing. In many cases, the systematic character of the errors is clear and consistent.

The kind of critical literacy examined in *Adult Literacy in America*, a national survey of literacy skills (Kirsch, Jungeblut, Jenkins, & Kolstad, 1993), represents a more advanced stage of this overall process. Thus, it is to be expected that learners in college writing courses will err in the production of formal research reports in systematic ways. The appropriate integration of suitable outside sources comes as a result of significant meaningful practice in the development of maturing literacy at this stage, just as the appropriate conventional use of plural or past tense forms does in the development of L1. The ability to read and synthesize data and use it to support an argument for a particular thesis is a complex and sophisticated skill which develops systematically over time and with errors and effort on the part of the learners. As learners move from early research practice with finding sources and patching them together in a first attempt at research to the more skilled efforts at logical argumentation that are seen in professional journal articles, their errors reflect growing mastery of the conventions of academic or professional discourse. The growth in ability is largely a byproduct of acquisition more so than learning, to use Krashen's and Gee's terms mentioned earlier.

Advanced writing courses, writing across the curriculum, writing in the disciplines, and professional writing courses such as those in legal writing, technical writing, and business writing, all have developed in higher education as strategies to support the developmental process. But within and beyond schools, errors in literacy development represent systematic and positive growth. Such errors are the natural byproduct of learners engaged in developing critical literacy as much as they are the byproduct of language development from the beginnings of "mama" and "dada." Across the lifespan, such errors may persist and become "fossilized," to use the terminology of L2 development, and are yet another reflection of the similar characteristics of these processes. If the abilities to understand and use language for critical evaluation are central to a democratic society, the errors users make in developing such skills must not block their continuing growth. The fullest realization of critical literacy may come at the end of formal schooling or well beyond that point as systematic errors gradually dissipate and are replaced with more consistent, conventional usage.

PSYCHOLINGUISTIC REDUNDANCY

Nowhere in the development of critical literacy does its consistency with other aspects of language growth become more clear than in the persistent attention to aspects of psycholinguistic redundancy. Redundancy is a complex feature of language that is especially pertinent to and salient in discourse, that is, in extended written texts. Although most readers might think of redundancy in the pejorative nonlinguistic way it is usually used, meaning unnecessary repetition, in its psycholinguistic sense, redundancy is quite different. It is the naturally occurring information overlap in language that helps to insure that the message sent by a writer is the one received by a reader. And although this redundancy certainly occurs within sentences, it also occurs and has a major impact on the efficacy and efficiency of language across sentences and in larger units of text. Scholars have suggested that, although it is also important in spoken forms, redundancy supports meaningful exchanges in these larger units of written language in particular (Haber & Haber, 1981; Horning, 1993; Smith, 1994). These larger units of text are the focus of critical literacy whether reading or writing.

In all aspects of language development including the development of critical literacy, learners' errors tend to focus on redundancy. In first language acquisition, for example, children's errors cluster first around syntactic markers of redundancy such as plural endings and past tense markers. Usually, sentences contain other indications of tense and number, as in utterances like "I have two foots," in which both "two" and "foots" carry the plural information. This is a simple form of information overlap. It is also a place where L1 errors frequently occur.

Children's interest in redundancy is clear in many other aspects of first language development. They like, for instance, to hear the same stories over and over again, often to the distraction of parents. Snow and Ninio (1986) argue that such repetition is an essential experience on the road to the development of literacy skills. Moreover, if parents are reading a story, they must read it the same way each time, including whatever embellishments they may have added to the text. Repetition is a simple form of redundancy which book reading provides, and children seek it out. When they become readers, it is often common for children to read certain books over and over. In my own experience, the book *Johnny Tremain* (Forbes, 1943) came into my life around second grade and stayed in it, read over and over through high school. Recently, I reread it yet again and still liked it.

Another example derives from a conversation between linguist Martin Braine, and his two-and-a-half-year-old child, which illustrates a number of the aspects of language development that have been discussed here. The youngster in this case asks for the "other one spoon." Braine tried "repeatedly but fruitlessly" over several weeks to get the child to say "the other spoon," and finally his daughter produced the utterance as requested. Then, having satisfied her parent, she said, "Now give me other one spoon?" (Braine, 1971, pp. 160-161). This example is particularly interesting because it illustrates a child working on a redundant form. We might conventionally say in this utterance either "the other one" or "the other spoon" but not combine them. The child is working on sorting out how redundant to be. Like other aspects of language acquisition, this process is immune, indeed resistant to, direct teaching. In this way, language acquisition is like the development of critical literacy as noted earlier. Gee (1991) suggests that its development may sometimes be impeded by direct teaching.

In second language acquisition, errors in learners' interlanguage forms also cluster around redundant features of language. Like L1 learners, L2 learners make errors on markers of plural and past tense, syntactic features that are often redundant in sentence structure. In languages in which articles and verbs may be marked for gender, learners will often omit or err on gender markings. There may be errors in the word order reflecting L2 learners' developing mastery of the word order of the target language (Broselow, 1988). Speakers of the language will understand the learners despite the errors because they cluster on redundant information, but redundant information is necessary and omitting it does not yield conventionally correct forms.

In emergent literacy, the impact of redundancy is again clear in learners' errors. Spelling patterns often show omission of letters that are not needed for phonological reasons (such as double consonants; Treiman, 1993). Samples of early writing may also show children fooling around with punctuation. Young children may write texts in which every word is followed by a period, or every sentence begins a new paragraph. Punctuation and paragraph forms are signals of structure that are highly redundant in nature. Like all redundant features of language, they help convey meaning and make written forms efficient and effective. Doing without these conventions makes interpretation significantly more complex. One has only to think of the Old Testament, written originally in ancient Hebrew, with little paragraphing, no punctuation, and no vowels, and the hundreds of hours and pages of scholarly effort that have gone into its interpretation. These scholars would have considerably less to discuss if the written forms were conventional and redundant.

Beginning readers often generate miscues due to their lack of awareness or attention to punctuation. At the beginning of literacy, it is difficult to attend to all features of redundancy in language simultaneously. As Smith (1994) observed, beginning readers are tied to the visual display on the printed page and develop a kind of tunnel vision as a result. Thus, they must focus on each letter sound or word combination before they can get at meaning. Beginning readers reading aloud will often fail to provide appropriate intonation patterns because they overlook punctuation markers that contribute redundancy to the written text. Miscues may also focus on plurals, gender markings, and subject-verb agreement endings, all of which are often redundant. In emergent literacy, whether the reading dimension or the writing dimension, children are attending to, working on, and piecing together the redundant aspects of language.

Learners moving through maturing literacy and toward critical literacy also tend to concentrate their errors around redundant features of language. Students in developmental writing courses are often so placed because they have not yet mastered the conventional features of redundancy essential to the written forms of academic prose. As in L1 and L2 development, the errors tend to be on plurals, tense, and perhaps gender markings. Such writers are at the beginnings of maturing literacy and must develop an awareness of redundant features of the decontextualized language used in critically literate text.

The errors beginning learners make in the development of the maturing literacy described by the national literacy survey (Kirsch et al., 1993) start with reading. College students beginning to learn research do too much "reaching out" as described by Sudol (1987)—too much information gathering in the library and in interviews with primary sources. They do not do enough "looking in," again in Sudol's terms—careful reading and interpretation of facts, statistics, and ideas. Not enough attention is devoted to the real essence of critical literacy, which goes beyond comprehension to analysis, synthesis, and evaluation.

College writers in the later stages of maturing literacy will also reveal their concern with redundancy in written forms of the language. Often, formal research and argumentative papers of the kind required in college writing lack the overall discourse structure needed to make a cogent argument. The needed discourse structure is redundant in nature: It warrants a thesis at the outset that is restated somewhere near the end. Each part of the argument, to be effective, needs to be clearly and overtly tied to the point of the paper overall. Writers who are maturing toward critical literacy will often err in these redundant characteristics of argumentation. In other kinds of texts, redundancy plays a different role that becomes more clear only in later life. Then, storytelling abilities, and especially the ability to retell stories (i.e., to make effective use of redundancy), are especially important in some cultures (Obler, 1993).

Redundancy involves both repetition and more sophisticated and complex forms of information overlap. Beginning writers rely a lot on simple repetition to build redundancy into their texts. Over time, as writers develop, they are able to make increasing use of the more complicated kinds of redundancy to enhance their writing. Skilled writers, professional writers, and scholarly writers of effective and cogent arguments are so judged because they have reached a stage beyond maturing literacy, a stage of critical literacy in which they have learned not only to read and understand prose texts, but also to synthesize and integrate information in documents; extract, manipulate, and draw conclusions from numerical information in texts; and, finally, write about their findings in a redundant way. These abilities are the ones examined for the Adult Literacy survey (Kirsch et al., 1993) and ones essential to full participation in our society. One mark, then, of a critically literate writer is the judicious use of assertion and reassertion of core ideas, synonyms, ties of sections of an argument to its overall point, and other subtle forms of redundancy (Ray, personal communication, February 17, 1997).

Knowledge and use of redundancy begins early in language acquisition, particularly in the involvement with written language in both reading and writing. Redundancy is a subtle and complex aspect of language, essential to the give and take of meaning but operating generally outside the conscious awareness of language users. Its complexity and sophistication suggest that skill in its use develops over time as people become more critically literate. Some of this development occurs before and outside school, as a byproduct of acquisition. Some of this development occurs in formal learning situations in schooling. And some of it does not develop until later in life and after formal schooling, when older people learn to tell and retell stories, capitalizing on the inherent redundancy of language to preserve their culture and memories.

CONCLUSION

If critical literacy represents, as I have been suggesting, an ultimate stage in language development, then its development must be seen as akin to other aspects of language development. Like L1, L2, emergent, and maturing literacy, critical literacy develops by stages that can be actively supported with teaching informed by an awareness of the stages in the development process and meaningful opportunities for practice both within and outside formal school settings. However, critical literacy must be acquired and cannot be pushed. Critical literacy is governed, like other language development processes, by the natural personality preferences of learners and may develop further much later in life as illustrated by some of the studies reported in the later chapters of this book.

The development of critical literacy will be marked by errors that reveal learners' underlying psycholinguistic processing, as L1 learners show the development of the rules of their linguistic competence, L2 learners reveal their Interlanguage system, children in emergent literacy make clear their awareness of text conventions, and those maturing in their literacy abilities work out the structure of discourse and the use of source materials. And, finally, critical literacy, like other aspects of language development, comes about as learners develop the ability to understand and use the inherent psycholinguistic redundancy that is a central feature of the written forms of language that are the base of critical literacy.

The implications of this view of critical literacy for formal instruction and literacy activities beyond school settings should be clear. Learners will pass through stages in the process of developing literacy abilities, and it must be understood that they move through this kind of process. Teachers' awareness of the stages of development can inform their classroom instruction and support their individual help for students at different stages. Facilitators of critical literacy in other settings will find an awareness of the developmental stages of the acquisition of literacy skills a useful focus. Learners work naturally in ways consistent with their personality preferences and preferred ways of doing tasks associated with critical literacy. Teachers can provide students with the strategies and skills of their nonpreferred dimensions of personality, offering them as viable alternatives that might work better on critical literacy tasks. Those working with people becoming critically literate in nonschool situations can foster the growth of literacy more effectively by keeping personality development and structure in mind.

Learners will make errors in their efforts to become critically literate. Teachers must see these errors as positive indicators of learners' developing awareness of the nature of critical literacy and as revealing their processing and production of written forms. Outside school, errors may likewise be seen as indicators of positive development. Finally, learners' errors will concentrate in the areas of language relevant to its redundancy. Knowledge of the varied forms of psycholinguistic redundancy can allow teachers to understand how learner errors arise and why, and to provide focused and useful instruction pertinent to the error patterns and redundant nature of written language. Some aspects of redundancy may be especially useful to literacy in later life, and language users may want or need to focus specifically on developing their capacity to tap the naturally occurring redundancy of language.

The development of critical literacy is essential in our society. It is a democratic goal, an educational goal, a necessary goal for all of us individually and collectively. Learners move toward critical literacy skills in formal education; critical literacy is the essence of education. Members of a democratic society need critical literacy to be full partici- pants in society and culture. Critical literacy is a most complex and sophisticated combination of human language abilities. Critical literacy is a human achievement that shares a staged character, the influence of personality preferences, and error and redundancy with other human language development in L1, L2, emergent, and maturing literacy. Understanding critical literacy as arising through these shared processes of linguistic development will allow teachers and others to foster the growth of critically literate citizens.

REFERENCES

Berkenkotter, C., Huckin, T., & Ackerman, J. (1989). *Social context and socially constructed texts: The initiation of a graduate student into a writing research community* (Technical rep. No. 33). Berkeley, CA: Center for the Study of Writing. (ERIC Document Reproduction Service No. ED 313 700)

Bloom, L. (1991). *Language development from two to three.* New York: Cambridge University Press.

Braine, M. D. S. (1971). On two types of models of the internalization of grammars. In D. I. Slobin (Ed.), *The ontogenesis of grammar: A theo- retical symposium* (pp. 153-186). New York: Academic Press.

Broselow, E. (1988). Second language acquisition. In F. Newmeyer (Ed.), *Linguistics: The Cambridge survey* (pp. 194-209). New York: Cambridge University Press.

Brown, H. D. (1994). *Principles of language learning and teaching* (3rd ed.). New York: Prentice-Hall Regents.

Brown, R. (1973). *A first language.* Cambridge, MA: Harvard University Press.

Byrne, B. (1991). Experimental analysis of the child's discovery of the alphabetic principle. In L. Rieben & C. A. Perfetti (Eds.), *Learning to read: Basic research and its implications* (pp. 75-84). Hillsdale, NJ: Erlbaum.

Chall, J. S. (1983). *Stages of reading development.* New York: McGraw-Hill.

Chomsky, C. (1969). *The acquisition of syntax in children from 5 to 10.* Cambridge, MA: MIT Press.

Chomsky, C. (1970). Reading, writing and phonology. *Harvard Educational Review, 40,* 287-309.

Daniell, B. (1996). Composing (as) power. *College Composition and Communication, 45,* 238-246.

Ehrman, M., & Oxford, R. (1989). Effects of sex differences, career choice, and psychological type on adult language learning strategies. *Modern Language Journal, 73*, 1-13.

Eimas, P. (1991). The perception of speech in early infancy. In W. S-Y. Wang (Ed.), *The emergence of language: Development and evolution* (pp. 117-127). New York: W. H. Freeman.

Forbes, E. (1943). *Johnny Tremain*. Boston: Houghton Mifflin.

Gee, J. P. (1991). What is literacy? In C. Mitchell & K. Weiler (Eds.), *Rewriting literacy: Culture and the discourse of the other* (pp. 3-12). New York: Bergin & Garvey.

Goodman, K. S. (1993). *Phonics phacts*. Portsmouth, NH: Heinemann.

Goodman, Y., & Burke, C. (1972). *Reading miscue inventory manual: Procedure for diagnosis and evaluation*. New York: Macmillan.

Haber, L. R., & Haber, R. N. Perceptual processes in reading: An analysis-by-synthesis model. In F. J. Pirozzolo & M. C. Wittrock (Eds.), *Neuropsychological and cognitive processes in reading* (pp. 167-200). New York: Academic Press.

Horning, A. S. (1987). *Teaching writing as a second language*. Carbondale: Southern Illinois University Press.

Horning, A. S. (1993). *The psycholinguistics of readable writing: A multidisciplinary exploration*. Norwood, NJ: Ablex.

Horning, A. S., & Sudol, R. A. (Eds.). (1997). *Understanding literacy: Personality preferences in rhetorical and psycholinguistic contexts*. Cresskill, NJ: Hampton Press.

Howard, R. M. (1995). Plagiarisms, authorships, and the academic death penalty. *College English, 57*(7), 788-806.

Jackendoff, R. S. (1994). *Patterns in the mind*. New York: Basic Books.

Jensen, G., & DiTiberio, J. (1989). *Personality and the teaching of composition*. Norwood, NJ: Ablex.

Jung, C. G. (1971). *Psychological types*. (H. G. Baynes & R. F. C. Hull, trans.). Princeton, NJ: Princeton University Press. (Original work published 1921)

Kirsch, I. S., Jungeblut, A., Jenkins, L., & Kolstad, A. (1993). *Adult Literacy in America*. Washington, DC: Office of Educational Research and Improvement.

Krashen, S. (1985). *The input hypothesis: Issues and implications*. London: Longman.

Kutz, E. (1986). Between students' language and academic discourse: Interlanguage as middle ground. *College English, 48*(4), 385-396.

Lawrence, G. (1993). *People types and tiger stripes* (3rd ed.). Gainesville, FL: Center for the Applications of Psychological Type.

Lynch, A. Q., & Sellers, P. A. (1996). Preferences for different educational environments and psychological type: A comparison of adult learners and traditional age college students. *Journal of Psychological Type, 39,* 18-29.

Morris, P. J., & Tchudi, S. (1996). *The new literacy: Moving beyond the 3 Rs.* San Francisco: Jossey-Bass.

Murphy, E. (1992). *The developing child: Using Jungian type to understand children.* Gainesville, FL: Center for the Applications of Psychological Type.

Myers, I. B. (1980). *Gifts differing.* Palo Alto, CA: Consulting Psychologists Press.

Myers, I. B., & McCaulley, M. H. (1985). *Manual: The Myers-Briggs Type Indicator.* Palo Alto, CA: Consulting Psychologists Press.

Nelson, K. (1981). Individual differences in language development: Implications for development and language. *Developmental Psychology, 17*(2), 170-187.

Obler, L. K. (1993). Language beyond childhood. In J. Berko Gleason (Ed.), *Language development* (3rd ed., pp. 421-449). New York: Macmillan.

Pinker, S. (1990). Language acquisition. In D. N. Osherson & H. Lasnik (Eds.), *Language: An invitation to cognitive science* (pp. 199-241). Cambridge, MA: MIT Press.

Quenk, N. L. (1993). *Beside ourselves: Our hidden personality in everyday life.* Palo Alto, CA: Consulting Psychologists Press.

Schumann, J. (1978). *The pidginization process: A model for second language acquisition.* Rowley, MA: Newbury House.

Scribner, S., & Cole, M. (1981). *The psychology of literacy.* Cambridge, MA: Harvard University Press.

Selinker, L. (1972). Interlanguage. *International Review of Applied Linguistics, 10,* 209-231.

Selinker, L. (1992). *Rediscovering interlanguage.* London: Longman.

Shaughnessy, M. P. (1977). *Errors and expectations: A guide for the teacher of basic writing.* New York: Oxford University Press.

Slobin, D. (Ed.). (1985). *The cross-linguistic study of language acquisition* (Vols. 1-4). Hillsdale, NJ: Erlbaum.

Smith, F. (1994). *Understanding reading* (5th ed.). Hillsdale, NJ: Erlbaum.

Snow, C. E., & Ninio, A. (1986). The contracts of literacy: What children learn from learning to read books. In W. H. Teale & E. Sulzby (Eds.), *Emergent literacy: Writing and reading* (pp. 116-138). Norwood, NJ: Ablex.

Stanovich, K. S. (1991). Changing models of reading and reading acquisition. In L. Rieben & C. A. Perfetti (Eds.), *Learning to read: Basic research and its implications* (pp. 19-32). Hillsdale, NJ: Erlbaum.

Sternglass, M. S. (1988). *The presence of thought: Introspective accounts of reading and writing.* Norwood, NJ: Ablex.

Sudol, R. A. (1987). *Textfiles: A rhetoric for word processing.* San Diego, CA: Harcourt Brace Jovanovich.

Sulzby, E. (1986). Writing and reading: Signs of oral and written language organization in the young child. In W. H. Teale & E. Sulzby (Eds.), *Emergent literacy: Writing and reading* (pp. 50-89). Norwood, NJ: Ablex.

Teale, W. H., & Sulzby, E. (Eds.). (1986). *Emergent literacy: Writing and reading.* Norwood, NJ: Ablex.

Treiman, R. (1993). *Beginning to spell: A study of first-grade children.* New York: Oxford University Press.

Critical Literacy and Large-Scale Writing Assessment: The Michigan High School Proficiency Test

Ellen H. Brinkley
Western Michigan University

Ronald A. Sudol
Oakland University

During its 1991 session, the Michigan State Legislature passed a bill that required all students beginning with the high school class of 1997 to pass a state proficiency exam in writing, reading, mathematics, and science. The original legislation called for students to pass the proficiency tests or be denied a high school diploma. Later legislation lowered the stakes so that all students could still receive locally issued diplomas, whereas those who passed the proficiency tests would receive state endorsements for the test areas. In response to the legislation, the Michigan Council of Teachers of English (MCTE, a state affiliate of the National Council of Teachers of English) was eventually awarded a contract by the Michigan Department of Education to develop the curricular framework and assessment plan for the Michigan High School Proficiency Test (HSPT) in Writing. (State affiliates of other professional societies were awarded contracts to develop the HSPT in Reading, Science, and Mathematics.)

Our participation in creating a standardized writing proficiency test for statewide administration compelled us, and the group of Michigan educators with whom we worked, to define literacy clearly enough to serve as a framework for deciding what students should write on the test and how we would judge what they wrote. Such a framework for the proficiency test in science, for example, would identify all the skills and knowledge students are expected to possess at certain levels. Test developers would then create test items based on those identifications. But what would such a framework for writing look like? The easy solution from the standpoint of test development might have been to identify elements of acceptable written products and to design easily quantified multiple choice test items accordingly. But such a framework would not have appropriately reflected the teaching, learning, and assessment of writing in Michigan classrooms; and we feared it would instead shift the curriculum toward an emphasis on isolated skills and drills.

As all of the contributors to this collection of chapters have shown, the concept of *literacy* is highly resistant to singular definition. Even when literacy is defined very succinctly, one can detect multiple layers of meaning. The National Literacy Act of 1991, for example, defines literacy as

> the ability to read, write, speak English, and compute and solve problems at levels of proficiency necessary to function on the job and in society, achieve one's goals, and develop one's knowledge and potential. (U. S. Department of Education, 1993, p. 8)

The key words—*read, write, English, function, job* and *society*—imply the kind of literacy many Michigan legislators may have had in mind when they passed the original exit test bill. Indeed, perceived lapses of literacy and numeracy committed by Michigan high school graduates had led representatives of business and industry to complain about public education, leading in turn to legislative action aimed at protecting the state economy from being damaged by underskilled workers. Vivid memories of the last recession and intense competition from foreign manufacturing are powerful influences in a state highly sensitive to economic ups and downs. The word "function" in particular helps to define one level of literacy that the public through its elected representatives sought to standardize and assess. Promoting functional literacy in order to improve the economic and social well-being of the community is an appropriate focus of civic action, supported by the key words in the U.S. Department of Education definition—*read, write, English, function, job* and *society*—that connect individuals to the world outside themselves.

The Department of Education (1993) definition of literacy goes on, however, with an additional set of keywords—*achieve, goals, develop, knowledge,* and *potential*—words that center on individuals without connecting them directly to their contributions to the economic and social well-being of the community. These words point not to functional literacy but to "critical" literacy—as implied by state legislators' hopes that Michigan students could achieve "world-class standards" and as defined in various ways by scholars and teachers cited elsewhere in this volume. In critical literacy, language is used not only to perform everyday tasks and to communicate effectively but to develop habits of mind and heart that give voice to original ideas; encourage intellectual, spiritual, and aesthetic development; and potentially lead to significant civic action.

By training, instinct, and experience, we were convinced that a writing assessment would need to be framed by such a full-bodied definition of literacy if it were to have a positive impact on teaching and learning. Thus, the assessment that emerged from this project measures functional writing skills on three separate pieces of writing, but it also includes such elements of critical literacy as reflecting on one's own writing processes, using writing to communicate about a subject other than English language arts, and writing to generate and convey original ideas that are thoughtfully developed and polished in response to a specific writing task. Developing the curricular framework and assessment plan that would reflect both functional and critical literacy involved collaboration among an array of stakeholder groups: K-12 classroom teachers and administrators, university teacher educators and rhetoric and composition specialists, state Department of Education testing and measurement staff, staff from a national testing company, legal consultants, state-level business and professional organizations, and members of the State Board of Education and State Legislature. We describe how those who fulfilled the charge of the contract renegotiated the culture of statewide testing development and explain how, by working contractually with the State Department of Education, we managed the test design process. We also discuss our experience of confronting head-on the conflicting roles of writing teachers in the culture of the classroom versus writing test developers in the culture of a professional community pulled by high stakes purposes that affected students and teachers, test contractors and the state Department of Education, and parents, legislators, and other members of the public.

This chapter, then, reviews the process of developing Michigan's writing assessment from the perspective of two university professors who provided leadership in its design and implementation. Our principal theme is that defining and measuring literacy within the context of standardization needs to be a negotiated process requiring deliberation, flexibility, and patience on the part of numerous stakeholders if literacy is to have any meaning beyond the lowest level of language functioning.

TEACHERS TAKING ON NEW ROLES

Distinguishing between functional and critical literacy is a useful academic exercise, but the distinction becomes problematic when we try to make valid connections between what goes on in classrooms and what can be assessed in a statewide program. The common assumption at the outset, based on some confusion about how Michigan's exit test might differ from tests in other states, was that functional literacy would inevitably be the focus on the assessment. Such an emphasis, however, made many teachers uneasy because the focus of language arts teaching is critical literacy, which is rarely assessed and more difficult to standardize. Thus, even before we responded to Michigan's Request for Proposals, conflicts about professional roles—as writing teachers and as potential writing test-makers—emerged.

In fact, the Executive Committee of the Michigan Council of Teachers of English had lengthy, professionally soul-searching discussions about whether we should even get involved. How could we in good conscience create another external test that would cost the state so much money? that would deny a diploma to some students? that would result in newspaper comparisons of school-district scores? None of *us* had lobbied the legislature to establish a high school proficiency test, but the state legislature had already mandated the tests. An Expert Panel had been commissioned and had issued a set of recommendations. We appreciated the state's decision to turn to professional content associations for the test design. If we did not participate, we felt sure the state would turn to an out-of-state national testing company. During the previous year we had watched the state develop what we perceived to be professionally indefensible teacher competency tests, so we knew how bad the proposed writing assessment could turn out to be. Might students in Michigan be better off, we wondered, if we did participate?

Participating was surely more difficult than not participating. How much easier in the long run it would have been to assume the worst about state testing and either reject the invitation or make an effort—almost sure to fail—to get the testing legislation revoked. Ultimately we decided to take the risky step of becoming involved, hoping against hope that by designing the test ourselves we could fight to create an appropriate performance assessment that would have a positive effect on students and their writing in Michigan's classrooms.

But once the decision was made to participate, new questions that were just as disturbing soon followed. How could we design an assessment that we as teachers of writing could defend from a curricular perspective but that would be legally defensible as well? Could we avoid casting our current theoretical assumptions aside as we struggled to design a high-stakes statewide writing assessment? How close to actual classroom practice might an assessment we created come? Fighting memories from our own past experiences with standardized tests, we dared question whether students might, for example, be permitted to talk to peers during the composing process, even in a testing situation. In moments when we felt less bold, we wondered how we might fulfill the psychometricians' demand for multiple measures/multiple items without creating merely a series of quick-writes and without using multiple-choice items.

In short, we wanted what White (1996) says that teachers want from writing assessment:

- Assessment that supports their work or at least does not deny its importance;
- Assessment that recognizes the complexity of writing and of the teaching of writing;
- Assessment that respects them as professionals and their students as individuals; and
- Assessment that will not be misused to provide simple, damaging and misleading information. (p. 14)

An assessment that satisfies these teacher expectations would be similar to classroom assessment—direct multiple measures honoring the writing process with ample allowance for discovery, revision, and feedback. To the extent that this kind of assessment replicates the classroom, however, it runs contrary to the interests of other groups, losing the benefits of standardization, for example, or losing in scoring reliability what it gains in validity (Sudol, 1996). Thus, White (1996) suggests that the effort to accommodate the needs of teachers raises these questions:

- How can large-scale assessments be consistent with teachers' judgments of individual students?
- How can students and teachers receive useful and constructive feedback from assessment?
- How can assessments support collegial work among faculty members and supportive relations between teachers and students?

- How can assessments provide or give the appearance of providing the data sought by other interest groups without becoming reductive or interfering with teaching and learning?
- How can teachers control writing assessment so that it is not used for purposes contrary to their interests? (p. 14)

Because statewide writing assessment was new to Michigan, we knew we would need a political consensus among English language arts teachers about what kind of writing should be included and how writing should be tested. Therefore, to design the test, we gathered together a group of 29 educators who represented a wide range of stakeholders and professional perspectives and experiences. Included were English language arts classroom teachers from a range of grade levels, composition and rhetoric specialists, special education teachers, principals, curriculum coordinators, teacher educators, state Department of Education liaisons, a linguist, and a psychometrician.

KEEPING STUDENTS AND THEIR PARENTS IN MIND

In the course of a career in school, students are subjected to a great deal of assessment including the usual run of quizzes and examinations; standardized test instruments focused on aptitude and achievement; measures of physical condition, behavior, and demographic factors; and studies of the effect of academic and social programs. From the point of view of students (and those who speak on their behalf), these indirect measurements primarily serve other constituencies. Even when the results of assessments take the form of specific information for students, such tests are often part of a larger system of sorting and categorizing that seems to benefit school authorities and the public more than the students. Because schools reflect the communities they serve, information about students reflects and becomes entangled with information about the community itself—and not always in helpful ways.

From the standpoint of students, White (1996) describes the following as needed in writing assessment:

- Assessment that stresses the social and situational context of the writer;
- Assessment designed to provide maximum and speedy feedback to the student;
- Assessment that breaks down the complexity of writing into focused units that can be learned in sequence and mastered by study;
- Assessment that produces data principally for the use of learners and teachers; and

- Assessment that focuses on critical thinking and creativity and that places surface features of dialect and usage in a large social context. (p. 22)

Writing assessment results are public information and therefore appear in newspapers. Often charts of school-district scores are clipped from newspapers and posted in real estate offices where they are taken to be an indicator of the quality of different schools and school districts. The "information" drawn from this process affects real estate values, exacerbating, in turn, discrepancies between school districts in terms of family socioeconomic levels. Parents who can afford to live where they like can choose for their children a school district with higher scores. Within this social context, the issues and problems that arise from students' and parents' perspectives include the following:

- How can writing assessment overturn the exclusive patterns of the past and open opportunity to the deserving in marginalized groups?
- What kinds of writing assessment display the least bias toward the underprivileged or the oppressed?
- How can writing assessment draw on and value the rich experiences of nontraditional students and still treat traditional students fairly?
- How can those scoring writing assessments overcome the various biases inevitably part of their privileged positions?
- How can assessment in context become part of learning and not be misused to exclude individuals or groups from educational opportunity? (White, 1996, p. 22)

FOCUSING ON THEORETICAL AND PRACTICAL ASSESSMENT ISSUES

Various tensions between theory and practice occupied us as we tried to form a consensus on what the assessment should look like. Clearly the assessment would need to reflect sound theoretical assumptions about writing processes, but the very nature of assessment demands constant attention to practical applications. On the one hand, the assessment would need to reflect actual classroom practices. We could not attempt to test students on what they had not been taught or had ample opportunities to practice. On the other hand, one purpose of the assessment was to standardize the criteria for assessing writing and to empower teachers and school districts in their efforts to offer the best possible writing instruction. So even though the assessment would need to reflect current practice, it would also need to have a positive influence on future practice.

We could avoid erring on one side or the other by articulating a few basic assumptions that were easy to agree to on both practical and theoretical grounds. Our understanding of a constructivist model of literacy learning provided a starting point: Learning is not passive and assessment should not be passive either. It is not enough for students to demonstrate that they can identify right answers. Students have a better chance to demonstrate what they know if they have to articulate that knowledge for themselves. But it is not enough for students just to be able to articulate someone else's ideas. Instead, we expect students to think critically and to use what they know to actually "make new meaning," that is, to demonstrate critical literacy.

These assumptions led inexorably—and quite easily—to the necessity for direct assessment of writing. Certainly assessing writing by scoring fully developed pieces of student writing comes closer to recognizing and encouraging critical literacy than using multiple choice formats. Although assessment professionals consider indirect, multiple choice formats to be highly reliable because they can effectively measure discrete skills, we know that this benefit also confines test formats to issues of functional literacy. Their very presence on the test, we felt, would have a deleterious and retrograde effect on future practice by supporting functional literacy at the expense of critical literacy.

The measurement experts argued long and hard in favor of using at least some multiple choice questions as a way of validating scores on writing samples. But the argument that it would be illogical to use a less valid form of assessment (indirect) to validate a more valid form (direct) prevailed. The measurement experts eventually agreed that the methods and procedures of holistic, analytic, and criterion-referenced scoring were sufficiently reliable to warrant basing the entire score on actual writing. Doing so, however, would require us to use multiple measures in the form of several samples of writing whose scores would be averaged, weighted, or combined.

A CURRICULUM AND ASSESSMENT FRAMEWORK

It is more becoming than expedient to claim that an assessment could match a curriculum, especially a curriculum designed to promote critical literacy. Yet the desire to do so is nearly overwhelming to conscientious practitioners. Once we had easily settled on direct performance assessment, several other more difficult issues needed to be confronted. What is broadly referred to as "the writing process" as the foundation of a valid writing curriculum is not susceptible in every detail to valid assessment. Two features of a good writing curriculum, for example, are conferring and time for incubation and revision. Measurement experts insisted that the need for a high-stakes assessment to be fair and equitable made it difficult to include any provision for peer conferences. Some degree of conferring is retained in the elementary and middle school versions of the writing assessment that have lower stakes for individual students.

The assessment is also subject to practical time limits. For reasons of equity and security, for example, the measurement specialists required that all drafting and revising be done in the same session, and all test takers must have the same amount of time in which to write. So the writing process that students use on the assessment is necessarily truncated when compared to the kind of process they would use under the guidance of effective writing teachers.

This process is not to be pinned down, although assessment tries to do just that. So the gap between curriculum and assessment is something we learned to live with. At the same time, however, we were determined to push the envelope of assessment as far as we could toward recognizing and honoring as much of a valid curriculum as practicality and equity would allow.

We were charged by the state to create an assessment that reflected existing state documents about writing—the Michigan Core Curriculum (1991) and the Michigan Essential Goals and Objectives for Writing (1985)—and the teaching of writing, although we were not bound by the limitations of the existing documents. We felt we needed to convey to teachers and other interested parties something of the open and recursive nature of writing. Thus, one member of our committee, after two days and long evenings of discussion, devised this graphic (Figure 3.1). The cursive loops that turn on themselves convey a graphic message of first generating ideas and language and then rethinking and revising throughout the recursive development of thoughtfully composed, significant pieces of writing.

We also struggled to articulate a definition of writing that had not been explicit in existing documents, a definition focusing on writing as a process of composing meaning for the following purposes: reflecting and exploring ideas and feelings, creating knowledge and meaning, communicating ideas, and/or validating learning. Most of us were experimenting with writing portfolios in our classrooms and were convinced of the value of permitting students wide choices of topic and genre in their writing. We also realized that the design of the test would strongly influence curriculum. Thus, we were determined not to assign writing in a particular genre or to require a specific organizational pattern.

Still, we wanted to convey to teachers and others a sense of the range of writing choices that students could avail themselves of as they

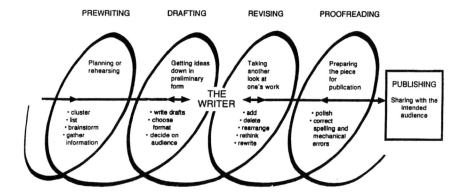

Figure 3.1. Writing as process

Note. Prepared for the Michigan Proficiency Examination Framework for Writing by the Michigan Council of Teachers of English (1993).

carried out the HSPT Writing tasks. After lengthy discussion, we adapted and extended Britton's (Britton, Burgess, Martin, McLeod, & Rosen, 1975) categories—expressive, transactional, and poetic—to suggest a wide array of writing possibilities and writing purposes (see Figure 3.2).

Throughout the process, issues and questions emerged that led our group—about half of whom were K-12 classroom teachers—to reflect on and distill our own classroom assessment practices. For example, early discussions about classroom practices often focused on questions that seemed relevant to writing assessment: Do we use writing portfolios? What do we ask or encourage students to write? What do we ask or encourage them to write about? To what extent are students permitted or encouraged to confer or collaborate with others about their writing? How much time, if any, do we provide for in-class writing? How do we test student writers' editing skills? To what extent can our students use computers for composing? What accommodations do we provide for ESL or LEP students? And how do we respond to and evaluate students' writing?

Writing:
Reflecting and Exploring Ideas and Feelings
Creating Knowledge and Meaning
Communicating Ideas
Validating Learning

A RANGE OF POSSIBILITIES

WRITER'S PRIMARY PURPOSE➔	EXPRESSIVE	INFORMATIVE	PERSUASIVE	IMAGINATIVE
Audience	self/trusted others	others in a specific situation	self and targeted others	others/self
Text Features	informal, often narrative...	factual, explicit...	argumentative, factual, rhetorical, strategic...	poetic, fictional metaphorical...
Sample Formats	journal entry, prediction, reminiscence, learning log, observation, prereading, reflection on writing/learning, accessing prior knowledge, personal reactions...	letter, memo, report, essay, news article, lab report, math story problem, chart, time line, survey, progress report, computer program, fact sheet, pamphlet, instruction manual...	editorial, essay, case study, campaign pamphlet, list of possible solutions or arguments, pro's and con's, problem solving matrix, letter to editor, debate, proposal, dialogue...	poem, play, story, dramatic monologue, quick write, role play, simulation, word play, fictional biography, TV scenario or script, news program, song lyrics, advertisement, cartoon...
Reader's Purpose	understand, identify with writer...	gain information, examine facts/ideas...	reconsider ideas, understand, decide...	enjoy, vicarious experience...

Figure 3.2. Writing possibilities

Note. Prepared for the Michigan Proficiency Examination Framework for Writing by the Michigan Council of Teachers of English (1993).

As important as these questions were, we all discovered that we had to look beyond the perspective of our own experience. We were charged with designing a required assessment to be administered to 110,000 Michigan 11th-graders. It would need to be unbiased and value the experiences of students from tiny rural school districts in the Upper Peninsula and from large urban districts downstate, students with special needs, and students with varying cultural and socioeconomic backgrounds. As we adjusted to this less comfortable state-level task, we reshaped many of the questions we had discussed earlier: Should we, could we require portfolios for 110,000 Michigan students? What might we ask all Michigan students to write and/or write about? Could we permit students to talk to each other about their writing during a "high-stakes" test? How much time should we provide in a testing situation for writing? Would we consider including a multiple choice section to test editing skills, as so many standardized tests have done and as testing and measurement specialists encouraged us to do? Could we permit 110,000 Michigan students to use computers on an assessment given within the proposed test window of one or two weeks? What accommodations should we recommend for Michigan's ESL and LEP students? And how should the writing of over 100,000 students be responded to and/or evaluated? What should the evaluative criteria consist of?

When all was said and done, and after some modifications by the Michigan Department of Education, Figure 3.3 shows what we created.

GETTING RESPONSE FROM OTHER STAKEHOLDER GROUPS

The Part 1 provision for gathering portfolio pieces emerged from conflict between writing teachers and the attorneys and psychometricians. Although most of us who were teachers of writing used portfolios in our own classes, we discovered from research of writing assessment in other states that what seemed so appealing in Vermont, for example, was not practical or even possible for us at this point in Michigan. Someone reminded us that there are more students in the city of Detroit than in the whole state of Vermont. And we discovered that Vermont's initial experience with portfolio scoring resulted in such low reliability that only school scores were, initially at least, being released (Viadero, 1993).

Believing so strongly in our own classroom experiences with portfolios, some of us wondered if, in spite of others' difficulties, *we* might be able to learn from other states' mistakes and overcome or avoid their problems. In reality, however, our optimism could not stand up to the attorneys' and psychometricians' insistence that high-stakes statewide testing, as initially legislated, could not deny students a high

Part 1—Reporting and Reflecting (30 + 5 minutes)

- Students will bring two pieces of writing to be included in their test folder.
- One piece must be from a class other than English.
- These pieces will be counted but not scored during the first years of writing assessment.
- Students will write about one or both of their portfolio pieces of writing and/or about their own writing process.
- This piece will be composed quickly.
- This piece will be scored as single-draft writing.

Part 2—Composing and Communicating Meaning:
Reading/Viewing/Writing/Talking Tasks (40 + 5 minutes)

- Students will read/view brief items focused on a theme.
- Students will write in response to a question posed about the items read and/or viewed.
- This piece will be quickly written, exploratory writing.
- This piece will be scored as single-draft writing.
- Students will discuss their responses with a small group of peers, followed by groups reporting ideas generated in groups to the whole class.

Part 3—Composing and Communicating Meaning:
Extended Writing Task (110 + 5 minutes)

- Students will compose an extended piece of writing.
- Topic and writing task will be linked thematically with the Part 2 items.
- Students will be encouraged to consider a variety of approaches to the writing task.
- Students will be encouraged to revise and edit this piece.
- This piece will be scored as a polished piece of writing.

Figure 3.3. Michigan High School Proficiency Test: Writing

school diploma—legally, a property right—on assessment measures that were still "experimental" in any way. The reporting and reflecting task in Part 1 is, therefore, a compromise. But it grew out of our classroom experience as teachers of writing because we understood that reflection and self-evaluation (a) builds on writing workshop experiences involving writing conferences and writing response groups and (b) helps students become articulate about their own writing strategies and processes.

In addition, Part 1 is task-oriented. The student enjoys the rare advantage of writing about something he or she knows more about than the reader—namely, his or her reflective analysis of an earlier writing experience. As such, the task is quite different from the typical assessment prompt that asks the student to address a topic or respond to a text. For example,

> Look over the two pieces of your writing that you have in front of you. Identify ideas or wording that you think work well in your pieces of writing and explain why they do.

The Part 2 writing task grew out of classroom writing-to-learn experiences in which student writers discover meaning by writing in response to materials read or viewed. As is true in classroom settings, students who take the HSPT can generate ideas for writing by actively thinking and writing about the brief items they view focused on a particular theme presented in the writing task. A Part 2 task based on the theme of "justice" might include a few quotations such as "Injustice anywhere is a threat to justice everywhere" (Martin Luther King, Jr.); "Justice becomes injustice when it makes two wounds on a head that deserves one" (Congo proverb); and "Justice cannot be for one side alone, but must be for both. . . ." (Eleanor Roosevelt). Also included as a spark to thinking about justice might be a "Peanuts" cartoon in which Linus and Snoopy are standing in the rain. Linus says to Snoopy, "Remember, it rains on the just and the unjust." In response, Snoopy thinks to himself, "But why us in-betweens?" Students are directed to write for 20 minutes on the question, "What does 'justice' mean to you?" by responding to the materials and relating them to their own knowledge and experience. After the writing, students can continue to generate and possibly to begin shaping ideas as they discuss the topic with their classmates.

Students continue to think and write in Part 3, this time in a more extended way about the theme and with a specific writing task. As we considered how to organize this major section of the assessment, we realized that in our classrooms many of us resist assigning topics and forms. But almost all of us include at least occasional common assignments for all students focused on a particular topic, which we believe is a reasonable real-world task, and felt comfortable with the compromise of specifying the topics but not a particular mode of discourse for the state HSPT writing tasks. Instead, we designed the Part 3 task to suggest several approaches students might take to the specific writing task, always including a final invitation to consider another approach of the student writer's choice. Working with the topic of "justice," students might be given the following specific task:

In dealing with people who have wronged others, some choose justice; some, revenge; some, mercy. Write a paper in which you examine how this choice affects the people involved in the dispute.

You might, for example, do one of the following:

explain why justice for you may not be justice for someone else

OR

argue whether some groups in our country have less access to justice than others

OR

consider a time when you felt a situation wasn't fair and you tried to get justice

OR

examine whether television and movies encourage revenge

OR

take any of several other approaches to discussing this idea.

Although our original intention was to provide scheduled breaks in the writing process for students to confer, we lost the battle to maintain this feature because of testing and measurement concerns about equity issues, that is, about individual students providing or receiving "help" that might skew their individual performances. We knew from classroom experience that even when students pick up ideas for their writing from others, what they create and how they handle and develop those ideas still result in original pieces. We were able to retain the time for student discussion of the topic in Part 2, however, because the discussion occurs after students have composed their quick-write response and before they know the specific writing task for the major piece. Thus, the activities of Part 2, including talking about the topic/theme, serve primarily as a prewriting experience in preparation for Part 3.

The length of the test brought resistance from another important stakeholder group. School administrators, particularly principals, insisted that our original timeline (providing 140 minutes for Part 3) was impossible and unnecessary. Principals felt enormously pressured when the legislature decided to tie state accreditation to test results, and they especially protested the proposed interruption of their daily school schedule to accommodate the long block of time requested for the new Writing test. The State Department of Education trimmed 30 minutes off our 140-minute recommendation. The current 110-minute block still draws considerable criticism, however. A recent statement Brinkley (1997) presented to a House of Representatives Education Subcommittee, therefore, included the following rationale:

Here's why Part 3 takes so much time: Michigan's Writing HSPT [High School Proficiency Test] is grounded in over twenty years of research that's been conducted by studying the habits of both student and professional writers. Researchers have discovered that good writing of significant, thoughtful pieces of writing usually takes a significant block of time (see Emig, 1971; Perl, 1980; Flower & Hayes, 1981). Research shows that few writers follow the model many of us were taught—that is, generate a thesis statement, construct a formal outline, then write five paragraphs. Many, if not most writers begin with a variety of possibilities, talk ideas over with a colleague or friend, and allow the writing to lead them to their central focus and to their best support and development. As thoughts emerge and are shaped, writers refine ideas and the language to express them. Eventually, they revise, edit, proofread and "publish" their writing (i.e., they mail a letter, turn in a report, or submit a completed assignment).

We are both involved with current discussions to design the next set of tests that begin in 2001. Because of school administrators' protests about the length of time required for testing, a further restriction on time is likely, probably involving the loss of another 20 minutes.

To confirm that the curricular framework and the assessment plan would be based on current classroom practice, we conducted nine site meetings around the state and gathered questionnaire data about current classroom practices. What we learned in those meetings was revealing in several ways. We sensed teachers' frustration at having to deal with one more thing that was being done "to them." They feared what we might create, and they came to the site meetings prepared for the worst: They came prepared to disapprove of the emerging assessment plan. When all was said and done, however, we were more often met with positive responses and thank yous from English language arts teachers, who felt affirmed as they recognized many of their own classroom strategies within a statewide test. One annoyed principal called early in the process to get information about the design of the test. Once he heard the description, he responded in amazement, saying, "Well, our students should do very well on this assessment. We already do all those things."

We occasionally were caught off guard and disappointed, however, when our own perspectives contrasted noticeably with the views of some other classroom teachers. Some seemed to favor writing as a linear, straightforward set of steps, and they feared that 11th graders would not write "lengthy responses" and thus wouldn't know what to do with 110 minutes. Interestingly, some teachers, especially those who had participated in Michigan's National Writing Project summer institutes—protested that 110 minutes was too short. More discouraging were negative attitudes that some teachers expressed about students and their abilities as writers. One teacher sarcastically questioned, "Is your purpose to test clear, concise, correct communication or thought processes?" (Apparently she approved of the first option but not the second.) She insisted, "Maturity of thinking is not a hallmark of the majority of my 10th or 11th grade students."

FROM GRADING IN THE CLASSROOM TO IDENTIFYING CRITICAL LITERACY

As teachers, many of us experienced one of our first teaching crises years ago when we faced our first batch of student essays. We believed that our primary responsibility was to read and grade these papers. We recognized that this task was part of what being an English teacher meant, but many of us were not prepared for how difficult that part of the job would be. Not that it was hard to identify spelling errors and disorganized paragraphs or to praise a persuasively argued thesis. Rather, an uneasiness gnawed at us when we tried to reconcile those supposedly objective tasks with the memories of evaluation tucked away from the days when we were students. Our job got more complicated when we began to hear our individual students' voices between the lines and to see their faces appear on the pages before us. For many of us, we resolved the crisis by swearing always to respond to individual student writing in terms of what would keep each student eager to write and learning to be a better writer—although we knew that doing so meant that we would never get papers "graded" quickly and that our book bags would always be filled with student papers.

Fortunately, conference sessions and writing projects eventually helped us discover ways to lighten the paper load somewhat. We discovered that it was not necessary or even wise to mark everything that we thought needed comment or correction. And we convinced parents that we did not need to read everything our students wrote, that as long as we felt compelled to read everything, our students would never do enough writing. We conducted writing conferences, taught students to do peer conferencing, and established writing centers so that face-to-face response could replace written response. Through it all, however, we were still faced with evaluating writing and writers. However, by this time, grading was a task we were better prepared to do because our judgments were informed not only by the pieces of writing students gave us to read but by our greater interaction with student writers.

In fact, grading in the insular environment of the classroom does more than assess. It enforces compliance with the rules and structures the teacher has established. Teachers may use grades to encourage, reward, and punish. More lenient grading at the beginning of a term may gradually be replaced by more stringent grading later. Conversely, tough grading at the beginning gets attention, and more lenient grading later may create the illusion that students are making progress. A student whose work shows improvement may get an inflated grade. A student who can do better but is not exerting enough effort can get a punitive lower grade. Some of these characteristics of writing assessment in classrooms reflect the teacher's role of mentor. Only the classroom teacher has the knowledge and authority to use the grading system to support instruction in these ways. But this supportive grading policy may sometimes be at odds with the demands of large-scale assessment. Despite its supportiveness it can be inconsistent, unfair, and arbitrary.

Indeed, in the matter of evaluating written work, teachers enjoy an extraordinary degree of autonomy. It is hard to think of another profession whose practitioners are able to do such critically important work without review by peers. It is true, of course, that teachers may be accountable to students and parents for their grading, but only under rare circumstances are they accountable to their colleagues. There may be collegial involvement in curriculum design and choice of textbooks, and teachers may occasionally visit each others' classrooms to observe methods. But second guessing their grading is almost always out of bounds. These observations are not intended to encourage fresh intrusion into the teacher's domain but simply to describe the professional practices that make scoring writing in a large-scale assessment problematic for its designers and threatening to both teachers and students. Students lose the nurturing context of the classroom. Teachers lose control. And others, remembering their own experience as students, might well expect large-scale anonymous scoring to be even more mysterious and whimsical than the grading of their erstwhile teachers. These concerns raise the specter of "subjectivity."

The notion that subjectivity would be in any way connected to a large-scale assessment raises hackles in these scientific and technical times. It is fairly easy to get people to agree about the value of direct testing of writing by having students actually write. The logic is plain, and it should follow just as plainly that such writing needs to be scored by qualified people. However, at this point in the argument people start to hedge their bets. They transfer their images of classroom grading with its message-laden pedagogical baggage to the large-scale assessment and assume the writing samples will be scored by thousands of teachers rendering autonomous judgments. Indeed, at one of our preliminary reports at a field site, a teacher remarked with bemused resignation, "I suppose this means I'm going to have to take home even more essays to read and grade," revealing a lack of understanding even among teaching professionals of how writing assessment can be standardized. Some teachers and administrators in the state seemed completely unfamiliar with large-scale writing assessment. One teacher commented, "I see no fair way to evaluate the writing portions. Three teachers + three papers = many grades."

The purpose of the statewide writing assessment was not simply to identify writing that was clearly incompetent and unsatisfactory because of minimal content or extensive errors, or both. Nor was the purpose of the assessment to identify writing that was exceptionally impressive, either because it made a dramatic and forceful presentation or because it displayed a flair for language, or both. There was no point in putting 110,000 students through this ordeal every year just to identify those who need remedial work or those who should get prizes. The focus of attention would have to be primarily on the vast middle group—that is, those whose writing was generally free of error and clear but superficial and those whose writing was generally free of error and clear but also more sharply focused and more richly developed. The distinction between those two groups is the distinction between literacy and critical literacy. If the assessment program was going to have an impact on teaching and learning, it would have to be along the lines of moving students from the second group to the third, from literacy to critical literacy.

RESTRAINED BY TESTING AND MEASUREMENT PURPOSES

Perhaps because of the teachers' conflicts about teaching versus testing roles, we frequently reminded ourselves that our primary goal was to do what was best for all the students in Michigan. We especially tried to keep this goal in mind during encounters with the attorneys and the psychometricians, whose concerns and agendas often seemed foreign to us as teachers. Specifically, the conflict of roles was most dramatic when we faced the challenge of determining how to design an assessment that would be legally defensible (Lutz, 1996). In spite of our charge by the state to design a performance assessment and not to create a minimum competency test, the attorneys and testing and measurement specialists seemed generally uncomfortable with performance assessment and kept reminding us of past court cases, as if the future had to be shaped primarily by what had been legally defensible in the past. In spite of the compromises we were forced to make or accept, in the end we successfully resisted some of the "suggestions" offered, especially the thought of creating a series of short quick-write prompts or including multiple-choice sections.

The testing and measurement people who worked closely with Michigan's Writing group did so from a variety of perspectives. One intermediate school district testing specialist worked as part of our management team. He represented a school district perspective, but also served as a helpful consultant who tried to understand our curricular concerns and helped us understand the testing and measurement constraints. The former head of the Michigan Assessment of Educational Progress (MEAP) also worked with us on an occasional basis in a similar capacity. Other testing and measurement persons, some of them with national reputations, advised all of the content groups and/or served on the state's technical advisory committee. Another testing and measurement specialist, employed by MEAP, met occasionally with us, usually to convey some message from the Department of Education and especially to try to convince us to stick to traditional methods. Generally speaking, however, the State Department of Education gave us considerable leeway during this phase of the process. White (1996) has identified the assessment characteristics that testing company professionals prefer:

- Assessment that produces scores quickly and cheaply;
- Assessment that reduces the complexity of writing and of the teaching of writing but that allows the data collected to imply complex measurement;
- Assessment that weighs heavily surface features of writing and dialect features of edited American English;
- Assessment that leads to the sorting of students according to existing social patterns; and
- Assessment whose meaning depends heavily on statistical explanations of sufficient complexity to invite misuse of scores. (p. 20)

Testing firms try to develop systems of evaluation free of the interpersonal elements of classroom grading. They routinely compare the results of direct and indirect measures of the same group of students and argue that a good correlation between the two indicates that the costly and less easily quantified direct measure could be scrapped. But the arguments favoring direct assessment of writing are so compelling, especially those arguments based on the linkage between assessment and teaching, that methods of direct scoring of writing have been closely studied and refined.

The many variations of direct assessment fall into two broad categories: analytic and holistic. In both types, trained readers assign numerical scores to student writing samples. Analytic scoring focuses on criteria that are scored separately. This method comes closest to replicating classroom grading because there is a clear linkage between the separate scores and writing instruction. The reported scores thus provide the kind of feedback students, parents, and teachers expect because the categories of analytic scoring can be designed to support a particular curriculum. On the other hand, because the categories are necessarily tied to written products, the numerical results give the impression that writing can be defined as the sum of separate elements of a text. If analytic scores were restricted to categories like "organization," "syntax," "diction," or "mechanics," the response in classrooms to these reported scores would fall short of advancing the kind of critical literacy that the Michigan framework sought to promote. This, plus the following reasons—greater time and expense required, the likelihood that many students' analytic scores would mirror their holistic scores, and greater difficulty in achieving satisfactory interreader reliability—led us to recommend holistic scoring for all three of the writing pieces.

PUBLIC AND POLITICAL AGENDAS

We realized the political nature of the rhetoric of scoring guides and descriptions of performance levels. Who would be well served? Who not so? We heard about scoring rubrics that identified students' performance using rigid, militaristic terms, such as "inadequate command" or "superior command," whereas others used much less harsh-sounding labels such as "apprentice" or "distinguished." We knew that we valued content and ideas at least as much as we valued use of writing conventions but were aware that many in business and industry might not. Therefore, we steered clear of analytic rubrics that heavily weighted students' performance based on surface features and grammatical conventions while slighting content, organization, and style.

We knew that our decision to use single holistic scores (an average of the two scores assigned by the readers) would well achieve the state's purpose of determining which students could produce proficient writing. But we realize in retrospect that we should have paid more attention to the public's need for more reported test information. Certainly students and their parents and teachers and administrators all need to know how individual students performed on the assessment. The outcry of these groups has now grown to such proportions that legislators are calling for more detailed score reporting. As writing teachers, we had considerable experience working with the need for feedback for students, parents, and administrators, but as writing test designers we have learned a new lesson about the public and political interest in students' performance. The state legislature has a stake in the test, because it was their mandate that created the tests in the first place. Now they too are feeling the heat when angry parents (and teachers, for that matter) complain about not getting enough information about individual student performance.

Our own situation was, of course, very political in many ways. With so many stakeholder groups trying to influence our decisions, we felt pulled in many directions. What is striking, however, is the fact that during the time we were discussing the test design, we were working under contract with the State. Thus, we were not simply assisting state employees to design the assessment. Instead, we had a contractual agreement to produce the curricular framework and assessment plan for the test and could, at least during this phase of the process, control the work of our committees and make the decisions. In our experience in Michigan we found it useful every now and then—when we felt pressured by some of the state's consultants—to say among ourselves, "Wait a minute; they are working for us; this is what we want; if it can't be done, prove it." Dealing with the multiple hidden agendas behind government action and policy, however, is a bit more difficult.

Although we operated in good faith, trusting that the tests we created could serve a positive purpose for many of Michigan's students, and although the testing company, ACT, operated from its own profit motive, the state legislators and the governor had a very different agenda in mind. Test results could be used to bring discredit to the public schools, demonstrate that the schools are doing a great job, increase or decrease funding, promote charter schools and voucher programs, take revenge on teachers' unions, or even all of these simultaneously.

In the end, the State Department of Education, not the Writing group, selected Michigan's labels for levels of proficiency. The labels selected—"proficiency," "novice," and "not-yet-novice"—have generated more criticism than perhaps any other feature of the state's tests. They are held up to ridicule in almost every conversation about the HSPT. Even worse, however, is the fact that the Governor has made public speeches identifying as a "failure" anyone who did not earn the "proficient" score and thereby did not qualify for endorsement. In doing so, the Governor and other commentators have taken an especially pejorative view of the "novice" category. A designation like "satisfactory" instead of "novice" might have generated less pain and misunderstanding. The distinction between "satisfactory" (or even "novice") performance and "proficient" performance corresponds, in fact, to the distinction between functional literacy and critical literacy, and the political heat produced in the aftermath of the first two administrations of the test demonstrates again the power and pervasiveness of idealized but singular characterizations of literacy.

THE EFFECTS OF STATEWIDE TESTING ON TEACHERS

An MCTE position statement that was distributed soon after the curricular framework and assessment plan had been submitted to the Department of Education reflected the ambivalence most of us still felt at that interim point:

> While we regret what we regard as a widespread overemphasis on large-scale testing, we have carried out the framework project because we care deeply about preparing students for whatever future they will face and because we believe that writing, because of its power to generate new knowledge as well as solve problems, can play a central role throughout our students' lives. (quoted in Brinkley, 1993, p. 3)

In retrospect, we realize that as designers of an external statewide writing assessment, we were stripped of our favorite roles. At every turn we had to focus on reconciling our familiar roles as teachers of writing with our unfamiliar roles of test-makers. For most of us as teachers of writing in student-centered classrooms, we like to think of ourselves primarily as observers, responders, listeners, encouragers, and coaches. We like to put off as long as possible the donning of the judge's robes. But as we became test designers, we had to accept a new role in an unfamiliar culture that was decontextualized and highly politicized.

ACHIEVING OUR PURPOSE

White (1996) suggests that if teachers controlled assessment practices,

> the ideal assessment would likely be an expanded version of classroom assessment—such as we see now in portfolios. Such an assessment would be performative and direct, include many kinds of writing, resist numerical reduction, be time-consuming and expensive, and incorporate such matters as revision, creativity, and discovery as part of the construct evaluated. (p. 14)

In many respects, this is the kind of assessment teachers in Michigan have created. It is technically not a portfolio assessment, although the test has a portfolio dimension.

On the other hand, White (1996) suggests that if the testing companies alone controlled and defined assessment practices,

> the ideal assessment would likely consist of a series of multiple-choice tests, with occasional impromptu essays added . . . mainly as window dressing and a public-relations effort to please the teachers. . . . The assessments would be passive and indirect, focus on surface scribal and dialectal features, allow numerical reduction, be efficient and cheap, and use correctness as a major part of the construct evaluated. (p. 20)

For the most part, this is the kind of test that Michigan teachers resisted, having realized the disconnection between what has been taught and what is tested and the influence such tests exert on the curriculum.

In many ways in Michigan we have achieved what White calls "the needed miracle." White realistically acknowledges, "The stakeholders stand at wholly different positions and are bound to see writing assessment from where they stand. And with so much at stake, they cannot shift position without sacrificing what they are and do" (p. 23). White then calls for stakeholder groups to learn the value of views other than their own. He calls for going "beyond the boundaries of the comfortable" in terms of professional niches: "those boundaries must be crossed if the future of writing assessment lies, as I believe it does, in negotiating and compromising among the interest groups involved" (p. 24).

Those of us from a variety of stakeholder groups who were involved in the development of the HSPT know well the boundaries that have been crossed and the negotiation and compromise that have taken place. Although we know some districts have created some indefensible test-prep programs, we also know that more students are using in-process journals as they reflect on their own writing processes. And more teacher-student writing conferences and writing response groups are taking place. More students are becoming articulate about writing, using retrospective journals turned in with their final papers, and are using writing to learn in many of their classes. More attention is being given in Michigan's classrooms to writing thoughtful, better reasoned arguments and carefully crafted sentences. In short, we believe that more students are using writing to challenge old assumptions and to consider new possibilities; that is, more students are becoming critically literate.

Unfortunately, Michigan citizens in general still know so little about large-scale writing assessment and how scoring can be done reliably that parents' letters to the editor frequently express skepticism about "subjective grading." Thus, the Michigan Department of Education, Board of Education, Governor, and Legislature face a continuing challenge to build stronger literacy connections with students, parents, teachers, administrators, and school board and community members—all of whom need information and assurance that they and their children are being well served.

REFERENCES

Brinkley, E. H. (1993, August/September). Michigan group designs assessment frameworks and is paid for its efforts. *Council-Grams* [News and information for leaders of the National Council of Teachers of English], pp. 1-3.

Brinkley, E. H. (1997, July 22). Statements presented to the Michigan House of Representatives Education Subcommittee on the High School Proficiency Test. Lansing, MI.

Britton, J., Burgess, T., Martin, N., McLeod, A., & Rosen, H. (1975). *The development of writing abilities.* London: Macmillan Education.

Emig, J. (1971). *The composing processes of twelfth graders.* Urbana, IL: National Council of Teachers of English.

Flower, L. S., & Hayes, J. R. (1982). A cognitive process theory of writing. *College Composition and Communication, 32,* 365-387.

Lutz, W. D. (1996). Legal issues in the practice and politics of assessment in writing. In E. D. White, W. D. Lutz, & S. Kamusikiri (Eds.), *Assessment of writing: Politics, policies, practices* (pp. 33-44). New York: Modern Language Association of America.

Michigan Council of Teachers of English. (1993). Michigan proficiency examination framework for writing.

Michigan State Board of Education. (1985). Michigan essential goals and objectives for writing. Lansing, MI.

Michigan State Board of Education. (1991). Michigan core curriculum outcomes and position statement on core curriculum. Lansing, MI.

Perl, S. (1980). Understanding composing. *College Composition and Communication, 31,* 363-369.

Sudol, R. A. (1996). Assessing writing: A response. *Language Arts Journal of Michigan, 12*(1), 59-63.

U. S. Department of Education. (1993). *Adult literacy and lifelong learning.* Washington, DC: U. S. Government Printing Office.

Viadero, D. (1993, November 10). RAND urges overhaul in Vt.'s pioneering writing test. *Education Week,* p. 1.

White, E. M. (1996). Power and agenda setting in writing assessment. In E. D. White, W. D. Lutz, & S. Kamusikiri (Eds.), *Assessment of writing: Politics, policies, practices* (pp. 9-24). New York: Modern Language Association of America.

4

Service Learning and the Literacy Connection*

Emily Nye
New Mexico Institute of Mining and Technology

Morris Young
Miami University of Ohio

Literacy may mean rather diverse things to different people. To me it meant the ability to stay healthy, thus survive and succeed, by being honest and open about the way I feel.
—Melissa [J3: 3][1]

*We would like to thank Caroline Taylor Clark, Anne Ruggles Gere, Deborah Williams Minter, Pamela Moss, and Carole Yee for their careful readings and thoughtful comments. The "Learning Communities" course was funded by a FIPSE grant.

[1]References after cited course material refer to unpublished project documents. Citations for these documents include the writing assignment and the page number (e.g., J1 = Journal #1, FP = Final Project, PP = Project Proposal). In all cases, the authors have received written consent to include these documents in published accounts of this project. All names have been changed to maintain anonymity.

In a course we taught at The University of Michigan, we worked to create a class experience that would bring together students' evolving concepts of literacy with the hands-on work of tutoring elementary and middle school children. We open with a quote from Melissa, one of our students, to suggest the very broad definitions and uses of literacy that we engaged in class. But we also find Melissa's comments compelling because she identifies how literacy provided a connection for her beyond the classroom and as a part of her everyday life. Other students in our class made similar remarks, contributing to a better understanding of their learning, development, and tutoring of literacy. The students' writings and experiences became the textual material for our class as we worked to see literacy not simply as a theoretical concept or practical skill but as infused in the daily lives and experiences of people. In this chapter we explore the connections students made between their lives, the lives of the children they tutored, and literacy.

Our course, "Learning Communities," was developed as part of a larger research project that focused on the effects of service learning on the university experience of undergraduate students.[2] Although offered through the School of Education, the course occupied a marginalized position in the university's economy of requirements because it did not provide distribution credits for any major and was an elective course for students. Students who enrolled ranged from freshmen to seniors, and they often cited their interest in performing community service for taking the class.[3] The course itself was designed to raise critical questions about how students learn, how we as teachers/tutors learn as well as teach, and how we are all involved in a collaborative process of education in one form or another. Students explored definitions and applications of the term "literacy" through participation in a weekly seminar and their work as literacy tutors at two after-school programs in Ann Arbor (a community center program for elementary students and a middle school).

The service learning format of the course brought together the theoretical ideas and discussions from our seminar with the practical experience encountered on-site.[4] The course addressed a wide variety of

---

[2]In their essay, "Learning Literacies," Minter, Gere, and Keller-Cohen (1995) discuss the changing and multiple conceptions of literacy held by the undergraduate students who participated in previous semesters of the "Learning Communities" course.

[3]There are many opportunities at the university for students to enroll in courses or programs that also perform community service. Our course was slightly different because of the combination of an academic seminar with tutoring in the community.

[4]See Anson (1992) and Herzberg (1994) for descriptions of similar service learning courses that integrate on-site tutoring work into an academic course. All three courses viewed the tutoring as an important component of the class but not the primary focus.

issues centered around the broad theme of literacy. Weekly reading and discussion themes included discussing the meaning of literacy, exploring the cultural contexts of literacy (using historical and anthropological texts), examining the use and representations of literacy in our contemporary communities, and considering the connections between race, class, gender, and literacy. In addition to these themes, we also introduced students to teacher research practices as a way for them to approach these complex issues about literacy and had them think critically about their work as tutors through journal writing and a final project based on their tutoring experience.[5]

Using teacher research practices to frame part of the course proved to be important because students found themselves in educational situations that required their immediate attention without any easy solutions readily available. Recent composition scholarship has theorized the classroom as a contact zone, "social spaces where cultures meet, clash, and grapple with each other" (Pratt, 1991, p. 34). Our course perhaps foregrounded the contact zone even more as students were placed in spaces very different than those they had experienced previously at the university. They found themselves in multiple contact zones where they had to negotiate what they perceived to be the competing interests of tutoring children with learning about themselves, and where they had to rethink their positions in the university because of their work in very different communities just beyond the borders of the university. They often expressed frustration with the situation, not knowing quite how to bring these different experiences together. One student, Arnelle, reacting strongly to what she saw as an emphasis on theory and on the *tutor's* learning, wrote in her journal, "I am there to help the students, so that's what I focus on. I'm starting to not like this class so much, and if I had the choice of whether to take it again: if I could go back in time, I do not think I would enroll." Another student, Rick, had a quite different perception of the class. He wrote, "A great deal of invaluable discussion came from the free debates about very touchy issues. It seemed that we had a lot of frank and yet very polite debates about very touchy issues. Most of the time if you have those kinds of discussions in class, people get upset."

The two afterschool programs at which undergraduates tutored were located just 10 to 15 minutes away from the university by car. Students and instructors carpooled, and the drives to and from the programs often became an additional site of discussion. The afterschool tutoring program at Eastside Community Center (operated by a nonprofit community organization) served about 40 students from Eastside

---

[5]See Appendix A for a course syllabus and a complete listing of weekly themes and teacher research material.

Elementary (located next door to the center). The children were usually referred to the program by the school or registered by parents who sought additional support and/or afterschool care for their children. Tutoring at Eastside was held Monday through Thursday for students in grades K-5. A full-time social worker (employed by the community center) coordinated the program and handled site logistics. Volunteers came from other schools and the community as well as from the University of Michigan. The coordinator matched each tutor to a child (or several children).

These tutoring groups met consistently for 15 weeks. Tutors usually helped their assigned children with homework, but grade appropriate worksheets were also available at the center for the tutors. Games such as Pick-Up Sticks and the ever-popular Connect Four were also available once the children finished their homework. The afterschool program at Southside Middle School was less structured than Eastside due to its status as a drop-in program. Southside has had an afterschool program for a number of years with a faculty member serving as supervisor. The children who came to the school library from 3:00-4:00 in the afternoon were there for a variety of reasons. Some were referred to the program by teachers who felt additional help was needed. Others were there because their parents wanted additional support for them or they had no one at home during the afternoon hours right after school. Because the children "dropped in" the undergraduate tutors worked with a number of different children and were not assigned to work one-on-one like the tutors at Eastside. However, the tutors often developed strong relationships with certain children and would work with them one-on-one if the situation allowed.

In describing the service learning course he taught, Herzberg (1994) raises several concerns that we also share and found emerging in our own class. One of Herzberg's main concerns is that students who participate in service learning courses often only develop a surface awareness of the social issues they encounter. He writes, "If our students regard social problems as chiefly or only personal, then they will not search beyond the person for a systemic explanation" (p. 309). When the students in our class express their interest in tutoring they are perhaps also expressing an unconscious desire to help a certain type of child. They expect to work with children who are having difficulties, and who need their help. It is this desire and construction of the child who attends tutoring (as opposed to the child who *needs* tutoring) that may keep the students from moving beyond the personal (or private) to the political (or public) reasons for educational disparity. To address this issue we read several articles in class that challenge the many labels often placed on children (e.g., Michaels; Polakow; Taylor & Dorsey-Gaines). And unlike Herzberg's class, which did adult literacy tutoring at a shelter, our students tutored at afterschool programs located at or next door to the schools. Although we also faced the difficulty Herzberg did in leading students "to transcend their own deeply-ingrained belief in individualism and meritocracy in their analysis of the reasons for the illiteracy they see" (p. 312), we also saw students begin to actively address systemic problems. This was due in part to the student's exposure to "agents" of the system—teachers, administrators, homework—and their effects on the children—both positive and negative—because the afterschool programs were located at or near the schools. The fact that we worked with children also accounts for some of the willingness to place responsibility with the "system" and not with the subjects; Herzberg's students believed the adults they worked with were at least partially responsible for their situations. Our students may not have developed the very deep understanding of the structural problems that Herzberg seeks, but they recognized the children were not responsible for their circumstances.

Even with this awareness, there was still a tendency to ask why a child was not achieving and to conclude first that it was a lack of effort and poor concentration. As the term continued, however, the students began to shift the "blame" and looked for other causes for their child's learning situation. Anson (1992) has described this as an ideological change, something that occurs in the students as they continue to work with the children and develop their own strategies for tutoring as well as their own methods of assessment and evaluation. Herzberg is right when he describes the discomfort students feel when asked to abandon their beliefs in equal opportunity and meritocracy: "Did they not deserve, did they not earn their place in school and society?" (p. 314). We found in our class that this was even more true when we discussed unstable and unfamiliar notions of literacy and raised the possibility that alternative dialects and discourses could function just as well. Some students resisted vehemently, arguing that a standard discourse and literacy was needed in order to have a society. How could students not react this way? After all, their presence in an elite university was affirmation that they had learned the standard discourse and literacy well, and had done what was required of them in order to attend the university. But as they continued to work with the children and to examine their experiences in their journal writing, they became more willing to let go of these markers of legitimacy and more likely to question in complicated ways the way our culture talks about literacy.

CONNECTING WITH LITERACY: DESIGNING THE COURSE

Our emphasis on journal writing and the reading of experiences, both past and present, allowed students to reformulate their ideas about literacy and education. We did not ask them to dismiss their past achievement in order to have them adopt new ideas about literacy. We did not ask them to rewrite their past to account for their current experiences. Rather we engaged what Bleich (1995) has called a "pedagogy of disclosure," a theory and practice of foregrounding an individual's history as "part of the process of presenting opinions, interpretations, and reports of other things" (p. 48). We asked them to use their memory in combination with the hope and promise they brought from their tutoring experiences to inform their readings of the use of literacy in our culture. We asked them to "disclose" portions of their lives in order to inform their practice. We asked them to recognize and reflect on their lives in order to see acts of learning and literacy in the children they tutored which, we hoped, would lead to more productive moments of learning and literacy.

Although our classroom discussions and car rides to the tutoring programs were important sites of disclosure, where students were able to interact more widely with others and their experiences, it was in the journal writing that we saw acts of disclosure more clearly bringing together the multiple experiences, sites, and ideas the students encountered. Part of our conception of the course was to have students develop a more personal view of literacy, to see it in everyday life and as working in more varied situations than they might expect. We designed journal writing assignments based on the reading material for the week but also asked students to draw together experiences from their past and from their tutoring as a way of discussing the week's reading (see Appendix B). We found that asking students to write about their tutoring experiences had several benefits. First, such reflection helped students to see and articulate what was happening on the tutoring site and in themselves. Second, this journal writing gave us a "window" to the students' thoughts and brought us closer to them.

The use of reflective writing has been examined by many composition scholars. Creating a reflective narrative asks a student to examine him-or herself. Carr (1986) argues that the coherence of the self is based in its narrative structure. Witherell (1991) urges teachers to encourage their students to construct such narratives:

> The teller or receiver of such stories can discover connections
> between self and other, penetrate barriers to understanding, and
> come to know more deeply the meanings of his or her own historical
> and cultural narrative. (p. 94)

Finally, Murphy (1993) points out that when we read our students' narratives, learning and teaching become connected. Murphy describes this connection as a kind of intimacy between teacher and student.

Horning (1997) discusses the uses of reflective writing in teaching writing. In a first-term college course, students reflect on their writing process by answering a variety of prompts such as, "A big problem I had in my writing was" or, "My personality did or did not affect a choice I made because of" When students explore these prompts, according to Horning, "they tell us the story of their learning through their reflections on the experience of doing so" (p. 7). Horning, Murphy, and others (Combs, 1995; Rubin, 1994; Witherell, 1991) argue that reflective writing shows us what and how our students are learning.

Recent discussions in composition studies made us aware of the dangers and ethical questions of asking students to disclose very personal and intimate experiences.[6] Thus, when we asked students to write about their experiences, we asked them to frame these discussions in terms of a learning/literacy experience and to make (critical) *connections* with the readings and their tutoring work. Journal prompts ranged from asking students to discuss a "memorable learning experience" to defining "what is literacy" to reflecting on their experience in the course. We evaluated the journals based on how well they integrated the readings, tutoring, and reflection, and we responded to the papers with extensive feedback and a check minus, check, or check plus. Although we employed Bleich's (1995) "pedagogy of disclosure" in our classroom, we also hoped that as students wrote their journals and consciously read their tutoring experiences through their own personal acts of learning and literacy that they would transform the "pedagogy of disclosure" into a pedagogical strategy of making connections not only in their own learning experiences but also with the children they tutored.

Prior to the start of the semester, we collected relevant articles and books about literacy, tutoring, and teacher research. We asked colleagues to share with us names of good sources. After much photocopying, classifying, and reorganizing, we divided the semester into the following categories: Introduction to Literacy and Tutoring, Introduction to Teacher Research, What is Literacy, the Cultural Contexts of Literacy, Portraits of Literacy, Literacy and the Community, Gender and Literacy, and Unofficial Literacies (see Appendix A). For introductory reading, we began with a general article by Pattison that, we felt, was accessible to students yet also challenged them to question the overly simple idea of literacy and the ability to read and write. We also included an article about tutoring, in the hope that students would begin to make connections between themselves and the "ideal" image of a tutor as presented by Stuckey and Alston.

---

[6]See Swartzlander, Pace, and Stamler (1993). See also Bleich (1995).

Next, we introduced the idea of teacher research so that students would see that they, as tutors and literacy workers, had legitimacy as questioners and researchers. Some students were very surprised at the basic concepts of teacher research, particularly those students with backgrounds in more traditional, quantitative investigations. Our initial idea was to supply students with tools for answering their own questions and then to shift to a more critical reading of several definitions of literacy. Two articles, one by Gee and another (in response) by Delpit, proved successful in generating a heated discussion about literacy. We tried to keep a balance of theory/practice articles in each section, so we included an article by Michaels. Students seemed to see how their literacy work with children could be the basis of "narrative" research. The following section, The Cultural Contexts of Literacy, was unsuccessful overall. Students were not particularly interested in the different cultural literacies presented, and they failed to see connections between what the authors described and what they were doing as tutors. The antiquity of the New England primer seemed to be a "turn-off." We later removed these readings from the coursepack.

The next section, Portraits of Literacy, featured an excerpt from Polakow's (1993) book, *Lives on the Edge*. The students said the reading was depressing and disturbing because of the images of poverty and the poor treatment of students by the educational system. Yet later, several students mentioned the reading in their journals as they wrote their own portraits of the children they tutored and constructed fuller pictures of the children's lives. We next provided students with more material on teacher research. At this point, the semester was half over, and we wanted the students to use the readings to help themselves find direction for their final projects. We included several readings from *Inside/Outside: Teacher Research and Knowledge* edited by Cochran-Smith and Lytle. Quite a few students (including Melissa, introduced earlier and who will be discussed later) found ways to incorporate their own questioning about their academic experience with what their tutees were undergoing in school. We also included an article by Anson.

In the final weeks of the class we tried to encourage our students to broaden their views of literacy. Two pieces of fiction ("The Lesson" by Bambara and "Alfred the Great") changed the pace of the class and provided an opportunity to explore larger issues beyond the Michigan classroom and tutoring sites. Both of these readings focused on the education experiences of African American students. We felt that our students were somewhat resistant to engaging in a dialogue about race and gender. This may have been because the African American students resented being the "token" ethnic group presented. Two readings by Gilmore, and one by Jordan, led to several interesting discussions about Black English.

We lacked a strong reading about gender and literacy, but we had students read a short story by Yamamoto. The story describes the relatively normal life of a woman who is able to hide her illiteracy until it eventually costs her her life. Our students interpreted this as a story about class as much as gender. Again, they seemed resistant to take a stand on the possibility of different literacy experiences for females versus males.

Finally, we had a section in the coursepack about Unofficial Literacies, which featured two articles by Hubbard, who examines the use of color in children's art (as a form of literacy), as well as note passing in a sixth grade classroom. Discussing these articles drew some interesting conversation and returned us to where we started: by redefining literacy. We continued to refine and revise the course over the next three semesters.

CONNECTING WITH STUDENTS: ARNELLE AND ALIX

One of the themes that emerged from the undergraduates' journal writing was the reading of the children's lives through their own experiences. Although our journal prompts often asked the undergraduates to think about past experiences to inform their ideas about literacy, the students themselves would take the next step and connect their own lives with the children they tutored. In disclosing portions of their lives in the journal writing, they often began to critically engage themselves, but this was mediated through the lives of the children they tutored. For example, issues of race or gender that emerged in some way in the lives of the children became opportunities for the undergraduates to discuss how these issues affected them. In addressing the difficulties or successes of the children they worked with, in trying to work through complex lives, the undergraduates often discovered the multiple constructions of their own identity. They did not necessarily see themselves reflected in the children (and in some cases made it a point to disidentify themselves), but the undergraduates did begin to understand that in their own education there were also complexities and complications, even in those "positive" experiences that helped get them to this point in their lives. The achievement of attending a major university often overshadowed or romanticized their past. As the writings of Arnelle and Alix reveal, they began to rediscover experiences in their lives that informed their tutoring as well as their learning.

Arnelle is an African American female who grew up in Detroit. She had attended both private and public schools. She appeared to be thriving in her University of Michigan experience. She was a junior majoring in communications, and she hoped to go into advertising. Arnelle tutored on Tuesdays and Thursdays at Southside Middle School and also volunteered through her sorority to tutor on Saturday mornings with a community program for African American students also at Southside.

This was the third class Arnelle had taken with Emily Nye. The other classes were a remedial writing course, followed by a term of first-year composition. She was invited to join "Learning Communities" because she and Nye had enjoyed working together in the past. Arnelle was an expressive and inquisitive student who was not shy about voicing her opinions. She liked to debate issues and argue, and her outspoken personality sometimes alienated her from others in the class. This did not seem to bother Arnelle. She had strong self-esteem and confidence in her abilities. Her journal assignment about a literacy experience revealed why:

> [when she was three] My father recorded me on tape so I could hear myself. . . . Hearing myself reinforced the fact that I had made a big accomplishment. Moreover, I feel that moment was kind of the start of something big for me. This was my realization of how "smart" I was. Therefore, by the time I started kindergarten, I had already internalized the fact that I was smart. [J6: 2]

In kindergarten, the guidance counselor would pull Arnelle from class to show off her intelligence. In particular, Arnelle impressed teachers with her extraordinary ability to count. She wrote:

> I [only] counted to 100 because when I tried to keep going, Ms. A. would make me be quiet. I figured, hey, if that impresses you, there's more. Likewise, with kindergarten class, I couldn't figure out why the teacher thought she was teaching us our names, addresses, and telephone numbers. Hey, that was each individual's personal common knowledge. Of course we know, I thought! [J1: 4]

Arnelle's view assumed that memorization was synonymous with intelligence and, furthermore, any child should be able to memorize. This became a recurring theme in her classroom discussions as she always complained about the poor ability of the middle school students to know their multiplication tables.

In her final project Arnelle describes an experience during her own middle school years that provides us with a clue about how she developed this attitude toward math. However, in this same description Arnelle begins to realize something about herself and her way of learning that moves away from this rigid attachment to memorization. She was competing in a national math contest, and had progressed to the playoff rounds. She and her opponent were tied, and her opponent was cracking under the pressure:

He got nervous and began to cry, so the boy used a sure proof tactic to make a comeback. He set a goal with a solution that he had memorized. Someone had taught it to him right before the playoffs in case he got into a tight fix (just as he did). . . . On the one hand, I felt bad for losing because I thought of the championships in terms of the champs being the smartest intellectually. It was not until I understood that learning does not mean memorizing that I realized that his win was pure luck. [FP: 3]

As Arnelle reflected on her education, she realized that education transcended memorization. Nye recalled Arnelle's disappointment when she failed to make the first-year composition class upon her entrance to The University of Michigan. In her final project for "Learning Communities," Arnelle expressed her revised theory about learning and then applied it to her work with Lawrence, the sixth grader whom she tutored. Arnelle reflected:

Until I came to the university, my reasons and goals for learning were the same: to please my family. Now that learning has taken on a whole new meaning for me, I actually expect to get some type of understanding or enhanced knowledge from whatever I am learning. While my reason for learning is to excel in my field of study, my goal is to reach an acme level in an advertising firm. In other words, the reason I am learning is to attain my goal; my goal being my reward for learning. [FP: 4]

She continued:

Although I did not learn early on, I know now what helps one to learn is knowing how they learn best: what motivates them to learn, what type of environment is most appropriate for them to study, their ultimate goal or what reward they expect to gain, etc. The objective of my project was to determine what helps my tutee . . . to learn best by observing his habits, his work, and taking a look at his family situation and how it influences him.

So [Arnelle and Lawrence's] next objective was to determine what helps Lawrence to learn and whether our conclusions were directed more towards Lawrence or whether they could be applied on a more universal basis. [FP: 4]

Arnelle proceeded to interview Lawrence in order to learn about his family and to determine Lawrence's attitude about learning. Her project broadened as she and Lawrence distributed a survey to 14 eighth graders "to see what they thought teachers could do in order to improve students' learning abilities." Their results showed that 10 students advocated doing more "in-class activities relevant to what they were studying." This brought Arnelle full circle to an observation she made about herself early in the term: "I learn best when the subject I am studying is relative to something in my life."

Arnelle was dedicated in her work with Lawrence and developed a close rapport with him. His academic performance improved. Through her tutoring, Arnelle was able to understand more about herself as a learner. The journal assignments afforded the opportunity to write and reflect about herself and her way of making "an impact on someone's life." Arnelle made these concluding observations:

> Education 317 taught different students various ideas about literacy. The one idea that was most enhanced for me was the idea of learning what helps a person to learn. Although I am not sure that there are areas in the educational and social arenas that play a larger part in the learning process in Lawrence's life, I am sure that helping Lawrence to recognize the importance of learning and how he learns best is a start in enhancing his education. [FP: 10]

Just as Arnelle learned more about herself through her work as a tutor, so did Alix. Alix is an African American female from an industrial, predominately white city in Michigan. Alix was a communications major in her sophomore year who was unsure of her career goal. In class, Alix sat with her friend, Yolanda. In fact, it was Alix who had recruited Yolanda into the class. The two students also tutored at Eastside Community Center on the same days and worked with two fifth graders, Mariah and Rose, who were also good friends.

In class, Alix was quiet and alert. She sometimes initiated class discussion and often responded to the instructors' questions. She responded as readily to comments from fellow students. Her classmates held a high esteem for Alix, perhaps because of her calm composure and articulate discourse. She was especially attuned to questions of race and gender. As a sophomore, she had already taken several introductory courses in the African American studies program, as well as courses in women's studies. Her comments in class were often informed by discussions in these past courses.

At Eastside, Alix was a stellar tutor. She and her tutee, an African American child named Mariah, developed an immediate rapport that resembled that of older-younger siblings. Alix was a creative tutor who initiated several different projects that transcended homework assistance. Often, Yolanda and her tutee, Rose, were included in tutoring activities. Occasionally Alix would exhibit some frustration when Mariah and Rose tried her patience with mischievous behavior. Working with Mariah, Alix seemed to see a vision of herself. This revelation was both enlightening and problematic for Alix. Excerpts from her journal outline how her perceptions of Mariah changed, and how she began to develop larger conclusions about education and identity.

Initially, Alix described Mariah as an intelligent child. She soon discovered that Mariah enjoyed school, was good in reading, but had a weakness in long division problems. Mariah described herself to Alix as "a good friend. I don't look for trouble and I don't like to fight." This comment suggested that Mariah was socially well adjusted. Indeed, she was popular in the tutoring program. Alix maintained this perception of Mariah until she discovered that Mariah tended to cheat at games. In class, we read an excerpt from Polakow's (1993) account of poor children in school. Alix thought about Mariah in the context of class readings:

> After speaking with Mariah about her academics, I asked myself why was Mariah more successful in school than the children in Polokow's article. Mariah was successful, to me, because she has never been labeled or singled out by a teacher. A reason why Mariah may have escaped being labeled could be her quality of life. Mariah lives the "American Dream." She lives in a house with both of her parents and her sister. Mariah never has to worry about where she will sleep or eat, in fact, she may have no worries. Actually, Mariah might not live the "American Dream" but a biased outsider might see her life this way.[J4: 2-3]

This view of Mariah shows that Alix is beginning to judge the child by her own life experience. One may detect an edge of jealousy in this excerpt. Alix has begun to challenge the "appearance" of Mariah as a social and successful African American fifth grader.

Alix's journal entries continued to scrutinize Mariah, by way of scrutinizing Alix herself. For her "Literacy and the Community" journal, Alix chose to describe a key event in her life: membership in her African American culture. She formulated a theory that associates literacy with cultural identity (or identity with cultural literacy). She called her family's move to a predominantly white community a "disturbing experience."

> [t]here was no one like me in the class. As a result, I always conformed to White America. I never forgot I was African-American and I didn't try to be white but I took up their culture instead of my own. I talked like my white friends, listened to their music, and imitated everything they did so I would fit in. I never thought that I was ignoring my own culture but I soon realized that I was and so were my teachers.

Mariah is more fortunate than I was because she has never been the only African-American in her class but I'm almost certain that her culture is not the "mainstream" but it has to be addressed by her teacher. I have Mariah do her academics like reading and writing, multiplication, division and science. But I also ask Mariah things about her culture, like who is Arthur Ashe or I ask her what is her favorite song. I try to tie culture into our tutoring sessions whenever I can. If I would have had someone tutoring me who represented my culture in grade school maybe I wouldn't have waited until high school to accept and appreciate my own culture. [J5: 1, 3]

By looking back at her own life, Alix has created a tutorial role that makes sense to her. She serves as a skills tutor, but also as a role model and cultural teacher to Mariah, Rose, and even Yolanda.

But as Alix continued to contemplate her role, she became disappointed. She questioned Mariah's intellectual development, as well as her cultural identity. In her final journal entry, she wrote:

[w]hen we started the program I saw Mariah as an intelligent girl, and I still do, but she is not ready to go beyond her grade level. I guess my expectations of Mariah were really high and she could not meet them. I have begun to just do fifth grade level things with her and she enjoys it because she hates challenges. I had to get used to the fact that Mariah did not want to be challenged and she only accepts new ideas when she understand its concepts. I found it disturbing that Mariah did not want to be challenged because as an African-American she will be met with nothing but challenges in her education and her life. [J8: 2-3]

Alix seemed especially disappointed in Mariah's attitude about being African American:

I'm not sure if their school does not discuss ethnic identities or if Mariah just doesn't pay attention to it. Someone had brought to my attention that Mariah's father is Indian but Mariah identified herself to me as African-American. The conclusions that I came to about Mariah is that maybe she doesn't know which culture to embrace— Indian or African-American. Eastside should try to raise the children's consciousness about all ethnic identities because it is very important for a child to know their culture because it will always be a part of them. [FP: 8]

Alix places blame on the larger school system for Mariah's deficient cultural education. In the end, she seems to "forgive"' Mariah and even acknowledges her own shortcomings:

> I was very much the same. . . . I had stopped raising my hand during class and I too had become concerned about my appearance. But I was in the fifth grade nine years ago, why haven't some changes been made?

> I hope that both of these girls enter a classroom where they will really be made part of it before they enter college. [FP: 9]

Her work as a literacy tutor caused Alix to rethink herself, her culture, and the broader question of education.

As Arnelle and Alix describe their experiences with the children they tutored, they also begin to interrogate larger constructions of culture and identity and the effects these constructions have on the children's education. Arnelle's discovery of the role learning styles plays in a person's education is also a discovery of how people are located in culture in various ways and how they must interact in the larger culture and its institutions. Alix's critique of Mariah becomes a critique not only of Mariah's personal construction of identity but also of how culture has constructed Mariah. As Arnelle and Alix work to understand how the children are located in culture and the implications of this, they are also becoming more aware of how they are located in the culture. The lives of the students and the lives of the children are intertwined as they share experiences together and work to understand these experiences.

CONNECTING WITH CULTURE: RICK AND MELISSA

Another move the undergraduates began to make in their writing was to use what they learned from their tutoring experiences to question what they saw as larger structural problems that affected the education of the children they tutored. Disclosing learning experiences from both their past and their present became an act of transforming those experiences into a pedagogical strategy that enabled the undergraduates to intervene in the children's lives.

Rick was a white male from the suburbs of Detroit. He was a junior who had changed his major several times. He was concerned (if not obsessed) about his career choice. Rick came from a family of teachers, but he had started college with the idea of becoming an engineer like his uncle. Rick seemed to be overwhelmed by homework for other classes, as well as family problems that arose during the semester. These obstacles challenged Rick but he managed to complete his journals and papers, and he enjoyed his tutoring experience. Rick was one of the more talkative members of the class. At Eastside, Rick worked with several children. He loved sports and athletics, and he established himself at the tutoring site by interacting physically through sports and games.

Being in "Learning Communities" gave Rick a license to explore some of his own questions about choosing a meaningful career. He engaged other members of the class in conversation about career counseling. As the term progressed, Rick struggled to find a topic for his final project. He continuously talked about his own career dilemma, and sometime during the term he announced his decision to go into teaching after all. In class discussion as well as in writing, Rick tried to understand why it had taken him so long to reach this "obvious" conclusion. He wrote:

> I wanted to be just like my Uncle Jack who was an engineer. I had no idea what he did, I only knew that my cousins had really cool toys. My whole life I was going to be an engineer for those two reasons. [FP: 2]

A recurring theme in the journal assignments asked college students to reflect on their own learning style and process. This proved particularly relevant for Rick. He wrote:

> I think any time I come into new surroundings or a new system I'm definitely a follower. I keep my mouth shut and learn as much as I can from others and from the information available. . . . Once I'm confident I've learned about something and have been around a while, I take more of a leadership and motivating role.

This came as a revelation to Rick, as he tested out the idea of learning from others and learning by experience (having "been around a while"). He wrote:

> The thing that strikes me most about the class is that it seems most of the learning came not from readings, but from in-class discussions concerning the topics raised in the articles and papers.
>
> Most of all I learned the relationship between association and learning. This is the most important concept in teaching. The idea that the teacher must relate the material to the students in a way that causes connections to the familiarities and knowledge of the student. Once these connections between the concepts and lives can be made, learning can occur. [J8: 1,4]

With this in mind, Rick found a way to apply his newly formed theory of "learning by association" to his dilemma of choosing a career.

He believed that children should have a program to show them what professions were really like,

> not just how much each position makes or what subjects are related to the field, but an in-depth look at them. If a child has a *purpose* and an *association* to the material in school, he or she will do much better in job related areas of study. [PP: 2]

Rick had most recently been a physics major and he thought like a scientist. He wanted to derive a method of testing a child's aptitudes that would, in the end, direct the child to a concrete career choice. Rick returned to his high school and spoke to his old guidance counselors. He brought back a prototype of an aptitude test, and he adapted it to his idea of "purpose" and "association."

Rick worked at Eastside with a third-grade boy named Tony. On several occasions, Rick mentioned that Tony reminded him of himself as a child. It made sense that Rick would try out his theory on Tony—"I kind of looked at this as a personality test". The course instructors were skeptical when Rick produced a questionnaire for Tony to answer, in part because it seemed to reinforce many of the constructions of education that they were trying to call into question. Rick stood his ground, administered the test, and wrote an interpretation in his final report. Rick was not surprised when Tony's test revealed the career goal of "teacher." He concluded:

> I found it really interesting that out of each of the five job clusters that Tony matched with, the job that repeated the most was teaching. Now Tony mentioned that he wanted be a teacher when he grew up. It seems like he's pretty well adjusted as to the alignment of his interests with his career decisions as a THIRD GRADER. I'm jealous! [FP: 13]

Whether or not Tony does indeed become a teacher, he will probably not forget his tutor Rick—or Rick's career test. Tony may have wanted to please Rick, or perhaps Rick's test was valid in more ways than one. The strong identification Rick started to have with Tony suggests that Rick did begin to see his own experience being acted out once again with Tony. Tony's test result not only provides him with a head start in Rick's estimation but also validates Rick's own career decision. Although this is problematic to some degree because of what seems to be Rick's self-actualization through the child he tutors, it also illustrates the strong relationships created in this tutoring situation and the concern by the undergraduate students for their charges: They want to help the children avoid the difficulties they have experienced in their own lives. If Rick had someone like himself as a tutor when he was Tony's age, perhaps he would have been more focused as a college student and teacher-to-be.

A final example of a college student who learned about herself through her literacy tutoring experiences was Melissa, a white female from the east coast. She was a freshman and unsure of her major. She enrolled in "Learning Communities" at the suggestion of one of the other students, Bob, who had been a volunteer at Eastside the previous semester and was also in the class. Melissa was a typical freshman in many respects, exploring various social and political activities on campus. She held a part-time job and was also involved with the student government elections. Although quiet in class, when Melissa did speak, she usually expressed a well-thought-out comment that showed that she had read the coursepack and was trying to connect ideas. Melissa's journal entries also tended to be articulate and reflective. She said that she enjoyed writing and kept a journal at home.

Melissa worked primarily with two children, Mary and Donald. She engaged in several creative projects with these children (especially with Mary), and she struggled to be an effective tutor. She enjoyed working with children (and she had done so before). Still, the tutoring experience surprised her. She wrote in a journal:

> We were and are their friends and role models, their tutors and their confidants. This was something that I did not fully expect at the beginning of the course. [J8: 1]

As the semester progressed, Melissa observed differences in the behaviors of Mary and Donald. In particular, she noticed Mary's low self-esteem. It was something that Melissa "thought about constantly."

> One possible explanation that I stumbled upon was the influence of the rigid gender construction in our society. [FP: 1]

Melissa went further to explore this idea. She brought to Eastside a collection of different popular magazines and asked Mary to pick out two images, one of a female and one of a male. She then asked Mary to pick objects that "belonged" to those images. Melissa reported that Mary compiled an "extremely stereotypically 'gendered' conglomeration of pictures and images." A lawnmower, tire, military scene, and male doctor belonged to the male image. A basketball, broom, vacuum, baby booties, and a woman cleaning windows belonged to the female image.

Melissa began to think about Mary in relation to her own experience as a college student. She wrote:

> We like to think that we live in a society that does not push or direct children on the basis of their sex or gender. Those who believe this is true are just wrong. I constructed a survey that questioned whether college-age women still experience the effects of gender-based stereotypes. [FP: 9]

Melissa "did more of my own research." She observed two university classes of similar size and gender ratio. One professor was male, and the other was female. She recorded the number of times a question was posed to the class, how many times males or females were called on to answer, and the number of times either gender called out the answer without being chosen by the professor.

Melissa found that in the class led by the male professor, 7 out of 10 questions were answered by males who shouted out before anyone was called on. In the class led by the female professor, the ratio seemed to be even. Melissa also observed that in the class led by the male professor, the female students tended to sit toward the back of the room:

> I feel this is a sign that the female students are aware (on some level) of the imbalance in the class and are intimidated by the professor. This pattern of male domination in the classroom was something that I was unaware of before I began to read about the role of gender in education. [FP: 10]

In Melissa's final paper, she attempted to articulate her theories on gender bias in education. She concluded by returning to Mary:

> Mary has these gender myths ingrained in her mind. They are there for a number of reasons: television, parents, etc. It is these mythical "ideals" that have contributed to her deteriorating self-esteem. [FP: 11]

Melissa's astute comment about the power of "mythical ideals" can be extended beyond her discussion of gender to other cultural constructions of race and class, all key terms in discussions about education. Although Rick and Melissa seem to take very different approaches in discussing their work (Rick seeks applied knowledge, Melissa develops a more theoretical discussion), they both articulate the importance of early intervention in the education of children. Rick and Melissa have an emerging understanding of the various cultural pressures the children face and transform this into a pedagogy that seeks to open up possibilities for the children. Perhaps Rick's tutee, Tony, will not grow up to be a teacher, but it is probably a career that did not seem like a possibility before. Melissa's tutee, Mary, will sadly still face the difficulties of gender discrimination, but with Melissa's help can see more possibilities for her life and perhaps continue the work she and Melissa have begun.

MAKING THE CONNECTION: SERVICE LEARNING PEDAGOGY

In the excerpts from the student journals we see how students use their acts of disclosure to perform complicated rhetorical acts of discovery through their writing. The students discover various identities they have created and used and strategies for learning and teaching. The students discover literacy and the complicated ways in which it operates. And the students also begin to bring together these different pieces of the "Learning Communities" experience, connecting theory with practice, the personal with the public, and their lives with the lives of others.

As teachers we asked ourselves: How could we help our students become aware of these moments? How could we help weave their discoveries back to the course theme of literacy? What acts of disclosure and connection do we perform to create an atmosphere of trust in which students feel free to converse with each other and write about their experiences on site and in class. Developing a pedagogy for a service learning course presents unique opportunities for answering these questions. It is the element and performance of service that changes the dynamic of the classroom and engages teachers, students, and the community service site in an experience that explicitly asks for connections. By responding individually (through journal comments) and collectively (class discussion), we do disclose portions of our lives in order to teach but also to experience learning ourselves, bringing our discoveries back into the discussion. As teachers we also share with our students (as tutors) those moments when we make a connection, however small but significant in the developing context for learning that it creates. In the conflicts and connections we begin to be invested in what we are doing, not because we are teachers or students but because we recognize the importance of literacy in our lives and that we are part of a larger community.

However, with this recognition and the decision to disclose parts of our lives in order to teach and learn about others and ourselves, we also choose to risk. In the course of developing an understanding about their learning and teaching, our students shared painful moments:

self-doubt and frustration in school, the divorce of parents, the death of a mother. But in sharing these moments the students also saw them as important, if not necessary, parts of their lives in how they interpreted the broad use of literacy in their learning. They began to understand for themselves what Brandt (1990) has described as necessary elements in the development of literacy:

> The most successful readers and writers are grounded in an immediate and particular context of need, which gives them purpose and direction to an act of reading or writing. Before skills or even background knowledge, literate people need a place to be literate—a place where they and others are asking the kinds of questions and doing the kinds of work that make reading and text-based knowledge purposeful. (p. 117)

Melissa echoes Brandt when she writes that literacy allows her "to stay healthy, thus survive and succeed, by being honest and open about the way I feel." Melissa also recognizes what literacy meant to the children at the community center when they found purpose for their reading and writing by making cards to comfort a friend, Jason, whose mother had just passed away:

> When the children are not genuinely interested in the work they are doing, they have no interest in doing it well. Who can blame them for that? Who wants to read about or write about something that has no relevance to their lives? Jason was relevant and they care about Jason. [J5: 1-2]

Jason was relevant, as were all of the children with whom the students worked. The students found purposes for their own literacy in working with the children. And the children found purposes for literacy, perhaps unknowingly, when the tutors shared their lives with them and made literacy and learning both a little more personal and a little more public. The transformative power of literacy, the "state of grace" to use Scribner's term (1984), becomes something more personal and commonplace, as we find literacy not in books or schools or culture alone, but among ourselves and in all of those things we make our own, and perhaps most importantly, in those things we share.

APPENDIX A: SYLLABUS OF WEEKLY TOPICS AND ASSIGNED READING

Introduction to Literacy and Tutoring:
Robert Pattison. "Hopefully into the Future: John Locke and Correct Usage." *On Literacy.* New York & Oxford: Oxford UP, 1982. 138-169.
J. Elspeth Stuckey and Kenneth Alston. "Cross-Age Tutoring: The Right to Literacy." *The Right to Literacy.* Eds. Andrea A. Lunsford, Helen Moglen, James Slevin. New York: Modern Language Association, 1990. 245-254.

Introduction to Teacher Research:
James Britton. "A Quiet Form of Research." *Reclaiming the Classroom.* Eds. Dixie Goswami & Peter R. Stillman. Portsmouth, NH: Boynton/Cook, 1987. 13-19.
Denny Taylor and Catherine Dorsey-Gaines. "Literacy and the Children at School." *Growing Up Literate.* Portsmouth, NH: Heinemann, 1988. 99-121.

What is Literacy?:
Lisa D. Delpit. "Acquisition of Literate Discourse: Bowing Before the Master?" *Theory Into Practice* Vol. 31, Number 4 (Autumn 1992): 296-302.
James Paul Gee. "What is Literacy?" *Becoming Political.* Ed. Patrick Shannon. Portsmouth, NH: Heinemann, 1992. 21-28.
Sarah Michaels. "Narrative Presentations: An Oral Preparation for Literacy with First Graders." *The Social Construction of Literacy.* Ed. Jenny Cook-Gumperz. Cambridge: Cambridge UP, 1986. 94-116.

The Cultural Contexts of Literacy:
Maurice Bloch. "The Uses of Schooling and Literacy in a Zafimaniry Village." *Cross-Cultural Approaches to Literacy.* Ed. Brian Street. Cambridge: Cambridge UP, 1993. 87-109.
Selections from *The New England Primer* (1727) and McGuffey's Reader (2nd ed. c.1857; 1st ed. 1885; 3rd 1857).

Portraits of Literacy:
Valerie Polakow. "The Classroom Worlds of At-Risk Children: Five Portraits," "Poor Children's Pedagogy," and "Lives on the Edge." *Lives on the Edge.* Chicago & London: U of Chicago P, 1993. 131-173.
Gordon Wells and Gen Ling Chang-Wells. "The Literate Potential of Collaborative Talk." *Constructing Knowledge Together.* Portsmouth, NH: Heinemann. 53-72.

More Teacher Research:
Chris Anson, "Academic Literacy Meets Cultural Diversity: An Analysis of Ideological Change Among Student Tutors in a Service Learning Program." *Academic Literacies in Multicultural Higher Education.* Eds. Thomas Hilgers,

Marie Wunsch, Virgie Chattergy. Honolulu: Center for Studies of Multicultural Higher Education, U of Hawai'i at Manoa, 1992. 32-41.

Judy Buchanan. "Listening to the Voices." *Inside/Outside: Teacher Research and Knowledge.* Eds. Marilyn Cochran-Smith & Susan Lytle. New York: Teachers College P, 1993. 212-220.

Michele Sims. "How My Question Keeps Evolving." *Inside/Outside.* 283-289.

Lynne Yermanock Strieb. "Visiting and Revisiting the Trees." *Inside/Outside.* 121-130.

Literacy and the Community:
Toni Cade Bambara. "The Lesson." *Gorilla, My Love.* New York: Random House, 1972. 87-96.

Perry Gilmore. "'Gimme Room': School Resistance, Attitude, and Access to Literacy." *Becoming Political.* 113-127.

June Jordon. "Nobody Mean More to Me Than You And the Future Life of Willie Jordan." *Harvard Educational Review.* Vol. 58, No. 3 (August 1988): 363-374.

Mary B. Smith. "Alfred the Great." *Ebony* (November 1992).

Literacy and Gender:
Hisaye Yamamoto. "Reading and Writing." *Seventeen Syllables and Other Stories.* Latham, NY: Kitchen Table: Women of Color P, 1988. 122-128.

Unofficial Literacies:
Ruth Hubbard. "There's More than Black and White in Literacy's Palette: Children's Use of Color." *Language Arts.* Vol. 67 (September 1990): 492-500.

Ruth Hubbard. "Unofficial Literacy in A Sixth-Grade Classroom." *Language Arts.* Vol. 65 (February 1988): 126-134.

APPENDIX B: WRITING ASSIGNMENTS

Guidelines for Student Journals
(with thanks to Luis F. Sfeir-Younis and Ratnesh Nagda)

In this course, we will be confronted with various new and old ideas, and many of them will be quite exciting and controversial. Opinions and views presented by your classmates and the instructors may be very similar to yours, or radically different from yours. We can benefit greatly in this course by critically examining our own and others' viewpoints, and increasing our understanding of the course topics. Below is a set of guidelines to help you in this endeavor. Please feel free to talk to us if you have any questions or concerns.

The ability to reflect and analyze experience is a survival skill. Unlike other journals you may have kept, your journal provides you with the opportunity to analyze and integrate our classroom activities, discussions, readings, and your reactions and observations about the material. We hope this journal will help process your experience, structure your thoughts and enable you to express and explore your own emotional reactions and intuitive insights. But this journal is more than a diary of what we do in the course. It should be a tool to help you apply course topics and materials to your lives; it should also be a tool for you to engage in the process of teacher-research.

The course spans 13 weeks, and we require 7 journal entries from you. The journals will be graded on a three-point scale (check, check-plus, or check-minus). Criteria for an acceptable journal will include evidence of reading and thinking. Weekly journal entries should include some integration of facts, ideas, feelings and your own experiences. Please hand in your journal entries at the beginning of class. We will review them and provide feedback. If you would like the option to improve your journal grade, you may revise up to *two* journals prior to November 16.

Formal Guidelines
- at least 3-4 pages, typed and double-spaced
- two copies of journal entry, submit weekly
- date each journal entry

Content Guidelines
You are writing for you; to help you think about, react, respond to and integrate what you are learning. Don't write what you think we want you to say. Write what you really think and feel, what is most helpful for you to come to some understanding about the question at hand.

Jot down notes regularly, such as after you finish a reading, or a tutoring session. Later, you can write a more polished entry. Write when your memories, thoughts, or reactions are fresh. The learning potential of your journal is greatly reduced if you wait and try to remember what you did and how you felt. Feel free to write additional journal entries; we would be happy to comment on them.

Re-read your entries periodically and comment on themes you see or on the ways you perceive your ideas and attitudes developing or changing.

You may want to include discussions of issues raised or presented in other classes, if they are relevant to the material in this course.

Journal Assignments
(from Fall Semester, 1994)
#1

This week's readings introduce ways that we examine literacy. James Britton's essay presents the notion of research as a process of discovery and learning. He suggests that teachers should see themselves as researchers. As researchers exploring literacy and the learning process, it is crucial that we put ourselves in the shoes of other learners. Take a first step (pardon pun) by writing this journal entry about yourself as a learner.

Approach this journal entry in two stages. First, think back over your life. What landmarks or milestones (such as events, or people) distinctly marked your path as a learner (for the better, or for the worse)? You may consider anything from your school, your family, or extracurricular life. Now list these milestones, as a timeline, or whatever comes to mind.

Finally, choose one particular incident from your list of milestones, and describe it more fully. How does this incident characterize you as a learner? To answer this question, you may have to grapple with other questions: How *do* you learn? What is your style of learning (leave-me-alone-I'll-figure-it-out-myself, or do I need explicit directions and hand-holding)? What is your attitude and philosophy about learning? What is it about the learning experience in this journal entry that most sticks with you and why?

#2

In this week's readings we begin to get an idea of the complexity of literacy and the difficulty in talking about it, much less defining it. What is literacy? Why do we need literacy? Why is it so important? Both Delpit and Gee discuss literacy in terms of discourse-dominant discourse, school discourse, home discourse, etc.—and how this discourse affects one's status in society. Michaels talks about how the different narrative strategies of children (and the perception of literacy/illiteracy it creates) can affect the type of education and classroom support they receive. Though we often think of literacy in terms of reading and writing, we see in this week's articles that reading and writing become more than just a set of skills/practices.

For this journal we would like you to discuss an observation or experience of a reading or writing practice. You can observe the children at the afterschool program, detail a personal experience, or any other reading/writing practice that you can describe fully. Your observation could be of something like the "sharing time" discussed by Michaels. Or it could be something like Delpit's description of Marge. But your journal should describe in detail the reading or writing practice, and then discuss the attitudes, the perceptions, the values, and so on, that seem to surround the practice. Is it an example of literacy? Why or why not? What does literacy mean to you?

#3

This week's readings focus on literacy in different cultural contexts (a Zafimaniry Village, colonial New England, 19th C. America). In each situation the community establishes different literacy requirements for its members. These requirements include subject matter, cultural values, type of skills/knowledge, etc. For the first part of your journal, discuss what seems to count as literacy in these different cultural contexts. What kind of literacy is valued? How do these communities teach literacy?

For the next part of your journal, find a "cultural artifact" from today. It could be a school assignment or a school textbook, an advertisement, and so on—something that seems to reflect our culture today and how it uses/views/teaches literacy. What kind of literacy requirements does our culture have? What kind of literacy is valued? How do we teach literacy today?

#4

In this week's readings, Polokow presents portraits of several children living in poverty. She describes many facets of these childrens' lives, including their family backgrounds, economic status, and how they fare under the influence of the "culture" of the school.

Polokow also writes about narratives of experience (of the classroom world) that speak to broader educational issues. Her examples of teachers who conduct these narratives provide another way of seeing that helps us come to a new understanding of "living on the edges."

Now, imagine that you are a "child watcher" like Valerie Polokow, or Denny Taylor, or Sarah Michaels, who is "sensitively tuning the classroom to the developing child's questions." For your journal assignment, interview your child so that you may construct a portrait of the child (or a child) you tutor. Try to weave together your interview with observations of the child at the tutoring site.

#5

In the story by Hisaye Yamamoto we see how a woman's life is intertwined with literacy even though she could not read or write. Are there moments of literacy in her life? How so? How has literacy affected her life?

For this journal write about a memorable literacy event/experience. Though this may seem similar to the memorable learning experience you wrote about for an earlier journal, try to focus on a literacy event/experience. Tutoring reading/writing. Being tutored. Writing a letter for the first time. Writing a story. Borrowing your first library book. Why was it memorable? What occurred which made it special? Why was it an example of literacy? What role has this literacy event/experience played in your life?

#6

According to Hubbard, "unofficial" literacy holds an important place in the classroom. This enforces the notion that students' lives and cultures contribute to the classroom community, and are, in fact, vital resources.

Now imagine that you can magically create the classroom, or school of your dreams. Think about what you've experienced at your tutoring site. Draw from articles in our coursepack as well. First define the parameters of this classroom or school (it can be for any age), and then describe the ideal facilities, teachers, students, curriculum, and whatever else this classroom or school needs to fulfill your objectives. What are your objectives? Be creative!

#7

We have traveled a long journey together in this course, exploring and experiencing ideas about literacy, learning, and communities. Take this time to look back on the term, reflecting on the most meaningful moments.

What are the most important experiences you have had through the course?

What are the most important things you learned about yourself?

What have been some obstacles you have overcome?

How can you apply what you have learned and experienced to other parts of your life as a learner, a teacher, or simply as a human being?

REFERENCES

Anson, C. (1992). Academic literacy meets cultural diversity: An analysis of ideological change among student tutors in a service learning program. In T. Hilgers, M. Wunsch, & V. Chattergy (Eds.), *Academic literacies in multicultural higher education* (pp. 32-41). Honolulu: Center for Studies of Multicultural Higher Education, University of Hawaii at Manoa.

Bleich, D. (1995). Collaboration and the pedagogy of disclosure. *College English, 57*, 43-61.

Brandt, D. (1990). *Literacy as involvement: The acts of writers, readers, and texts*. Carbondale: Southern Illinois University Press.

Carr, D. (1986). *Time, narrative, and history*. Bloomington: Indiana University Press.

Combs, B. (1995). Student self-reflection: What, why, and how? *English Record, 45*, 19-27.

Herzberg, B. (1994). Community service and critical teaching. *College Composition and Communication, 45*, 307-319.

Horning, A. (1997). Reflection and revision: Intimacy in college writing. *Composition Chronicle, 9*, 4-7.

Michaels, S. (1986). Narrative presentations: An oral preparation for literacy with first graders. J. Cook-Gumperz (Ed.), *The social construction of literacy* (pp. 21-28). Cambridge: Cambridge University Press.

Minter, D., Gere, A.R., & Keller-Cohen, D. (1995). Learning literacies. *College English, 57*, 669-687.

Murphy, R. (1993). *The calculus of intimacy*. Columbus: Ohio State University Press.

Polakow, V. (1993). *Lives on the edge*. Chicago: University of Chicago Press.

Pratt, M. L. (1991). Arts of the contact zone. *Profession, 91*, 33-40.

Rubin, L. (1994). Learning about reflection. In L. Flower, D. Wallace, L. Norris, & R. E. Burnett (Eds.), *Making thinking visible: Writing, collaborative planning* (pp. 223-227). Urbana, IL: National Council of Teachers of English.

Scribner, S. (1984). Literacy in three metaphors. *American Journal of Education, 93*, 6-21.

Swartzlander, S., Pace, D., & Stamler, V.L. (1993, February 17). The ethics of requiring students to write about their personal lives. *Chronicle of Higher Education*, B1-2.

Taylor, D., & Dorsey-Gaines, C. (1988). *Literacy and the children at school. Growing up literate* (pp. 99-121). Portsmouth, NH: Heinemann.

Witherell, C. (1991). The self in narrative: A journey into paradox. In C. Witherell & N. Noddings (Eds.), *Stories lives tell: Narrative and dialogue in education* (pp. 83-95). New York: Teachers College Press.

$$5$$

A Change of Course: Creating a Context for Reforming Literacy Education

Lu Huntley-Johnston
Elizabeth Ervin
University of North Carolina at Wilmington

Models for progressive literacy instruction—for example, writing workshops in which all students are fully engaged and enthusiastic, or service learning classes in which students are inspired to become activists—are often so different from teachers' present situations that we do not know how to begin to approximate them. As teacher educators, we experience not only our own anxieties about implementing extensive literacy reforms, but also those of our students. We needed a way to expose our students to nontraditional images of literacy instruction and to equip them with strategies for realizing these models over time. So we began to reconsider the curriculum of one persistently perplexing English education course at our institution, Writing for Teachers. This course was designed in the early 1980s as an introduction to writing process theory and practice for prospective K-12 teachers, and since then has developed in ways that reflect progressive scholarship in composition and literacy studies. But despite our commitment to the purposes and goals of Writing for Teachers—and despite the broad acceptance of process approaches to writing at the college level—we continue to be stymied by our students' allegiance to traditional attitudes about writing, students, and teaching.

In general, the preservice students who enroll in Writing for Teachers lack writing practice, dislike writing, have had unpleasant experiences with writing instruction, and/or understand writing as something done only for school. Many demonstrate extreme passivity as learners. Because of their prior experiences with literacy education, many of them resist progressive pedagogy, are skeptical about the possibilities for implementating progressive theories, and seek to reduce pedagogy to "recipes" or methods. Britzman (1991) maintains that these attitudes can be linked to pervasive cultural myths about the work of teachers that "partly structure the individual's taken-for-granted views of power, authority, knowledge, and identity" and "work to cloak the more vulnerable condition of learning to teach and the myriad negotiations it requires" (p. 7). Later in this chapter we discuss the cultural myths of *teacher as expert, teacher as self-made,* and *everything depends on the teacher;* at this point, however, we note that our students internalize these myths in varied, but predictable ways. Some, for example, subscribe to the notion that experience alone will yield good teaching. Others believe that students hate to write so much that their primary focus as teachers will be motivation. Still others are convinced that all of their teaching decisions will be made for them, that they will only be reacting to and enacting someone else's curricular mandates; depressingly, many seem to embrace this role. In short, our students have remained largely unconvinced that literacy studies as represented by Writing for Teachers can translate into K-12 classroom application: They perceive university preservice courses as "theory land," unrelated to the "real world" of the classroom.

It was this dissonance between our students' vision of literacy instruction and our own that led us to develop "Sharing Worlds: Preservice Teachers Meet Veteran Teachers."[1] The purpose of this project was to illuminate connections between literacy theory and practice by introducing preservice students to progressive literacy instruction through the practices of exemplary veteran teachers. Our goals—to promote more effective preservice instruction in university English educa-

---

[1]This project was made possible by a Charles L. Cahill Award from the University of North Carolina at Wilmington and a Classroom Projects Grant from the North Carolina English Teachers Association. Grant monies funded teacher stipends, payment for teacher substitutes, and the costs of videotapes and other materials.

tion/literacy classes, provide ways for veteran teachers to construct and share their knowledge with future professionals, and facilitate dialogue among preservice and veteran teachers—led us to redesign Writing for Teachers, this time with veteran classroom teachers playing a central role. We selected six veteran K-12 teachers to participate in Sharing Worlds, each of whom have National Writing Project experience, extensive teaching expertise, and familiarity with the literacy and learning theories we study (e.g., Bomer, 1995; Brooks & Brooks, 1993; Calkins, 1994; Cambourne, 1988). We arranged for each teacher to attend our university class sessions and demonstrate or make a presentation about classroom practices that promote successful literacy development among their students. These visits and subsequent discussions often agitated our students, forcing them to reexamine their preconceived ideas about teaching, writing, and how children learn.

Restructuring Writing for Teachers did not create additional assignments for our students; it did, however, provide additional context and background for the assignments already in place. The most extensive of these asked preservice students to conduct, over the course of the semester, a case study of a student writer of the approximate age they were preparing to teach. This project involved interviews, classroom observations, and writing sample/artifact analysis. Sharing Worlds exposed students to alternative conceptions of literacy instruction that sometimes affected their interpretations of their data; however, because they did not always have a direct impact on these case studies, we do not cite them in this study. A series of short response papers was also central to the course. In previous semesters, students were required to write these papers in response to ideas from course texts, posing questions based on their reflections on literacy teaching and learning. Once we incorporated teacher visits into the course, we asked our students to prepare for visits by reading relevant chapters in our course texts and to integrate personal reactions to the teachers, key moments from the presentations, and relevant passages from the course readings into their response papers. During the semester students completed a minimum of five response papers, copies of which became the primary data source for this study. Other data included our field notes and reflections, videotapes of the teachers' presentations, and a variety of written artifacts.

As Sharing Worlds progressed, we noticed that three of the veteran teachers elicited especially animated responses from our students, and so we focus our discussion on them. Alice Oakley, an eighth grade teacher with 15 years' teaching experience and a MA in literacy studies, told our classes that the majority of her students are learning disabled, "and if it [a workshop-based writing pedagogy] can work with them, it can work anywhere." Alice seemed to fit preservice students' image of the quintessential language arts teacher: enthusiastic, caring, a little eccentric. Moreover, she expressed herself in such a way that suggested that her pedagogy is fully developed, even though other conversations with us made it clear that this was not the case. Susan Harris has taught high school English for 10 years; she has completed a master's degree and is currently working on a doctorate in English education. Unlike Alice, Susan structured her presentation to illustrate the ongoing process of learning to teach; she embraced reflection as a necessary component of her developing pedagogy and admitted to our students that she often struggles to make her practices consistent with her beliefs. Preservice students were impatient with the ambiguity of Susan's discussion, perhaps because it challenged their assumptions about experience and expertise and put pressure on them to name their pedagogical beliefs and influences. Our students' uncritical acceptance of Alice and rejection of Susan were somewhat mitigated by Gail Brown, a kindergarten teacher with 13 years of teaching experience. Gail's presentation was as reflective as Susan's and suggested a similar pedagogy; her classroom demeanor, however, was more like Alice's, thus opening our students to Gail's central theme of teaching as intellectual work.

Through their responses to these teachers, students revealed the degree to which they struggled with reflection and problem posing, and in this study we examine the ways these struggles manifested themselves in their use of language, their tendency to reduce pedagogy to tricks and resolutions, and their a priori adherence to cultural myths about teaching. Our narrative also features several "vignettes of complexity"—the first of which appears next—that represent pieces of the Sharing Worlds story that cannot be neatly integrated into the whole. These vignettes are intended not only to illustrate patterns of resistance, doubt, and questioning that characterize the process of becoming a teacher but also to suggest issues in teacher education that we believe would benefit from further inquiry.

Lu's class: When I read Anne's response paper on freedom and responsibility in the classroom, it felt like I was being kicked in the stomach. Her perception of the teacher's intricately structured literacy pedagogy, centered on student responsibility, was that this teacher's approach was "a farce." Anne distrusted what she termed "a form of reverse psychology used to get [students] to do something they don't want to do." Being self aware of her role as a student writing an assigned response paper, Anne said, "I feel forced to do something which bores me and seems pointless and irrelevant." The assignment to respond to what she was learning in our class was just another form of the "freedom game." If she weren't forced by this game, "[she] wouldn't do much thinking or analyzing at all." Her honest, articulate response left me dazed, wondering about the source of Anne's frustration. In her mind, teaching must be a form of manipulation and I, the supreme manipulator. When I invite students to think and analyze and it gets interpreted as coercion, I have to wonder—what keeps the mind in chains?

AUTHORITATIVE DISCOURSE: THE PEDAGOGY OF WHAT WORKS

Preservice students typically enter Writing for Teachers eager to apply their developing vocabulary of educational terms to discussions of literacy instruction. They feel especially comfortable using terminology they hear so often that the meanings seem self-evident. As teacher educators we want to take advantage of this prior knowledge; however, we observed in Sharing Worlds that terms like "teaching philosophy," "student-centered classroom," and "whole language" are used inconsistently and imprecisely by preservice students and veteran teachers alike. Preservice students often used such terms uncritically, allowing them to "stand in" for complex educational theories or phenomena that they were unprepared to think about in depth or detail. Veteran teachers presented us with a different set of language problems: Often they drew upon a language that, although familiar, suggested a more conservative or vague pedagogy than they actually espoused; at other times, conversely, their discourse was so unfamiliar that students dismissed it as "too radical." The result was that our classroom discourse was so pervasively overdetermined that it was difficult at times to know what anyone was talking about.

This problem was introduced during the visit of our first veteran teacher, Alice Oakley. A student asked Alice what she meant by the term "constructivism," but unable to provide a satisfactory definition or explanation, Alice backed away from the theoretical discussion, saying simply, "It works for me." In the class discussions and written responses following Alice's visit we began to notice the allure of these words. Several students in Lu's class said, "I started seeing that this can work." In Betsy's class, Celia expressed her conviction "that if given time, it will work in a kindergarten class." Although we were pleased that students were getting confirmation that what we were studying about writing workshops could be implemented with success in the classroom—this, after all, was one of our main goals in Sharing Worlds—we were concerned that many students depended on a vague and superficial discourse to articulate their emerging pedagogies.

In her response paper, for example, LaShonn commented, "I think when the students are actively engaged in their learning, the rest will fall into place." And Jennifer wrote,

> During the lecture Ms. Oakley emphasized the importance of having
> a personal teaching philosophy. She tells us that forming a philoso-
> phy is time consuming yet a very worthwhile undertaking.
> Teachers, like herself, who have a clear teaching philosophy that
> they are impassioned about have a very stable grounding to anchor
> themselves and their teaching methods from. Ms. Oakley warns us
> that if we don't feel strongly about our philosophy, it won't work.

It is unclear what LaShonn and Jennifer mean by "falling into place" and
"not working." At this point, they are unable to realize—partly we argue
because they are echoing Alice's language—that becoming a teacher
depends not on a fixed philosophy but on the constant reexamination of
our practices. Furthermore, when we interpret these written comments
in the context of others made during our classes, it becomes clear that
preservice students' conceptions of sound pedagogy are still shaped
profoundly by things like classroom management concerns—more
specifically lack of resistance: If students are not complaining and seem
to participate willingly, if other teachers are not objecting, then "it" is
"working." Sarah, a preservice teacher featured in Vinz's *Composing a
Teaching Life* (1996), demonstrates clearly how limited this language is.
She admits that she

> explores different teaching techniques to see if they will "work."
> "Work" for me right now means that the kids don't complain and
> are busy and orderly. "Work" mostly means busy work—turning
> every activity in. I end up with too much grading, but I can't figure
> out how to motivate them. (p. 21)

This view of successful teaching is given confirmation when experienced
teachers use language that does not specify an alternate vision.

The problem with "the pedagogy of what works," of course, is
that it does not mean anything. It is one of those phrases that seems so
commonsensical that it does not need to be questioned or even
explained. It manifests the cultural myth that teachers are self-made by
valorizing the notion that good teaching is strictly intuitive and ineffa-
ble, something that cannot be identified or articulated. As such,
Britzman (1991) argues, this orientation is powerfully reductive: It
"diminishes reflection on how we come to know and on what it is we
draw upon and shut out in the practice of pedagogy" (p. 230). The larger
danger of this orientation, Britzman says, is that it "cover[s] its own theoretical tracks . . . and encourages the stance of anti-intellectualism" (p.
231). If "it works," then why think about it any further? There is plenty
that does *not* "work," after all.

Alice's pedagogy is sophisticated but her language exemplifies what Bakhtin (1981) calls *authoritative discourse*. Britzman adapts this term to her study of the professional development of teachers, arguing that authoritative discourse establishes "normative categories" to which it "demands allegiance. . . . It is 'received' and static knowledge, dispensed in a style that eludes the knower, but dictates . . . the knower's frames of reference and discursive practices that sustain them" (Britzman, 1991, pp. 20-21). Although Alice has gradually transformed her teaching to account for more progressive literacy theories, she spent her early professional background as a very traditional teacher. Remnants of this background remain embedded in Alice's language, and we wonder if the contradiction between her language and her pedagogy may neutralize her message, thus preventing preservice students from recognizing how, specifically, her classroom differs from more traditional ones.

Students were also under the influence of authoritative discourse as they responded to the teachers' visits. Gail Brown, for example, made passing reference to teaching "phonics and other important stuff" during her presentation; her point was that phonics is part of her holistic approach to literacy but that she does not teach it as an isolated part of her curriculum. April, however, interpreted Gail's reference to phonics as endorsement of a more traditional paradigm for literacy pedagogy. She wrote of how pleased she was that Gail taught phonics, adding: "By no means will phonics stop all illiteracy or raise everyone's reading level, but the use of phonics helps students become better readers as well as critical thinkers." April's frame of reference on effective literacy instruction has been so strongly shaped by the authoritative discourse of "phonics" that her understanding of Gail's point about integrative reading approaches is precluded from the start. Clearly, authoritative discourse exerts power even at the level of single words, causing progressive teachers to sound traditional and influencing students to hear things that are not really being said.

In contrast to Alice, Susan Harris self-consciously adopted a discourse identified as *internally persuasive* (Bakhtin, 1981), which according to Britzman (1991), "admits a variety of contradictory social discourses" but "has no institutional privilege, because its practices are in opposition to socially sanctioned views and normative meanings" (p. 21). Internally persuasive discourse "celebrates the ambiguity of words" and "is opened during times of spontaneity, improvisation, interpretive risks, crises, and when one reflects upon taken-for-granted ways of knowing" (Britzman, 1991, pp. 21-22). Susan's presentation seemed to disturb students on several levels. She did not discuss assignments or assert the value of specific practices, but rather focused her attention on our students—their lives as learners and prospective teachers and the ongoing decision-making processes by which they would refine their pedagogies. Her presentation included an activity that invited students to identify key influences or "stepping stones" in their lives as learners, to freewrite about one of those influences, and to use the material from the freewrite to generate one or more questions about teaching. Many of our students struggled, resisting the opportunity to reflect; some wrote down Susan's influences and questions as she modeled the activity. Others went so far as to blame Susan for being vague in her expectations because they simply did not know how to process a discourse as generative and dialogic as hers.

Betsy's class: When our class met after Susan's visit, I asked students why they had seemed reluctant to pose questions, why they had seemed so uncharacteristically quiet and non-participative during her interactive presentation. "I really thought she was trying to teach us something," one student said derisively. "I thought that activity she did was a gimmick," another added. "She danced around her answers," one young woman complained as others nodded in agreement. "She didn't help me to understand and didn't give me enough information to find my own answers."

But by far the greatest source of discomfort was what my students termed the "student-centeredness" of Susan's presentation. "I guess I've just never experienced that kind of classroom before," several students shrugged (with the unmistakable implication of "and I hope I never will again"). Others described in detail a "student-centered" class they were currently taking that seemed "out of control," confidently concluding from this single experience that student-centered classrooms don't work. When I challenged my students on this conclusion, I learned that their image of a student-centered classroom was essentially that of a prison run by the inmates: students would decide what— indeed if—they wanted to learn, and the teacher was either too lazy to "teach" or was reduced to the role of doormat. When I pointed out that ours was a student-centered classroom, students seemed confused. I reminded them about our mini-lessons, showed them our syllabus——how I had created a predictable structure for each week, but how I had left many of our reading assignments open so that I could respond to students' questions as they developed. No, they insisted, student-centered classrooms don't work, and only lazy teachers try to enact them.

The degree to which our classes functioned as sites of linguistic struggle was more apparent during the Sharing Worlds project than in previous semesters. The dialogue between and among preservice students and veteran teachers became increasingly layered with complicated language patterns as the semester progressed. Bringing individuals together from the university and the public schools created language struggles for us, too, as we reacted and commented to response papers, prepared mini-lessons, and facilitated class discussions. The clash of authoritative and internally persuasive discourses led to linguistic overdetermination, imprecision, and ambiguity, but also provided ample material for critique. These conflicts made us more conscious of the hold that cultural myths have on our students as they attempt to forge pedagogical beliefs and a teaching identity.

IDENTITY, PERSONALITY, AND THE PERILS OF REFLECTION

In their initial responses to veteran teachers, students in our classes paid an inordinate amount of attention to personalities. Words like "confident," "enthusiastic," "dynamic," and "charismatic" were used not only to express admiration for teachers whose presentations they especially enjoyed, but also to assess the committedness or skills of those teachers—as when Britt commented that "being perky and upbeat all the time is one aspect of the whole [process] approach." Furthermore, students were more inclined to take seriously the ideas of teachers whose personalities were compatible with their own self-concepts.

It is certainly reasonable that students would desire to see something of themselves in a teacher whom they admire and, moreover, as Vinz (1996) remarks, that they would use "their own personalities, commitments, styles of action, and decision making" to shape their pedagogies in principled and imaginative ways (p. 186). However, this identification becomes a matter of concern when it reduces teaching to personality, which Britzman (1991) attributes to the cultural myth that teachers are self-made:

> In the supposedly self-made world of the teacher, pedagogy is positioned as a product of one's personality and therefore is replaced by teaching style. . . . The mistaken assumption is that somehow, teaching style metamorphoses into knowledge. In this discourse, teaching style becomes like a costume: one tries on different personae until the right one is found. Such a metaphor reduces pedagogy to its most mechanical moment . . . [and causes] the mystification of the process whereby teaching style develops and its contradictory effects. (p. 232)

This cultural myth suggests that students can bypass reflection as long as they don the cloak of an acceptable teaching "style." They adapt to the styles of other teachers whom they like or admire, even if in the process their own identities and beliefs are displaced.

Many of our students were critical of the implications of mythologizing teaching style, particularly after interacting with several teachers in Sharing Worlds. Suzette exemplifies this attitude:

> My first encounter with Gail Brown should have prepared me. She was walking down the crowded hall towing a little wagon full of "teacher trappings." It occurred to me that in just a few months that would be me, wagon and all. Just the similarity of both of us pulling our materials on wheels [Suzette is a commuter who carries her books and supplies in a rolling suitcase] was uplifting and seemed to make a "click" with my progress towards becoming a teacher.
>
> Mrs. Brown's theory of teaching and her approach to writing gave voice to my own theories of teaching and writing. For some time now, I have been trying to articulate what my theory is but it seemed to be stuck inside my head. I knew what I believed but was simply unable to express it.

Suzette continues by commenting on specific features of Gail's presentation, using them to generate an extended definition of literacy. She vows at the end of her written response "to reflect more on [Gail's] presentation in the next few months to get a better view of how her philosophy incorporates the things that [she] believe[s] about how children learn." Unlike many of her peers, Suzette does not stop with a superficial identification with personality, but rather uses the details of Gail's appearance as clues that lead her to a more critical consideration of the content of the presentation and the beginnings of her own definition of literacy.

Lu's class: So much talk about teachers' personalities made me uneasy throughout Sharing Worlds. My discomfort began during our class brainstorming session following Alice's presentation, when students generated the following observations: "her energy inspired the students"; "enthusiasm—not stuck in one style, excited about what she's teaching"; "confidence in herself and her teaching"; "believes in her philosophy strongly which gives her confidence." Since I consider myself a pretty serious classroom teacher, I began to feel self-conscious about how students perceived me and my abilities: do they interpret my deliberateness as lack of enthusiasm, my willingness to share in the question-posing process as lack of confidence or authority? These concerns resurfaced when Susan visited our class. I was immediately drawn to Susan because the teaching influences she identified in her presentation—feminist theories of knowing, for example—were so similar to my own, and because her personality and classroom ethos, too, reminded me of myself. When so many of my students expressed their disapproval of Susan, I couldn't help but take their criticisms personally. I had tried after Alice's visit to introduce the question of how personality affects pedagogy—asking, specifically, whether a teacher has to be espe-

cially dynamic or openly "confident," to engage students in a writing work-
shop, and wondering aloud whether my personality is conducive to the kind of
pedagogy I want to espouse. I was fearful about bringing up the issue again,
concerned that by identifying so personally with the issue I might appear to my
students as (gulp) lacking confidence.

Even when students tried to be critical of the relationship between personality and pedagogy, their thinking often stalled, perhaps because they lack what Vinz (1996) calls "a language of reflective inquiry"—that is, a discourse that helps them to strategically rehearse meanings as they "confront multiple and contradictory beliefs" about literacy teaching (pp. 26-28). Martha exemplifies this predicament. From her experience as a tutor in a computer lab, Martha considered herself adept at changing roles, but wondered whether she would have to "entertain" her students in order to keep them "excited" about her classes:

> Is being able to change roles so quickly part of my personality? I have seen teachers that can not change roles so quickly. Does that mean that they are ineffective teachers? Personality is part of a person and a person does the teaching. So I want to conclude that, yes, personality is a major factor in teaching.

Martha begins to question the ways in which her personality and prior learning experiences might affect her teaching, but she is unable to move beyond tautological reasoning as she explores these connections. Because Martha does not yet have a language to make explicit and reflect on her puzzlement, the struggle between authoritative and internally persuasive discourses remains latent, and the cultural myth of the self-made teacher goes uncritiqued.

Tracie reaches a similar impasse when she writes, "I feel more focused and even more confident about myself as a future teacher. I no longer feel I must be like someone else. There is a place for my personality and qualities. It's up to me to find it." Unlike some of the students we have cited, Tracie does not feel the need to identify strongly with a "model" teacher. But neither does she know how to proceed with introspection, believing that she can find "a place for [her] personality" only by looking outside herself. This inclination is a byproduct of the myth of the teacher as expert, in which teachers seem to exist fully formed and finished, and the processes of "how we come to know, how we learn, and how we are taught" (Britzman, 1991, p. 230) are hidden from view, not recognized, or not attended to.

Based on her work with preservice, beginning, and experienced literacy teachers, Vinz (1996) suggests that a language of reflective inquiry includes *retrospection,* "the stories of . . . experiences"; *introspection,* "look[ing] inward and [thinking] through the meaning of . . . stories"; and *prospection,* "look[ing] toward the future" (p. 27; emphasis in original). We observed similar modes of inquiry in our students' responses to the Sharing Worlds teachers, but generally these occurred in isolation. Celia, for instance, found one presentation "enlightening in [the] sense that *it helped me to begin doing some self examining. I realized that I had to look at my own authoritarian personality and be aware of it when I am teaching. I can see myself in a classroom* dictating to the children about what they need to do to get the work done, without giving them choices" (emphasis added). Celia's desire to "do some self examining" is indeed a promising start; however, she does not yet have the language to go beyond naming what she sees as a flaw in her personality that might prevent her from practicing teaching in the way she would like.

Few of our students, in fact, engaged in sustained introspection or retrospection, despite the fact that we spent considerable time at the beginning of the semester reflecting on our experiences with writing and with school. Most seemed to prefer the prospective mode of inquiry, often graphically underscoring their commitments to future activities. Amy, for example, vowed that "[W]hatever I do as a teacher, I *'will'* keep in mind to find at least one positive point about each student's paper"; similarly, Chell wrote, "My students *will* read every day, either in class or at home for 30 minutes, and I will respond to what they have read" (emphases in originals). In one response paper, Sharon projected herself into her future professional life in the following ways: "I began to think of what I wanted to make available to my own students. . . . I think I would like to have an easy to read, large print vocabulary stand, lots of creative supplies, carpet squares for out of seat work, and encouragement banners located at eye level for my students"; "I see myself doing lots of collaborative exercises but also setting certain traffic patterns to my available resources and placing those resources in specific areas of the classroom"; "I do not see my students scattered around the classroom doing their own thing."

Although Sharon has a very specific image of her future classroom, she seems trapped in a discussion of activities and logistics rather than pedagogy. She can envision her classroom down to the last detail of where the dictionary will be stored, but falters when she tries to articulate the underpinnings of her decisions: "Is it appropriate to have small crates with glue, markers, and scissors located in the center of a group of student desks, or is that inviting conflict and disruptions into the learning environment? Would I allow my students to freely get up at any given time to check the vocabulary stand or have a certain time during each lesson to allow students to use it?" Without any detailed retrospection or introspection—considering, for example, why students moving freely around the classroom strikes her as disruptive, or whether her desire to do "lots of collaborative exercises" is incompatible with her desire to avoid conflicts among students—Sharon is unable to reflectively inquire into her pedagogical goals and purposes.

Vinz (1996) acknowledges that the challenge for many preservice students and teachers "is to develop a means of inquiry that prepares [them] to deal with the daily pedagogical struggles without disguising them in the 'tricks of the trade' discourse" (p. 265)—what we have previously called the "pedagogy of what works." Certainly, teacher educators can guide preservice students through careful introspections and retrospections, showing them the ways in which our experiences influence our attitudes and actions and demonstrating ways to intervene in those processes by making them explicit and subjecting them to critique. But we believe that it is also useful to examine why our preservice students might be drawn to the prospective mode of inquiry in the first place. As illustrated in Sharon's, Chell's, and Amy's writing, prospective discourse can sound like a mantra or even a prayer: *I will, I must, I need to, I see myself.* Such formulaic utterances can be reassuring, for they signal a kind of resolve, but because the rationales behind the resolutions go unspecified and there is no accountability for action, they can also be empty. Retrospection and introspection could initiate the necessary groundwork to support such claims but because these reflective processes are more likely to challenge fixed ideas and destabilize certainties about teaching, many students resist or avoid them. In this way, prospective discourse represents another example of authoritative discourse, which is "received" and "dispensed" in ways that are sometimes invisible to knowers (Britzman, 1991, p. 21).

Allegiance to authoritative discourses about teaching is encouraged by a variety of sources, including preservice "methods" courses. In *The Making of a Teacher*, Grossman (1990) provides a detailed example of the first day of a class called Curriculum and Instruction in English: the professor describes the course to students as "a crash course in survival" that "places a lot of emphasis on activities," and describes the major textbook, furthermore, as "kind of a cookbook of activities" (p. 115). Grossman (1990) sees the class as a model of "principled practice," in which the professor focuses on "practical dilemmas and strategies," but "spen[ds] a good deal of time outlining the theoretical knowledge and assumptions underlying various instructional strategies and providing both a historical and scholarly context for classroom practices in the teaching of English" (p. 119). We find the example problematic, however, largely because the professor's discourse of "cookbooks" and "activi-

ties" might interfere with students' consideration of more complex pedagogical questions, just as the mere mention of the word "phonics"
obstructed April's more thoughtful consideration of Gail's whole language pedagogy.

Because prospective teachers fear that they must possess not
only disciplinary content knowledge but also pedagogical content
knowledge, they "look to teaching methods as the source rather than the
effect of pedagogy," thus perpetuating the view that methods are ends
(Britzman, 1991, p. 227). Their expectation is that "methods can be
applied like recipes and somehow remain unencumbered by the specificity of the pedagogical act," (Britzman, 1991, p. 227). But by adhering
to the normative discourse of "tricks" or "recipes," preservice students
are "prevented from attending to the deeper epistemological issues—
about the construction of knowledge and the values and interests that
inhere in knowledge" (p. 228). We have found that preservice students
are often frustrated and confused when we try to engage them in an
examination of why recipes are valued within teacher education, or
when we encourage them to recognize and critique moments of tension
within their professional preparation. The authoritative discourses of
schooling do not allow for such complexities, and thus preservice students experience a clash of expectations. Britzman (1991) writes:

> [E]ducation course work that does not immediately address "know
> how"or how to "make do" with the way things are and sustain the
> walls we have come to expect, appears impractical, idealistic, and
> too theoretical. Real school life, then, is taken for granted as the mea-
> sure of a teacher education program, and, as such, the student teach-
> ing semester is implicitly valued as the training ground, the authen-
> tic moment, that mystically fills the void left by so-called theoretical
> course work. (p. 49)

Intervening in our students' unexamined attraction to gimmicks sometimes feels like a lonely mission. We persist because authoritative discourse maintains its authority if it is not challenged, a fact which we
ignore at *our* peril.

DISRUPTING CULTURAL MYTHS: TOWARD AN INTERNALLY PERSUASIVE DISCOURSE

Throughout this chapter we have been using terms like "authoritative
discourse" and "the pedagogy of what works" to suggest the intractabil-

ity of Britzman's (1991) cultural myths and our students' susceptiblilty to those myths. In this section we illustrate in more detail the ways in which students and veteran teachers embraced "internally persuasive discourse" to disrupt and revise what Britzman (1991) calls the image of the "teacher as rugged individualist," which is supported by the cultural myths of *teacher as expert, teacher as self-made,* and *everything depends on the teacher.* More than just an approximation of *our* professional beliefs, the kind of critique we saw our students engaging in as a result of Sharing Worlds represents the beginnings of a radically different orientation toward schools and classrooms, toward writing pedagogy, and toward themselves as teachers. We have waited until this point to more fully define and illustrate these myths in order to highlight the contrast between students' being trapped by mythical thinking and being critical of such thinking.

The Myth of the Teacher as Expert

According to Britzman (1991), this myth regards knowledge as the accumulation of classroom experience, which "becomes the key to controlling knowledge and imposing it on students as a means of control" (p. 229). It allows no awareness of pedagogical complexity and perpetuates the expectation that teachers be certain in their knowledge and that knowledge itself be fixed and certain. Knowledge is reduced to simple "answers"—often expressed by the discourse of "recipes" and "what works"—and uncertainty is perceived as bad. Sandi embodies this myth when she writes, "It is my firm belief that the teacher should guide the education of the class since they are the ones with the advanced education. This is not to say students have nothing important to say, but as educators, teachers must inform us with the knowledge that goes beyond the students' knowledge." This myth seems most prevalent among students who resist seeing themselves and teachers in general as learners. Kimberly, for example, asks, "Why is it necessary for me, as a teacher, to be a scholar before I am a teacher? Shouldn't I be more concerned with making scholars of my students than myself?"

Some students, however, were able to be more critical of this myth. In her final response paper, April tried to come to some general conclusions about the course and Sharing Worlds. But instead of listing activities or assignments or offering platitudes about her need for experience, like many of her peers, she said,

> As I work through these ideas I may find that they aren't all meant for my classroom, but they have given me a chance to think of myself as a teacher as well as improve as a student. Not only have I

had experience with how hard it is to be a student but also how difficult it can be to think of myself as a teacher. I believe I have some
new views of teaching that will be [significant] as I embark into my
final frontier.

April's use of the phrase "final frontier" suggests that she sees teaching
as a journey rather than a destination and that she expects to continue to
learn as a teacher. Furthermore, she is beginning to question traditional
dichotomies that separate the needs and responsibilities of teachers and
students: Both, April realizes, must be learners. Janie, likewise, begins to
reconsider the "experience is knowledge" aspect of this myth:

> Unfortunately, I think some people believe that a college diploma
> indicates that your knowledge reservoir is full and you now have
> the full authority to impart all you know to the world. I think that's
> what I've been thinking, too. I thought that my experience here at
> [college] would supply me with all the answers and make me the
> kind of teacher that I would be for the next 20 years. The fact that I
> need to continue scholarly pursuits makes so much sense now. How
> can I ever understand how a child learns if I stop learning? How will
> I help them as they struggle with new information if my learning
> skills are rusty and unused?

What is remarkable about Janie's realization is that she is aware she had
been inhabiting a myth. She is self-conscious about the ways her thinking about teaching have been influenced and is capable of revising her
assumptions.

The Myth that Everything Depends on the Teacher

Like the myth of the teacher as expert, this myth attempts to minimize
complexity by equating learning with control, stripping multiple meanings and tensions from the classroom experience and encouraging teachers to blame themselves for their failures rather than to reflect on the
social situatedness of pedagogical practices (Britzman, 1991, pp. 223-
226). Moreover, it holds that all learning is solely the responsibility of
the teacher. The following passage from Martha, a response to Susan's
presentation, so powerfully illustrates the simultaneous ubiquitousness
and elusiveness of this myth that we quote her at length:

> I didn't see a glow in Susan's face. I felt as if she was going through
> the motions of teaching rather than actually trying to lure us into her

presentation. Was it her tone in voice or was it the things she said? I remember one incident in which one of my classmates asked Susan about reaching difficult students, and Susan's response made a very strong first impression on me. It was interesting that Susan was upset about an evaluation a student wrote about her. The student stated that Susan did not try hard enough to lure her into the class. Susan stated that her first reaction was that she gave this student every opportunity to be lured into the class. Susan took to the defense. I guess that could be a first reaction, but for me, it would not. My first reaction would show deep concern about how I failed to reach this student, not how I gave her every opportunity. And what did Susan mean by every opportunity? I wished that I had asked her what she believed was the problem in that she failed to lure this student into her class. . . . [S]he had not found the right tools to reach that child yet. I know Susan mentioned that next time she would evaluate the students more thoroughly before jumping to conclusions, but for some reason I struggle with the sincerity of her answer. I felt as if she was just saying that because that was the right thing to say.

Susan failed with luring me into the presentation and I could only speculate why. Maybe it was her lack of enthusiasm. I was falling asleep, so I began to wonder if that is what happens in the classroom. Do her students get bored with her as I did? I was not bored with Alice. Her enthusiasm alone made me listen to what she had to say. I figure anyone who is excited about doing what they do is worth listening to. Susan lacked that enthusiasm for me. I then began to wonder if she felt that she did not have to display any enthusiasm because we were college students? If that is so, is she not showing enthusiasm to her high school students because they are high school students. I do not believe it should make a difference what grade level you teach. If the teacher does not show any enthusiasm in their subject, then why should the student feel the need to be excited about learning it?

Martha's repeated characterization of teaching as "luring"—manipulating, tricking, enticing—is itself worth noting. But we want to call attention to the sentence, "Susan lacked that enthusiasm for me," which offers some insight into Martha's acceptance of the myth that everything depends on the teacher. Although she might be trying to say that *in her opinion* Susan lacked enthusiasm, Martha also, perhaps unconsciously, suggests that the teacher has to embody enough energy for everyone's learning—to have enthusiasm *for* me, on my behalf—and if she does not, she has failed everyone.

Some students began to challenge the idea that everything depends on the teacher. Sharon believes that "Taking myself, the teacher, out of the spotlight and having my students solve problems and discuss issues amongst themselves will lead to new ideas and realizations of differing opinions." Nikki asserts that she "will still 'teach' my students but they will have a say in what and how I teach. I like the idea of students teaching other students, but not all the time." Both Nikki and Sharon understand that although the teacher assumes responsibility for establishing a structure for learning, that structure does not always have to cast the teacher as the central figure.

Myth of the Self-Made Teacher

Similar to the previous myths we have discussed, this myth reduces knowledge and experience to stable, uncomplicated phenomena. At its core is the idea that teachers learn on their own, unaffected by historical forces and institutional structures. Within this myth, "only the strong survive." When Bridget says, "I hope after 16 years of teaching, I can say that I love teaching with a passion and it will show all over my face like it did with Gail," she suggests that "passion" is a kind of essential quality among "true" teachers that not only survives *in spite of* experience but also "shows" on one's face.

Other students demonstrated an inclination to look outside themselves, but not for answers or secrets to the "right" teaching personality. Rather, these students seemed to be trying to construct a professional community, one that included the visiting teachers, the authors of our course texts, and the Writing for Teachers classes themselves. Sometimes this construction of community took the form of rejecting previous pedagogical influences. Teresa, for example, seemed simultaneously overwhelmed and inspired by the various texts and teachers that informed the content and structure of the course: "[They] have had a tremendous impact on my decisions as a future teacher. I consider each presentation, [Writing for Teachers], and all previous classes as 'stepping stones' that will [be reflected] in my . . . teaching." Tracie seemed especially aware of the process of developing a professional community as she tried to define herself in relation to others: "We're not only reading the texts but we're also meeting the people who are there on the front line everyday. What we learn from them helps us realize what it is that we must do to prepare ourselves for teaching." Through Sharing Worlds, Tracie was able to "identify some of [her] fears about teaching and listen to how others handle those same fears." Several preservice students declared that "borrowing" the experiences of veteran teachers enabled them to exemplify and make explicit their own intuitive understandings of literacy learning and teaching.

These students' efforts to think in ways not bound by cultural myths mark fragile but significant beginnings of an internally persuasive discourse—one that takes "interpretive risks" and "reflects upon taken-for-granted ways of knowing" (Britzman, 1991, pp. 21-22). Although they do not perceive the influences of traditional schooling and attendant authoritative discourses, our students are nonetheless practicing new ways of thinking about teachers and students. The larger process of literacy learning that the teacher-presenters encouraged, however, is still something some students are simply unable to imagine. Wendi embodies this rigid stance as she maintains that "it is the responsibility of the teacher [*everything depends on the teacher* myth] to give the students the tools they need to improve their writing (i.e., a background in grammar and sentence structure). . . . A college graduate should have the skills of an accurately literate, well-educated member of society." Wendi's response paper suggests not only that her beliefs about teaching and learning are set, but also that in the end, students, too, are self-made experts. Fortunately, as we have illustrated, many of our students' papers show promising signs of a more complex attitude about teaching and learning.

Despite this emergent critical orientation and the reassurances of our visiting teachers, most of our students continued to express anxieties about teaching in schools where writing workshops are not the norm. Kim says, "I am greatly concerned that after I spend time learning how to teach workshopping . . . I will not be able to use it when I student teach." Debby, a nontraditional student who entered the class after completing student teaching, notes that during her student teaching "none of the teachers I encountered used the writing workshop." Our students, especially those who student teach at secondary levels, find that traditional approaches to literacy development are prevalent, and a preoccupation with state testing drives the curriculum.

Karma's questions remind us of realities we as teacher educators cannot dismiss: "We all study the 'new theories' and give them lip service in our education classes, but how many of us actually change our ideas, our 'eternal truths' of what teaching actually is? How many of us will really implement these strategies and ideas in our classroom?" (Brooks & Brooks, 1993, p. 113) One one level, Karma's questions are disappointing: We want our students to engage in cultural critique, not resign themselves to cultural forms defined by authoritative discourses. On another level, however, there is something significant about the fact that students like Karma have begun to articulate such difficult questions, attempting to define the status of their knowing in relation to the course texts and the teaching futures they envision. It is on this level that some of our students show that their interactions with the veteran teachers may have unsettled heretofore fixed ideas about teaching. Although this disturbance alone cannot dispel myths and transform discourse, it can begin a process of change.

THE FINE ART OF PAYING ATTENTION

We realize that the influence of Sharing Worlds on our students' developing perceptions of themselves as teachers is minimal compared to the influences of the larger culture. Vinz (1996), for example, points out that negative or idealistic portrayals of teachers are prominent in the very literature taught in English classes. What is insidious about these portrayals—and those that appear in television shows, movies, popular music, and so on—is that they can obstruct the development of a positive teacher identity. As Vinz (1996) writes, "[E]ntertainment gets a laugh by playing on stereotypes rather than interrogating them. I am concerned that real teachers in real classrooms become implicated in the social construction of teachers through popular portrayals" (p. 19). We share this concern, which is why we maintain the importance of encountering nonstereotypical images of literacy educators, such as those who participated in Sharing Worlds, and engaging as a class in the kinds of cultural critique that allow us to examine those stereotypes. However limited such an endeavor might be, it is a necessary step toward enacting more comprehensive reforms.

Knowing, then, that one course cannot have a fully transformative effect on our students, we can still name behaviors and attitudes that we believe advance the progress of preservice students: reading and writing with deliberateness, learning to tolerate complexity, developing a teacher-researcher orientation, and adopting an internally persuasive discourse. Our observations echo those described by Perry (1970). Perry identifies nine "positions" occupied by students as they advance through college, beginning with dualistic thinking, moving through various stages of uncertainty and diversity of perspective, and eventually asserting commitments within "a relativistic world" (pp. 9-10). Within Perry's scheme, "The good teacher becomes one who supports in his [or her] students a more sustained groping, exploration, and synthesis," and whose evaluation attends to "more than discrete rights and wrongs, [extending] through time to assist discrimination among complex patterns of interpretation" (p. 211).

Sharing Worlds has highlighted for us ways in which the Writing for Teachers class—from assignments to conceptual terminology to our own pedagogies—is a fitting context for setting in motion the intellectual practices Perry advocates. The response paper assignment invites preservice students to be exploratory and use their experiences as students to inform their thinking about teaching. As they read and write, we ask students to look not only for points of connection with their beliefs or experience, but also points of tension, where their thinking is challenged; through this process they can begin to consider more critically their own school and literacy histories. By examining their learning histories more deliberately, students can recognize and expose cultural myths associated with schooling. The case study project—inquiry about a student writer—provides an even more tangible opportunity for preservice students to investigate the complexities of writing instruction. From the earliest stages of the project, as they formulate and revise research questions, students are forced to question their assumptions about students and writing (e.g., that students do not like to write or only write for school purposes). Most students find this process challenging, but unlike the response papers—in which students often preempt fuller inquiry by offering pat resolutions or tautologies—the case study provides a greater incentive for students to explore writing and learning in a more dynamic way. These kinds of assignments, we believe, are vital in initiating what Ray (1993) calls "a researcher's model of mind, characterized by intellectual uncertainty, a self-critical attitude, and openness to new ideas and practices" (p. 51).

Identifying patterns in our students' thinking about the course content has helped us to clarify our own goals and pedagogies for Writing for Teachers. We now realize, for example, that students do not know what we mean by reflection. Thus, if we expect them to reflect more deeply on their literacy experiences or the implications of their pedagogies, we need to use what Vinz (1996) calls a *language of reflective inquiry*, nudging students beyond prospective modes of discourse to retrospection and introspection as well. Furthermore, if we want students to be able to recognize and interrogate cultural myths about schooling, then we need to assist them in naming those myths. We might begin by discussing Britzman's (1991) myths about teaching and then inviting students to identify other cultural myths. These refinements represent what we call the *metapedagogical:* naming our purposes as we put them into practice. By laying open the workings of our own pedagogies, we submit them to ongoing critique. In addition to developing *our own* metapedagogical languages, we believe that a central goal of Sharing Worlds must be to assist veteran teachers in developing *theirs.* Making explicit the whys and hows of their teaching rather than reducing it to "what works" can support veteran teachers' professional development by making them more self-conscious about their knowledge and creating new contexts in which they can directly influence the professional development of preservice students.

We have also come to recognize ways in which Sharing Worlds could be revised to be more effective for preservice students and veteran teachers alike. One is to strive for depth rather than breadth by inviting the participation of fewer teachers. Our students found it overwhelming to meet and reflect on so many different teachers with so many different approaches, and we believe that this limited their responses to a superficial preoccupation with personalities or activities rather than pedagogies. In the future, we will select three teachers instead of six and ask them to visit our classes at least twice during the semester. Our hope is that sustained relationships with these teachers will encourage our students to move beyond impressions toward more thoughtful questioning and critical reflection. We also foresee this process being reinforced through distance learning: By "visiting" public school classrooms via fiber optics, classes like Writing for Teachers could see examples of progressive literacy instruction in action over a longer period of time. This is only one of many possible ways that exemplary teachers such as those who participated in Sharing Worlds could be made key partners in developing and modeling teacher education.

Betsy's class: I fear that "the teacher should be a learner" has become a cliché—one more phrase that we use without understanding the myriad challenges it presents. All of my students embrace the idea, but recently Melissa raised some hard questions for me. Melissa told our class about the elementary teacher she was observing: "She was reading a story about chameleons, and she kept pronouncing it like shameleon. *And then she wrote it wrong on the board:* cameleon! *The students knew it, too; they were pronouncing it right." I asked Melissa why this bothered her if she believed that teachers didn't need to know it all, and she couldn't answer. Neither could I. I thought about how much pressure I feel to* convey *as well as* model *effective literacy instruction in Writing for Teachers. Sometimes I feel like I'm more preoccupied with whether my students* notice *that I'm modeling what we're reading about than with whether I* am *modeling what we're reading about. As an untenured professor, I'll admit that I'm concerned about my teaching evaluations—the Student Perception of Teaching forms, or SPOTs, as they're called at my institution. On these forms, students will not infrequently assess my "knowledge of course subject matter" as "fair" or even "poor," and I suspect that it's because they don't recognize my approach as knowledgeable. "Being a learner" is a risky role for teachers. For a lot of students and administrators, modeling learning looks a lot like modeling incompetence.*

In the past we expected our students to assert connections they were making among theories and practices, course texts, and personal experiences. Now our emphasis is on reflection, which we believe promotes self-conscious, thoughtful practice—what Vinz (1996) describes as "seeing ourselves seeing" (p. 103). Tremmel (1993) maintains that this idea of seeing both simplifies and complicates his work with student teachers. He realizes he is "not dealing with any great mystery that requires a high-tech, high-dollar solution"; rather the task is to help students "pay attention" (p. 448). As simple as this sounds, it means "confront[ing] what is going on in [the] mind" and that ultimately "one must have the skill and the courage to begin to know the self" (p. 449). As difficult as it may be to "teach" the habits of paying attention, we find reasons to be hopeful. For the behaviors and attitudes we have promoted through Sharing Worlds are not limited to the literacy classroom; they have value outside the classroom, too. Living more consciously—more reflectively, more deliberately, with a greater sense of our own agency and greater openness to possibility—will make teachers and their students better citizens of the world as well as better citizens of a classroom. If we practice behaviors with an eye toward the democratic promise of literacy instruction, we can live more artfully both inside and outside school.

REFERENCES

Bakhtin, M. M. (1981). Discourse in the novel. In M. Holquist (Ed.), *The dialogical imagination* (pp. 341-42). Austin: University of Texas Press.

Bomer, R. (1995). *Time for meaning: Crafting literate lives in middle & high school.* Portsmouth, NH: Heinemann.

Britzman, D. P. (1991). *Practice makes practice: A critical study of learning to teach.* Albany: State University of New York Press.

Brooks, J. G., & Brooks, M. G. (1993). *In search of understanding: The case for constructivist classrooms.* Alexandria, VA: ASCD.

Calkins, L. M. (1994). *The art of teaching writing* (rev. ed.). Portsmouth, NH: Heinemann.

Cambourne, B. (1988). *The whole story: Natural learning and the acquistion of literacy in the classroom.* New York: Scholastic.

Grossman, P. L. (1990). *The making of a teacher: Teacher knowledge & teacher education.* New York: Teachers College Press.

Perry, W. G. (1970). *Forms of intellectual and ethical development in the college years.* New York: Holt, Rinehart and Winston.

Ray, R. E. (1993). *The practice of theory: Teacher research in composition.* Urbana, IL: National Council of Teachers of English.

Tremmel, R. (1993). Zen and the art of reflective practice in teacher education. *Harvard Educational Review, 63,* 435-458.

Vinz, R. (1996). *Composing a teaching life.* Portsmouth, NH: Boynton/Cook.

When a Micro-society Meets Its Partner: A Search for Critical Literacy Opportunities Through Service Learning Initiatives

Dan Fraizer
Springfield College

The word *literacy*, like the word *culture*, becomes a complex and difficult concept as educators, politicians, technocrats, and other power brokers invest it with meanings often convenient to their purposes, concerns, or interests. In order to cut through the hyperbole we might imagine literacy "simply" as "basic" reading and writing, but such oversimplification can be risky. For example, an unquestioned acceptance of "literacy" as the primary determinant of success or failure in school can focus the collective attention of decision makers on some idealized form of literacy, which may then be misconstrued to create arbitrary and narrowly defined educational requirements.

Acknowledging and articulating the complexity of literacy, on the other hand, has afforded scholars the opportunity to ask difficult and probing questions about the social and cultural contexts in which reading and writing activities take place. Two of the most well-known scholars in this regard are Graff (1979), who examined schooled literacy in 19th century Canada; and Street (1984), who examined forms of literacy in Iran.

Street (1984) was one of the first to describe the ideological model of literacy, which

> stresses the significance of the socialization process in the construction of the meaning of literacy for participants . . . it distinguishes claims for the consequences of literacy from its real significance for specific social groups [and] treats skeptically claims [of] "openness," "rationality," and "critical awareness" [due to increased literacy levels achieved through the schools]. (p. 2)

Street's comparison of various forms of literacy taught in religious, commercial, and governmental sites in Iran in the 1970s shows how difficult it is to make generalized claims about the value of any idealized form of literacy.

Street's claims echoed those of Graff, who had completed his own historical examination of the goals and outcomes of literacy instruction in several Canadian cities. Graff (1979) argued that schooled literacy did little to directly benefit the working classes and primarily reinforced class divisions by associating literacy with middle-class behaviors and values. Graff concluded that literacy can only be understood in context: "It can be established neither arbitrarily nor uniformly for all members of the population" (p. 292).

These works and those of others, including Brodkey (1986), Cook-Gumperz (1986), and Graff (1985), have shown literacy to be not only context based, but inherently ideological in the sense that literacy is never neutral but always meant to address actual or perceived problems or situations. Sometimes this understanding leads scholars to conclude that literacy is primarily a weapon used to exercise control (Stuckey, 1991). But the ideological model of literacy can also suggest opportunities to challenge the status quo. In his discussion of literacy "crises," for example, Trimbur (1991) sees narrowly conceived literacy issues as "pretexts for educational and cultural change that renegotiate the terms of cultural hegemony, the relations between classes and groups, and the meaning and use of literacy" (p. 281). In other words, opportunities exist to challenge authority by asking difficult questions about the power relations inherent to all discussions of literacy. Such discussions preclude all other claims of inherent "value" in literacy.

The label *critical literacy* may help to reveal some of these power relations. The risk is that "critical" may also be understood to be of significant, even pivotal importance. For example, compared to what has been called *functional literacy*, "critical" literacy suggests an ability not only to read and write in order to "function" in society, but an ability to use reading and writing in order to discriminate and assemble meanings in subtle and complex ways. This could suggest a form of "higher order" thinking, because it implies an ability to interpret and use written forms of language in order to make distinctions that are perhaps lost on the majority of readers and writers.

In this chapter I am less interested in privileging some idealized and hierarchical complexity as a defining characteristic of critical literacy and more interested in describing the interaction of two specific groups of socially and culturally diverse students in order to explore the potential for responding to critical literacy situations. Drawing on Freire's (1970) concept of "problematizing the existential situation" (p. 218), as well as work done by those often labeled "critical educators" (Freire & Macedo, 1987; Giroux, 1983, 1992; Shor, 1992), a critical literacy situation would create opportunities for students to "read their world" (Freire & Macedo, 1987) through their interaction with other diverse groups of people while also undertaking reading and writing activities that encourage them to do the following:

- create personal and differentiated meanings from their experiences with others;
- explore dominant power relations among various groups of people and work toward more socially democratic relations among these groups;
- question or challenge traditional or "received" sources of knowledge (such as textbooks, documents, official policies); and
- pose or reframe problems, rather than attempt to solve problems without examining underlying assumptions about what constitutes a problem.

The focus in a critical literacy situation would be on culturally and socially specific struggles over power and meaning as they are articulated through language. Because I also assume that the struggle to express and communicate through language (a process) is more meaningful to learners than the mastery of idealized language conventions (a product), a critical literacy situation must start with the assumption that multiple literacies coexist as a result of an ongoing struggle for meaning and power. Lankshear and McLaren (1993) argue that:

> Literacy must not be seen as referring to something singular, like an essential technology, a specific skill, or a universal phenomenon

such as print or script. Rather, reading and writing consist in myriad
social and socially constructed *forms*. . . . For many social settings we
do better to think in terms of litera*cies* rather than literacy. (p. xvii)

Multiple literacies exist across a wide range of privileged and
non-privileged social contexts, or what Lankshear and McLaren call
"indices of the dynamics of power" (pp. 12, 13). My attempt here is to
show how some literacies—especially school-based, content-driven
ones—are privileged over others. I do this not to justify a particular hierarchy of literacies, but to show how different literacy objectives of different groups might be linked so as to influence one another in more socially democratic ways through their mutually beneficial interaction. I first
describe one set of school-based literacy objectives that bring together
college students and elementary school children. These literacy objectives
in turn enable other literacy goals and activities to be undertaken through
a college service learning program and create opportunities for critical literacy activities across a range of sites and situations. My argument is that
the interaction of different groups with different literacy objectives
enriches and nurtures literate activities of all kinds, even as it makes
absolute definitions of and proclamations about literacy more difficult.

STRUCTURES AND RELATIONS OF POWER: SPRINGFIELD COLLEGE AND DEBERRY ELEMENTARY SCHOOL

Springfield College is a small- to medium-sized 4-year college located
within a medium-sized, old New England city. It was originally constructed by the YMCA and has a long history of supporting sports and
health-related programs and a philosophy of educating the "mind,
body, and spirit" of its students. In recent years, the college has expanded its health and human service programs and now places great emphasis on preparing students for service-related careers. The college is interested in developing relationships with organizations and institutions
within the city of Springfield that will benefit both college students and
city residents. One of those relationships is with a nearby public elementary school, the DeBerry School.

As one of five magnet schools in Springfield, the DeBerry School
is currently developing a curriculum built around a "micro-society
through technology" theme. DeBerry School seeks to collaborate with
Springfield College in order to help realize some of the goals of this curriculum. One of the most visible programs involving Springfield College
students is a federally funded service learning initiative. Service learning
attempts to give students an opportunity to perform what is usually

known as community service, while connecting this service to the college curriculum. Service learning is a method:

- under which students learn and develop through active participation in thoughtfully organized service experiences that meet actual community needs;
- that is integrated into the students' academic curriculum or provides structured time for a student to think, talk, or write about what the student did and saw during the service activity;
- that provides students with opportunities to use newly acquired skills and knowledge in real-life situations in their own communities; and
- that enhances what is taught in school by extending student learning beyond the classroom and into the community and helps to foster the development of a sense of caring for others (National and Community Service Learning Act of 1990, 1991).

The DeBerry School is a significant service site at Springfield College, especially through an initiative called "Partners." In the Partners Program, college students pair up with selected DeBerry students on a weekly basis. They first visit the elementary school to help DeBerry students with their homework. Then college and elementary students travel the short distance to the college, where they play games, get to know one another, and eat dinner together at the college cafeteria. Over time, college students and elementary school children develop close personal relationships that often cross significant cultural and social boundaries. This "border crossing" has also been facilitated in other service learning situations (see Hayes & Cuban, 1996).

About Springfield College Students

Approximately 3,000 students attend Springfield College. Most are resident students who attend classes during the day, with a smaller number of weekend students, who are typically older, returning students enrolled in the School of Human Services. Whereas the weekend students are often city residents who interact with people of color and life in an urban setting on a regular basis, most of the resident students are young, come from suburban communities, and are White. Their life experiences are generally limited to their teenage years, and most of these students' exposure to urban settings and people of color is limited. Attending college in the city of Springfield, an urban center comprised of Black, Hispanic, and White residents, creates an opportunity to experience diversity on a daily basis. However, many college students never leave the campus to experience this diversity, which contributes to divisions between the college and the surrounding neighborhood.

About DeBerry Students

DeBerry School is the focus of ongoing concern. The school is located in an inner-city "contested" area of mostly Black and Hispanic residents, and students are primarily drawn from the surrounding neighborhoods. The Springfield Public Schools have directed much attention in recent years to fighting "White flight" to private and parochial schools. Test scores (Iowa Test of Basic Skills) at DeBerry are low, and literacy efforts are complicated by the need to teach in both Spanish and English.

The cultural differences between Springfield College students and DeBerry School students are significant. Most Springfield College and DeBerry School "partners" come from different communities and families and have grown up with different kinds of experiences and expectations. There is also a significant age gap. Nevertheless, participants from both groups do find common ground as the college students attempt to support the younger students in their efforts to succeed academically and as the younger students begin to look to the college students as role models. These relationships create the potential for reading and writing activities that transcend more narrowly defined literacy practices.

FORMAL SCHOOLING LITERACY OBJECTIVES: KEEPING AN EYE ON THE PRIZE

One of the difficult conceptual problems associated with literacy of all kinds is that although practitioners tend to think of literacy in terms of activities, those not immediately involved in these activities tend to think of literacy in terms of the finished product. For most teachers and students, literacy is usually something to do, whereas for policymakers and other concerned citizens, literacy is something to *have* in one's possession, often in order to justify the expense of books, teachers, and schools. It is not enough that students and teachers engage in reading and writing activities of their own choosing, especially when these activities attempt to value and accept the forms of language students themselves use (Collins, 1989; Goodman,1987; or consider the recent attempt by the Oakland, CA school district to value what is now called "Ebonics"). Educational institutions seem destined to attend to reading and writing outcomes that meet the expectations of those groups most invested in the schools (Graff, 1979). Historically, urban schools in particular constrained literacy to its most narrow forms, even as they exhibited the greatest diversity in student populations (Borman & Spring, 1984; Kaestle, 1973). Educational inequities are now clearly evident due to inadequately funded public school systems all over the United States, especially in cities where tax revenues continue to erode while suburban schools prosper (Kozol, 1991). In response to this reality, public schools in many cities have chosen to develop and market "magnet" schools with "specialized" curricula in order to attract both students and federal dollars. This is the case at the DeBerry School, which received a three-year grant to fund the planning and implementation of a "micro-society" theme. According to the program description, the school will:

> offer a specialized micro-society through technology curriculum that would not otherwise be available to students in this district. The specialized curriculum will integrate the study of mathematics, science, history, geography, English, foreign languages, art, and music, and will strengthen students' reading and vocational skills. The micro-society school will be one in which students build a society in miniature.

The goals of this society-in-miniature are to emphasize "working, being productive, generating savings, investing capital, trading, negotiating contracts, making and marketing goods and services, forming corporations and partnerships, and deal-making" (program description). The society imagined here, then, is first and foremost identified with the values of the stereotypical American entrepreneur. This is not a society imagined through the eyes of someone like Fidel Castro in Cuba, or even the eyes of someone like Lyndon Johnson, whose "Great Society" programs of the 1960s meant to take care of the less fortunate and promote the common good through a variety of government-funded services, including literacy programs. On paper, this societal vision values the accumulation of capital and the development of services meant to assist in capital accumulation, albeit couched in the language of self-sufficiency. Public services or civic responsibility, to the extent they exist in this vision, seem intended to provide the stability and order necessary for capital accumulation to take place.

The DeBerry School curriculum is meant to be linked to this vision of American society by offering both "basic curricular" and "micro" activities that prepare students for "positions" in the micro-society. For example, a student would go through an interview process with teachers and other staff in order to hold positions of prestige such as a

CEO. Workshops by staff educate children about leadership opportunities, and children submit business plans that describe the products they will create and market. Various "strands" are intended to help students prepare for these positions. They include "Mathematics and Business," "Science and Technology," "Social Studies and Government," and "Literacy." The intent of at least three of these "strands" is clearly to match traditionally "academic" subjects with so-called "real-world" applications. But what about literacy? Why is it not paired with a "real-world" application? Probably because in this vision, literacy (as opposed to reading and writing) is valued more for its facilitation of general educational goals rather than any particular site in the "real world." Here is the micro-society definition of literacy: "In today's fast paced world, literacy means much more than reading and writing. Literacy includes facility with technology and mathematics and full participation in our democracy" (program description). Although it is unclear how facility with technology and mathematics is related to full participation in democracy, there is a sense that literacy is somehow important enough and big enough that this will become apparent. Literacy becomes a handmaiden to the other strands, assisting with the "real work" to be done in business, technology, and government. There is also a sense that, through their implied connection to the "real-world" strands, literacy activities will lead to an awareness of real world consequences. One "strand specialist" recorded these comments from students:

> "If we get hurt, will we be paid?" "Can we share money?"
> "We have to pay taxes?" "That's not fair! You mean that if I
> don't come to school I won't get paid?"

As with any reading material, these program descriptions need to be appreciated in context. The readers of this document are most likely parents and other adults who either intend to send their children to DeBerry School or who are in a position to evaluate the program itself or the program proposal. There is very little in the program description, however, that describes actual reading and writing activities. Although the "micro-society" program may or may not be a success by any number of criteria, it is unclear from these materials alone what sorts of reading and writing actually take place. When literacy is commodified as a product to be marketed to parents or official decision makers, rather than lived as an experience, little is likely to be revealed about the nature of the experience. Literacy as a product for sale may serve more as a smokescreen, obscuring or smoothing over social, economic, and cultural influences on actual literacy activities.

Micro-society After One Year

How much of an impact has this initiative had after its first year? It is clear from my own observations, interactions, and interviews with DeBerry students, teachers, and Springfield College students that the micro-society curriculum is in place and that most of those who are aware of it or have some experience with it think it is a good idea. Teachers are enthusiastic because the children are enthusiastic. DeBerry students clearly understand the economy of earning and spending micro-society dollars and look forward to earning them. For example, one business is "Josey's Jewelry," which "hires employees" to make jewelry, giving students a popular place to spend the dollars they "earn" at their various jobs. Other "business ventures" include "the Ultimate Science Store," "The Wood Shop," and "Puppet Place." Hallways at DeBerry School exhibit pictures of children holding up micro-society dollars, selling beverages, and making crafts.

From the DeBerry students' perspective, the atmosphere is perhaps similar to a Saturday morning yard sale. Micro-society is fun because it gives students a chance to do something different than their usual classwork and to take pride in their status and positions of responsibility. For example, elections held during November gave students a chance to be excited about voting and to think about who among their peers they would vote for.

Discussions with adults (teachers and college partners) about the micro-society are more serious in tone. Responsibility was often cited as an important outcome. One college partner described DeBerry School as "an oasis" and valued the micro-society for what it would teach students about "the real world." Status linked with responsibility was also a valued outcome for adult participants. In one instance, a DeBerry student who had just qualified for a job as a CEO of a micro-society company became very excited about his new job, until he realized he did not know what a CEO was. He was told by a college partner that a CEO was someone with a lot of responsibility who was in charge of the company and that CEOs often make enormous salaries in comparison to average workers.

Whether viewed seriously or as fun, nearly all comments about the micro-society were positive. One college Partner noted that "the set up [of DeBerry School] gives the students a sense of belonging and a feeling of community." Even though the program may be on its way to becoming a success, it is more difficult to describe its impact on children's reading and writing abilities, except in primarily functional ways such as being able to read and follow directions or count money.

WHEN PARTNERS DO LITERACY ACTIVITIES AT DEBERRY SCHOOL

College students who become involved in the Partners Program act as tutors/mentors to public school students one day a week, for 12 weeks during the semester. Partners spend about three hours a week together, of which about 45 minutes is spent on homework. Because the rest of the time spent together focuses on recreational activities and dinner, this homework/tutoring session often provides the chief opportunity to engage in reading and writing activities. Site coordinators (experienced Partners) support and assist new Partners during this time, and training sessions are held throughout the semester that teach tutoring strategies and motivational techniques. These training sessions focus on general considerations such as how to stay student oriented, how to praise students, and how to help them to stay on task. DeBerry students are pretested and posttested at the beginning and end of the semester to assess their progress, and each DeBerry student must be rated by his or her college Partner after each tutoring session to determine whether his or her social behavior was appropriate. If a DeBerry student does not put forward a significant effort in these tutoring sessions, he or she can be taken out of the Partners Program. Because the program is so popular, a waiting list is ready to provide new DeBerry students if this happens.

Because evaluation through the standardized testing of the Iowa Tests of Basic Skills is the most generalizable and visible literacy goal to all, homework activities often require students to do practice work meant to improve test performance. The Iowa Tests, designed for grades three through eight, "are designed to measure how well a student has learned the basic knowledge and skills that are taught in elementary and middle schools, in such areas as reading and mathematics" (Definition of "Iowa Tests," 1996, p. 1). It should come as no surprise that much of the interaction I observed involved completing worksheets with math, spelling, and reading comprehension problems culled from textbooks. College Partners attempt to create a "get down to business" atmosphere, and they praise students for the amount of work they can complete, the number of correct answers they get, and their avoidance of "tricky" problems that "will get you on a test." College students act as role models in these sessions to the extent that they show they know a very specific form of literacy: how to read, write, and do math in order to do well on tests.

Most of the tutors I spoke with expressed concern for their Partner's ability to do well on tests, but not for the use of these tests to determine success. They also expressed frustration with the degree of cooperation they received from DeBerry teachers. Although teachers "started out" providing homework materials and even writing personal notes to tutors, teachers seemed to "lose interest" after a while, often providing no work or correspondence in students' folders. College Partners would then resort to board games or other social activities. In interviews I conducted with College Partners, several speculated that the commitment of teachers to an inner-city school was negatively affected by teacher pay rates that were less than suburban public schools or private schools. In general, disillusionment with urban schools among many (not all) future teachers was apparent (see Flippo, Hetzel, Gribouski, & Armstrong, 1993).

However aware of such structural influences some of the college partners may be, their involvement has been structurally limited to a personal, one-to-one relationship. Larger *institutional* or *programmatic* issues, such as questioning the credibility of tests, are seen as outside their responsibility or capacity to change, even when working toward such change might further both the program and the individual's goal of helping his or her partner develop reading and writing abilities.

Most teachers at DeBerry School appear to be appreciative of the support they receive through the Partners Program. Responsibility for renewing a commitment from some teachers to improve communication with Partners about homework assignments should clearly rest with program coordinators and DeBerry School administrators. This is not the most important issue in this case, however. More importantly, this problem serves as an example of a school-based decontextualized literacy situation, with the same sort of questionable, even manufactured concern in evidence that was apparent during the fabricated "literacy crisis" of the 1970s (see Trimbur, 1991). At that time, declining test scores were cited as evidence that literacy itself was in decline. Trimbur reviews the work of others who show multiple factors influenced a "decline" in test scores, including disenchantment with schooling and the increase in numbers of students from different demographic groups taking tests such as the SAT. Greater and more varied educational opportunities and experiences for a larger number of students may have affected literacy activities but did not point directly to a literacy "crisis."

Similarly, a literacy "crisis" with racist undertones may be unnecessarily manufactured at DeBerry School. Iowa Tests of Basic Skills scores are used by the Springfield Public Schools to compare one school within the district to another, even though one of the authors of the test argues forcefully that "the primary purpose of tests like these is not to compare Cedar Rapids with Des Moines, or any other school. . . . The primary purpose . . . is to furnish information to three people—the parent, the teacher, and the child—about his or her relative strengths and weaknesses" (Rogahn, 1997). Nevertheless, low test scores at DeBerry School, with its higher than average Black and Hispanic enrollment, are used to suggest the school has serious problems.

In any case, the perception of academic difficulties serves to at least partially justify the involvement of the Partners Program. A primary literacy site is established (DeBerry School), with a target population (Partners participants), and a general goal identified (do better on academic reading and writing). Literacy resources (tutors) are made available, and the interaction of diverse groups of people is valued as a bonus outcome. However, the form of literacy practiced is poorly articulated, and those involved are often isolated in pairs so that each participant eventually relies on his or her own notion of what activities are appropriate. As individuals communicate less as a group, they become more isolated from one another, and the reading and writing that is done becomes less meaningful to anyone except in an often arbitrary sense of being done "correctly" or not in order to have a supposed impact on test scores. Participants continue to be involved in spite of this poorly conceived study hall approach because, in this case, the program is about more than reading and writing. Relationships develop as both College Partners and DeBerry students continue to learn from one another, but not particularly because of an engagement with reading and writing. Interest in reading and writing for reasons outside an abstracted sense of academic success atrophy. Literacy as an *activity* becomes sterile, even if students' reading and writing abilities improve as a result of other factors such as children's exposure to positive role models who seem to value reading and writing.

How, then, might literacy become a more personally meaningful activity to all participants, and how might these participants develop their reading and writing abilities by becoming involved in critical literacy opportunities? Some of the work on reading and writing in service learning situations provides a clue.

LITERACY PRACTICES AND SERVICE LEARNING AT SPRINGFIELD COLLEGE

Many College Partners seem to accept "worksheet" literacy activities with their DeBerry partners, not because they think they are interesting or educational, but because they recognize their own educational experiences in the use of such decontextualized practices. They may be limited, then, by their own background and understanding of the value of reading and writing. Because they are in school and have spent most of their lives in school, school-based literacy acquisition probably influences how they define their literacy objectives. Literacy development may also be understood by Springfield College students with the assistance of a metaphor, such as physical development (something of great importance at Springfield College), so that literacy development may be seen to require the same commitment to repetitious drill and strain as, say, pumping iron (see Novek, 1992, for an exploration of various literacy metaphors). College Partners really do want their DeBerry Partners to do well, but they may be unable to see beyond their own "ideologies of literacy" (Lankshear & McLaren, 1993) to imagine how DeBerry students might value and develop reading and writing for their own intrinsic reasons, as well as for extrinsic reasons other than tests. College life reinforces highly formal and stylized literacy practices by linking all reading and writing activities to assessment. Assessment is in turn linked to career opportunities. College students in general are perhaps ideal participants for teaching and reinforcing test-bound literacy practices that are linked to school success, but are not especially well equipped to help primary school students use reading and writing in order to reflect on their experiences with others, especially if they do not use reading and writing to help them make sense of their own experiences in life.

Service learning gives a student the chance to perform a valuable community service *and* to learn something in the process. Service learning also tends to be most often associated with learning about the community and the needs of particular individuals within that community, so that often reading and writing activities become secondary. For example, much emphasis is placed on students' perceptions and understanding of the groups with whom they interact, whether it be inner-city school children (including their learning styles), nursing home residents, or ethnic groups (see Flippo et al., 1993; Heinemann, Obi, Pagano, & Weiner, 1992). Writing is usually a part of service learning in one of two ways. Bacon (1994) has distinguished between "writing *about* service experiences [compared to] writing *as* service" (p. 14) in order to identify two usually different goals: writing as a way of reflecting on the service experience compared to writing materials that are then used out in the community. Cooper and Julier (1995), on the other hand, have argued that this approach is too dualistic and that both goals can be accommodated through community and classroom goals that reinforce one another and give students the chance to learn (and write) about their community situations in preparation for the writing (or teaching about writing) they do *as* service. In this way, the writing and reading students do allows them to "revisit both their prior experience in volunteering . . . as well as their current participation with a community agency" (p. 80).

A First Step

Among one recent group of Partners participants, writing about service created the necessary preconditions for breaking away from an ideologically bound, school-based understanding of literacy development. Whereas College Partners in the past had signed on in order to "be involved in the community and do some good," this group committed themselves to the program specifically as part of a class requirement. In an education course called "Early Childhood Development," students' involvement with Partners was linked to the course curriculum. As students studied, for example, particular stages of child development, they applied theoretical concepts from the course textbook to what they were observing in their DeBerry School partner's behavior. These observations were then systematically recorded in regular journal entries.

Students witnessed and recorded examples of "learned helplessness," "Gardner's theory of logical skill," "heteronomous vs. autonomous morality," and other child development concepts. Even when students did not employ educational terms or concepts, their descriptions of particular child behaviors and language gave the professor an opportunity to label these behaviors using educational or psychological terms in his or her marginal comments on the journals, thereby bringing theory closer to practice. Because Partners also interacted with parents, these college students were able to observe and write about parenting styles ranging from "authoritative" to "permissive/indulgent." Sometimes, parents and children exhibited a combination of parenting and learning styles, showing students that the categories they learn from their textbooks may not always label individuals as neatly as textbook authors present them. In this sense, students had the opportunity to challenge received sources of knowledge as well as articulate personal and differentiated meanings through their journal observations (two important qualities of critical literacy).

Rather than study the textbook and listen to lectures alone, isolated from the reality the course content describes, students used writing to help them process (and occasionally challenge) what they were reading in the textbook *and* observing out in the community as they performed their service. Literacy became contextualized in a significant and unique way as a meaningful *activity*, rather than as an abstracted "ability" or "skill" to be valued for poorly articulated reasons by often unknown authority figures such as test makers. More importantly, once the College Partner has this kind of literacy experience, he or she should be better prepared to help his or her DeBerry Partner have a similar experience, so that both groups read and write in order to learn from each other, rather than as unequal and narrowly defined "expert" and "beginner." Rather than be content to spend most of their time filling out worksheets and depending on DeBerry teachers whose commitment to the service learning project may be wanting, College Partners could be helped to initiate literacy activities with DeBerry students similar to those they experience as a result of their service learning literacy activities. Springfield College Partners in the Early Childhood Education class used written language to express their feelings, frustrations, and understanding of academic concepts in relation to real-life situations. DeBerry students should also be able to use written language to explore their feelings about the Partners Program and what they learn through their exposure to college students. They should do so in ways that do not focus primarily on written correctness but on writing involvement.

Specifically, why couldn't DeBerry students also write in a journal about their experiences with their Partner? Most DeBerry students learn much about what it is like to be a college student, and for some their exposure to a College Partner provides an important role model at a critical age. Many DeBerry students begin to formulate ideas about what they want to be and imagine themselves in college in order to realize those goals. Obviously, the micro-society curriculum also reinforces this kind of thinking in children, but through models conceived in narrow, socially idealized ways.

Although program development may address some of these concerns, my argument here is that *literacy, specifically writing,* can play an instrumental role in helping service learning participants to not only reflect on their experiences but also to pose community or institutional problems more clearly, explore power relations, and challenge authority productively. Literacy activities can help service learning participants who work in schools to process what they learn, as well as experience a learning process that may enable them to learn differently in the future. This is not only personally empowering but holds the potential for challenging the ways outsiders define literacy, or even a microsociety, for their own purposes.

Critical Literacy Opportunities

A more probing and collaboratively imagined reflective journal for all service learning participants is one way to begin creating and extending critical literacy situations. While the journal is an important place to apply textbook or course-related concepts, it can also be a safe and thoughtful place to begin to explore the situations in which service learning participants find themselves. Observations of a given situation need not be confined to how they illustrate the content of any given course. Herzberg (1994) has argued that community service, even when it is linked to a course curriculum, does not necessarily lead to an understanding of "the nature of the problems that cause these organizations to come into existence" (p. 308) or, in this case, the causes for the need for Partners to exist at DeBerry School. Herzberg worries that students' service experiences allow them to see that the people they serve are "just like themselves," but that "questions about social structures, ideology, and social justice are [not] automatically raised by community service" (p. 309).

Although the journal can and should be a place where students can talk about their experiences in terms of how they are personally affected by their interaction with people and programs, it should also be a place where students use writing to probe and better understand their service situations in larger terms. Problems or situations that arise for any given individual can be first described in the journal, but also contextualized by asking how that problem came into existence in the first place, thereby revealing larger structural issues and problems.

For example, one college student described an experience playing a board game with her young partner and several others. The game was "Life," and the players came to a section where they had to choose between the "career path" or the "college path." All the players except for this particular child chose the "college path." When asked why she did not choose the college option, she responded by saying she would become a waitress and make a lot in tips. The College Partner reflected in her journal that she either had low expectations of herself or just wanted attention. No comment was made by the professor, in this case, to invite the college student to examine other social or cultural reasons why this child might think attending college was out of her reach, such as her perceptions of who went to college based on her experience with Partners.

In a different case, a College Partner remarked in her journal that she thought "inner-city" children "grow up a great deal faster than my younger sisters and brother or I did." To support this, she cited her young Partner's reference to a romantic relationship between two college Partners ("You know they are doing it"). The professor's comments first raised the question of whether the child knew what she was saying, and second, suggested that "some would argue inner-city kids grow up slower, not faster." Here an opportunity existed to explore not only family and peer influences on behavior, but community and neighborhood influences by asking what sorts of generalizations can be made about inner-city children and what factors are relevant to children's development.

How might Partners begin to see not only their own role in a situation and the roles of those close to the children, but also the impact of community and other social forces on people's lives? One place to begin could be to encourage peer responses to one another's journals. Other service learning participants might "dialogue" with another person's journal, posing questions and making comments that expand on initial comments. In this and other similar ways, Partners might be able to move beyond the basic "worksheet" literacy initially assigned to them, beyond the "course concepts" literacy that is an often stated objective of service learning courses, and eventually beyond ideologies of the individual to more institutional and structural explanations. We should be asking not only what participants *do* at a service learning site, but why and who benefits. Students might, at this level, use reading and writing to probe the most basic and foundational assumptions that support the programs they are meant to serve. Some insights and solutions to community problems might never be discovered otherwise.

Finally, creating critical literacy situations holds the potential for social transformation, when the *collective* understandings of a group of service learning participants take literate form in order to communicate with those who might be in a better place to actually affect changes if they better understood institutional and programmatic problems in more thorough ways from the bottom up. Literacy and language activities in general should be seen as instrumental to understanding and evaluating not only individual students, but the one world in which we all live.

REFERENCES

Bacon, N. (1994, Spring). Community service and writing instruction. *National Society for Experiential Learning Quarterly, 14,* 27.

Borman, K.M., & Spring, J.H. (1984). *Schools in central cities/Structure and process.* New York: Longman.

Brodkey, L. (1986). Tropics of literacy. *Journal of Education, 168*(2), 47-54.

Collins, J. (1989). Hegemonic practice: Literacy and standard language in public education. *Journal of Education, 171*(2), 9-34.

Cooper, D., & Julier. L. (1995, Fall). Writing the ties that bind: Service learning in the writing classroom. *Michigan Journal of Community Service Learning,* pp. 72-85.

Cook-Gumperz, J. (1986). *The social construction of literacy.* New York and Cambridge: Cambridge University Press.

Definition of "Iowa Tests of Basic Skills." (1996, September 11). Internet: http://www.edweek.org/context.glossary/iowatest.html.

Flippo, R., Hetzel, C., Gribouski, D., & Armstrong, L. (1993, April). *Literacy, multicultural, and socio-cultural considerations: Student Literacy Corps and the community.* Paper presented at 38th annual Convention of International Reading Association, San Antonio, Texas. (ERIC Document Reproduction Number ED 356 466)

Freire, P. (1970). The adult literacy process as cultural action for freedom. *Harvard Educational Review, 40*(2), 205-225.

Freire, P., & Macedo, D. (1987). *Literacy: Reading the word and the world.* South Hadley, MA: Bergin and Garvey.

Gee, J. (1991). The narrativization of experience in the oral style. In C. Mitchell & K. Weiler (Eds.), *Rewriting literacy: Culture and the discourse of the other* (pp. 77-101). New York: Bergin and Garvey.

Giroux, H. (1983). *Theory and resistance in education: A pedagogy for opposition.* South Hadley, MA: Bergin and Garvey.

Giroux, H. (1992). *Border crossings: Cultural workers and the politics of education.* New York: Routledge.

Goodman, K.S. (1987). *Language and thinking in school: A whole language curriculum.* New York: Richard C. Owens Publishers.

Graff, H. (1979). *The literacy myth.* New York: Academic Press.

Graff, H. (1985). *The politics of literacy.* London: Macmillan.

Hayes, E., & Cuban, S. (1996, April). *Border pedagogy: A critical framework for service learning.* Paper presented at American Educational Research Association Conference, New York. (ERIC Document Reproduction Number ED 393 992)

Heinemann, H., Obi, R., Pagano, A., & Weiner, L. (1992). *Effects of using early pre-service field experiences in urban settings to prepare teachers to meet the challenges of teaching in multicultural urban schools.* (ERIC Document Reproduction Number ED 344 868)

Herzberg, B. (1994). Community service and critical teaching. *College Composition and Communication, 45*(3), 307-319.

Kaestle, C. (1973). *Evolution of an urban school system.* Cambridge, MA: Harvard University Press.

Kozol, J. (1991). *Savage inequalities: Children in America's schools.* New York: Crown.

Lankshear, C., & McLaren, P. (Eds.). (1993). *Critical literacy: Politics, praxis, and the postmodern.* Albany: State University of New York Press.

National and Community Service Act of 1990. (1991). In R. Wilts-Cairn & J. Kielsmeier, *Growing hope* (p. 17). Minneapolis, MN: National Youth Leadership Council.

Novek, E. (1992). Read it and weep: How metaphor limits views of literacy. *Discourse and Society, 3*(2).

Rogahn, K. (1997). Author of basic skills test says scores shouldn't be compared. Internet: http://www mesa.K12.az.us/~research/hoover.html.

Shor, I. (1992). *Empowering education: Critical teaching for social change.* Chicago: University of Chicago Press.

Street, B. (1984). *Literacy in theory and practice.* Cambridge: Cambridge University Press.

Stuckey, J. E. (1990). *The violence of literacy.* Portsmouth, NH: Heinemann-Boynton Cook.

Trimbur, J. (1991). Literacy and the discourse of crisis. In R. Bullock, J. Timbur, & C. Schuster (Eds.), *The politics of writing instruction: Postsecondary* (pp. 277-295). Portsmouth, NH: Boynton/Cook.

7

Student Literacy Partnerships Through Community Tutorials

Mary M. Salibrici
Syracuse University

In the small rural township where I grew up in the 1950s, two one-room schoolhouses still stood. I was enchanted, convinced they existed to capture my imagination. Fascinated by the time I was five by the idea of playing school and being a teacher, I gradually became even more intrigued by the prospect that at one time children of all ages were collected together into one room in order to learn. Later I discovered from family lore that this was indeed how one of my grandfathers had been taught in the 1870s. What an unusual way to go to school, I thought, especially compared to my own experience of travelling by bus to a large central district and joining other children my own age in one of many separate grades from kindergarten through 12th.

Perhaps this was my first introduction to cross-age, interactive learning. At least the one-room schoolhouse concept parlayed itself into my pretend activities because when I did play school with my brothers, I had to figure out ways for us to work on make-believe problems together because of the difference in our ages. At any rate, much as I would like to find a romantic correspondence to this childhood memory, the

reality is that my much-later experience doing writing-across-the-cur-
riculum projects and using the process paradigm in my writing classes is
more likely what led me to create the community tutorial as a literacy
outreach project for my writing students.

I believed the emphasis on interactive and discovery-based
learning between college and high school students would lead my students to recognize writing as an applicable and accessible skill. Critical
literacy certainly includes the successful development of reading and
writing abilities through practice in summarizing, synthesizing, and
making claims about the texts students read and write. In this respect I
concur with the definition of literacy as proposed by The National
Literacy Act of 1991:

> the ability to read, write, speak in *English*, and compute and solve
> problems at levels of proficiency necessary to function on the job
> and in society, achieve one's goals, and develop one's knowledge
> and potential. (U.S. Department of Education, 1993, p. 8; emphasis in
> original)

My interest, however, was in figuring out what our definitions of critical
literacy might mean in practice. If we propose that critical literacy
includes the ability to solve problems resembling those students actually
face in the world, then how are we creating such experiences for them
while they are in our classrooms? I contend that critical literacy is best
developed in discovery-based, collaborative environments. In other
words, critical literacy emerges within a learning situation that challenges students to understand problems, discover solutions, and collaborate with others in working out those solutions. Students need to face
practical situations requiring them to act on their ideas.

Of course, the groundwork for this literacy principle was laid
early in the 20th century by John Dewey, and later reinforced by Jerome
Bruner's (1960) work. Dewey (1916) advocated an instructional process
that would build on students' genuine situational experience, one in
which the students would be actively invested and in which genuine
problems would develop. Dewey worried that:

> As a consequence of the absence of the materials and occupations
> which generate real problems, the pupil's problems are not his; or,
> rather, they are his only as pupil, not as a human being. (p. 156)

Critical to the learning process, according to Dewey, is the opportunity
for students to be actively and cooperatively engaged in their individual
learning power. Dewey's cooperative learning model was based on the

notion that diversity could flourish at the same time that common purpose could be established in a classroom:

> The two elements in our criterion both point to democracy. The first
> signifies not only more numerous and more varied points of shared
> common interest, but greater reliance upon the recognition of mutu-
> al interests as a factor in social control. The second means not only
> freer interaction between social groups . . . but change in social
> habits–its continuous readjustment through meeting the new situa-
> tions produced by varied intercourse. (pp. 86-87)

For Dewey, growth meant process, a cooperative undertaking whereby
students would release their individual interests and talents for the community's welfare. Good educational practice would require an understanding of the intrinsic activities and needs of any given individual, be
capable of translation into cooperative forms of instruction, and broaden
the student's outlook as he or she concurrently learned to take various
new connections or consequences into account.

Bruner (1960) later provided another perspective on this notion
of discovery-based learning:

> Mastery of the fundamental ideas of a field involves not only the
> grasping of general principles, but also the development of an atti-
> tude toward learning and inquiry, toward guessing and hunches,
> toward the possibility of solving problems on one's own. (p. 20)

Bruner goes on to say:

> The best way to create interest in a subject is to render it worth
> knowing, which means to make the knowledge gained usable in
> one's thinking beyond the situation in which the learning has
> occurred. (p. 31)

If we want our students to write well, therefore, they have to do writing
as writers in real situations, in the same way that in our science classes
we should design activities so that students do biology as biologists. The
personal responsibility that exists at the heart of such a learning experience can only emerge, I believe, in the kind of interactive and problem-
solving activities that place students in the middle of discovering their
own ability as learners, problem solvers, chemists, readers, writers, and
so on. These experiences then help them develop attitudes toward learning that will serve them well elsewhere. Cooperative, interactive, discov-

ery-based learning, in other words, leads to stronger possibilities that students will develop portable literacy skills.

The community tutorial project provides opportunities for college juniors in my upper division writing class to collaborate with 11th grade English students from a local city high school. The students investigate the nature of the writing process by mentoring high school students who are involved in their own writing projects. They then document these investigations through case studies. Final reflective essays further ask that the college students make connections between the work they have done with the high school students and their own growth as writers throughout the semester.

The project began to take shape after I discussed its possibilities with a high school English teacher whom I met during a strategic planning session for a local city high school. We seemed to be on the same wave length when it came to innovative teaching practices, and at the time I was particularly interested in weaving some kind of community outreach into my work as a composition teacher. Scheduling experiments were about to begin at her high school, so we knew that we could count on block or double periods to accommodate visits by college students during class time. I then asked for a teaching section that would coincide with the morning periods when my partner would be teaching her 11th graders. During the first semester of our project, I also received a faculty instructional grant that covered some of my transportation and copying expenses.

My first task at the beginning of this project in Spring 1996 was to provide students with the necessary background to think, read, and write about the writing process so that they could then mentor high school students working on a particular writing project. In short, they needed a crash course in mentorship and problem solving. The first six weeks of my course, therefore, consist of reading about the writing process through a variety of texts, including excerpts from Aristotle's *On Rhetoric* (1991), Emig's *Composing Processes of Twelfth Graders* (1971), Lamott's *Bird by Bird* (1994), and Elbow's *Writing Without Teachers* (1973), writing short essays to define and summarize information about the writing process; developing a long-term personal project as a way of comparing individual progress to process theory; and working in small groups to practice peer response methods (see Appendix for course syllabus and assignments).

The centerpiece of the class is, of course, the case study, a form utilized by various professional communities and one that inspires habits of critical thinking, cooperative learning, and problem solving. Students have the option of volunteering for the high school project or choosing their own case study topic and forming their own study groups. The volunteers for the community tutorial/case study attend weekly sessions at the local high school over a six-week period. The actual tutorial sessions are organized into small groups, with each college student responsible for mentoring four to five high school students. The main goal of their case study experience is to determine how writers actually engage in a writing process and how that process relates to the finished product, at the same time that they are actually mentoring the high school students who are working on a writing assignment.

Volunteers for the high school case study meet and discuss the project in advance with the high school teacher. She makes a visit to the college classroom on the week before tutorials actually begin in order to explain the nature of her class and to describe her students. During this visit the students receive a calendar from the high school teacher that outlines various assignment deadlines, actual written assignments, and a list of the students who will be in their groups. It seems important to the college students to have this time with the high school teacher because they can ask specific questions about students and assignments, as well as begin to develop a line of communication about the project with someone other than me. Students continue meeting together in their small group as the project moves along because they need to plan their weekly strategies, to troubleshoot together about specific concerns, and, finally, to share and revise their case study drafts.

Helping the high school students with their writing projects and investigating the writing process of these students at the same time is the heart of the community tutorial project. The students take extensive notes after each tutorial session, discuss what happens in our regular debriefing trips back to campus, and meet with me individually to discuss specific problems as they arise. Additionally, through their contact with the high school English teacher, the students have access to all reading and writing assignments given to the high school students as well as copies of their drafts and final written texts. High school students also complete an initial survey of questions related to their writing habits and expectations, and the college students develop further interview questions to receive more personal and academic information about them. In short, the college students have plenty of data to complete an analysis.

Another special feature of the course asks the students to complete a personal writing project on a topic of interest to them, one that they develop through the semester as independent from the regular work of the course. Progress reports are turned in periodically to indicate how these projects are coming along. At the end of the semester we work on a final reflective essay in which students bring together everything they have learned through the initial reading and writing assignments, the case study, and the personal project. Students are able to look retrospectively at what they have accomplished and then write about the way they understand their own personal and professional writing process. Do they have a fuller perspective on their own writing abilities by the end of the course when the reflective essays are completed and a stronger sense of themselves as able producers and editors of texts? Thinking about the intersection of the community tutorial project and the personal project in a final reflective essay provides an opportunity for recognizing how strengthened writing ability has taken place.

Because they are responsible for coordinating and facilitating small writing response groups through the mentoring project, college students develop strong problem-solving skills in the act of working with individual students as well as a small group. Working with small groups requires the students to apply the concepts of revision and peer response as we have been practicing them in our class. In fact, this small group practice builds quite well on the commonplace literacy notion of "each one teach one." As college students identify and implement the mentoring strategies that work best for individual students, they concurrently enhance their problem-solving, assessment, and management skills. By engaging high school students in these "real-life" small group tutorials and then writing up their experiences in case studies, a form that serves them well later within the range of their proposed professions, college students begin to recognize writing as a useful, applicable, necessary, and accessible skill. Their involvement in such a discovery-based, interactive learning experience directs them easily toward productive application and self-assessment of the skills they are practicing.

The high school students, sometimes quite uninvested in their work for English class, usually bond quickly with the college students and often work ardently to apply the advice they receive about ongoing writing projects. Although they are unaccustomed to the procedures or possibilities involved in peer response, many of them are ultimately able to examine their own writing progress as it relates to the feedback they receive from peers in their small groups and from their college mentors. The fact that the college students exist in the classroom as mentors and, furthermore, as role models is undoubtedly the most prominent and successful feature of the project for the high school students. They witness the work of older students who use writing regularly and for real purposes in their college work.

Yet, how can I gauge whether the community tutorial is a successful literacy project for my student volunteers? What are the clues indicating that the project teaches my students about writing's usefulness and applicability, that it has the potential to help them learn and work in other domains? One insurance is to make the participation optional. The course is designed so that no student in my class feels compelled to join the high school students as the only way to achieve success. In the first week of classes, when I explain the syllabus and requirements, students are given several choices for completing the case study assignment; the high school project is only one option. Students may also develop case study projects that look at workplace or other kinds of academic writing. However, during each semester that the community tutorial has been offered as an alternative, I have had a full slate of volunteers on the first day of class and for a variety of reasons.

Some students are intrigued by the prospect of visiting such a setting as a way to revisit what they remember from their own high school days. Some have vivid negative memories of their own high school English experiences, so they volunteer with an altruistic spirit of hoping to change that possibility for others. Occasionally a student will volunteer for the project to test out an interest in teaching. Once a student even joined as a way to check up on his two brothers who just happened to attend the same high school. Whatever their reasons might be, it is important to me that the high school version of the case study assignment be presented as optional, so student engagement is accompanied by some sense of personal investment.

The community tutorial project also requires that the college students propose a particular problem or focus, something that provides them with a specific angle of study in addition to helping high school students with their writing. Are they interested in the way personal interests are developed and represented in writing, and, if so, how can they use their position as college mentors to study this idea in a way that will still help the high school students become more successful writers? Is the idea of revision and the writing process an area of concern, and, if so, can they use their college mentor position as a way to learn more about how revision functions and thus help students become more successful writers? Whatever the focus or problem might be, it is important that they begin with a specific idea and then develop a strategy for accumulating data as well as mentoring students. This is no small task and certainly a challenging one as they figure out how to study the very students they are also dedicated to helping.

As the time for the actual high school visits draws near, therefore, the college students need to establish ideas for small group and peer response activities, determine the instruments they will use to collect information and monitor progress, as well as figure out how they will come to know the high school students quickly enough so that everyone in the group will feel comfortable in such a working environment. Of course, as mentioned earlier, the early visits with the high school teacher and a review of the high school assignments, in addition to developing strategies using our own classroom work as a model, assist them in responding to this part of the challenge. They write up interview questions, meet with the other college mentors to devise ice-breaking activities, and assemble a variety of possible peer response techniques. Nothing can truly prepare them, however, for the real test of the experience: what to do when students aren't prepared or when they fail to respond—in short, when their plans fall through. The glitches that are bound to emerge as the project unfolds finally put to the test their critical abilities to accomplish such a task through problem solving and then to represent their work in writing. Here is discovery-based, interactive learning at its best. They figure out what to do as various problems emerge, operating from their theoretical understanding about how writing works as we have discussed it in class, but more importantly, discover and invent what works best based with the individuals, the behaviors, and the projects as they unfold within the groups.

What they learn about their high school students as writers is only surpassed by what they learn about themselves as thinkers and writers, and this unfolds organically and interactively within the project and again later as they compose their case studies and final reflective essays. In fact, because they discover a high school setting that is not primed with model students ready for their work and because this experience is one that continually challenges their discovery and problem-solving skills, their writing usually focuses on how the ideas they started with alter dramatically as the project unfolds. The most notable learning experience is, in fact, the way the college students ultimately discover something about the nature of their own writing as a result of what the high school students accomplish (or fail to accomplish) with theirs. The community tutorial project promotes learning about writing as well as writing performance, so it is important that students have time to reflect on what is happening to them and to examine ideas that emerge as the tutorials progress. Through my own observations of their tutorials, their informal chat sessions, case study write ups, and final reflective essays, I find that students usually need the entire length of the project for an in-depth understanding of their own writing to evolve.

The community tutorial is, in fact, not an ideal interactive situation. The 11th graders are diversified in many ways besides race and gender. Some of the students are enthusiastic and prepared; many are not. Some of the students are eager to provide responses in small writing groups; just as many are not. Some of the students are willing to think about the importance of writing to learn; some could care less. The task set before these college mentors—to help high school students improve their writing—is very real and not always comfortable.

Stacey,[1] for example, is an education major who began her community tutorial project with a rather skeptical attitude about the value of

---

[1]All student names have been changed.

revision but with great enthusiasm about the connection between the project and her future career as a teacher. She wanted to learn how to reach students, and her investment in this project was tied to this deeply felt professional goal. Two occurrences, however, dramatically altered her views about the importance of revision to a writer. In the first instance, early in the course, she decided to write poetry for her personal project as an opportunity to explore her feelings about various people who are important to her, but she acknowledged right away her unwillingness to change even a single word of any poem. It had to be good enough when it hit the page, or so she believed at first.

In the second instance, she began to work intensely with one particular high school student, Drew, as he struggled to compose one successful college application essay during the course of the project. His early drafts, she explained to Drew, were too ordinary and generic. As the weeks of interaction went by, Stacey gradually learned that Drew had many unique characteristics, including speaking three languages, living on three continents, and surviving a violent physical attack. She finally enabled him to see how revision could significantly improve his early drafts and how using his incredible life experiences would create a vivid impression on a college admissions office. However, it took the entire 6 weeks complete with periodic interest lapses by Drew before Stacey's point was understood.

Stacey's various pieces of writing for the course tell the story best. In the early reports on her personal project, for instance, she explains her own view of revision:

> I have a tendency to write with little consideration for revision, although it's not because I feel my work doesn't need it. Rather because after I've written something I am often no longer very interested in going through it again. . . . How do you edit a poem? It's like trying to edit my feelings. That's an odd thing to do! I guess I could rethink my chosen words and see if any better ones fit, but I feel as though that will take away from what I was trying to say.

However, by the time she was ready to submit her last report about the progress of her personal project she noted:

> I decided to give revising a poem a try. I read the one I wrote about my significant other again and decided I wasn't crazy about it. It didn't really say what I wanted it to say. I looked at it line by line. I changed most of the wording and some of the organization. I realized that while I was changing what I was saying my feelings hadn't changed, and isn't that a significant realization considering my cre-

ativity seems to stem mainly from emotions. I guess what I'm trying to say is that maybe it is okay that one revises. . . . I didn't lose the essence, I don't think anyway, I just enhanced it.

As she lives and works through this internal yet active process of understanding her own work, she is also interacting regularly with Drew in the community tutorial and trying to help him complete his own writing project. Her case study notes:

Drew . . . seemed to have little interest in this [college essay] assignment, often leaving for the bathroom for ten or fifteen minutes. However, in the end there lies a difference that separates him from the rest of the group. He opened up to me that very last day. He began to tell me of all those things that happened in his life, that for some reason he choose not to write about. I think his comfort level with me increased. I think he also began to see that these essays could be a lot deeper given the wealth of [his] life experience. This was a turning point, though I never got to see the product of it. For me, it is enough to know that he sees the difference between what he was writing, which shouldn't necessarily be tossed to the wind, and what he is capable of writing, both because of his experience and his talent.

Stacey could see the connection between her original use of writing as mostly functional and Drew's similar idea; in the beginning both were writing simply to get something written. Revision will not seem very important to a writer, after all, if the main reason for writing itself is simply to get it finished.

Yet, uninhibited by deadlines or an imposed topic for her personal project and combined with her gradual understanding of Drew as a writer, Stacey ultimately develops a new awareness about what it means to write well. Her final reflection for the course explores what she learned about herself through working with Drew:

It was of great interest to me where [Drew] got his ideas to write about and why he chose certain ones over the others. He really began to open up to me on the last day of the sessions. I think he viewed writing a lot like I did in the beginning, as a means to an end. . . . However, I think this student and I brought something to each other. I helped him with beginning to realize his process beyond those traditional steps one uses when writing, and he helped me to see a lot of my own personal progression [with revision].

What intrigued me about Stacey's work as the semester progressed was the way in which she began an internal discovery about the characteristics of her own writing through interacting with someone who seemed rather uninvested in writing for most of the project. She achieved something with Drew at the end, she hoped, but in fact she was teaching herself something quite important as well about the act of writing.

A similar experience awaited another student, although with slightly different consequences. John, a political science major whose plans include law school and an FBI career, approached the community tutorial project with great enthusiasm because, as he said, "my 11th grade English class was the best one I had in high school." Clearly, he hoped to give back to others what he felt he had gained himself. His particular focus was to find out how personal issues are represented in what we write, an idea that emerged from a sense that his own writing was always just a means to an end, a form of communication for school and work projects and nothing more. The idea that writing might represent something more than this occurred to him as he completed his personal project, a journal about his relationship with his father. He had begun to recognize the way his father was central to all his life choices, and the personal project allowed him to explore that connection, often in difficult ways. Frequently he explained that this was a type of writing he had never done before. The opening of his final case study essay problematizes the issue:

> Do all of our writings exemplify our motivations to act or even write a certain way based on personal experience? We all may have our own personal creative writing process, but in the end when we chose a topic to write about, doesn't it generally reflect on a reaction to a life experience that has helped construct us?

Questions like these began to emerge in the early progress reports John wrote for his personal project, along with many new ideas and emotions. At the same time, his small group of high school students was working on college application essays from a variety of perspectives. One female student, Jill, wrote at length about her desire to pursue a career in social work. John decided to investigate more about her personal background. Was there a connection, he wondered, between her personal life and the nature of her writing?

As it turned out, she came from a very difficult and often violent background; however, rather than turn violent and difficult herself, she had developed successful counseling techniques that she relied on when helping her friends and family members sort out their problems. This had, in fact, been her role within her circle of friends and family, and she wanted to translate this strength into a professional career. John concludes:

Because of her hardships she is determined to take preventative action and to try and help people that have similar problems. She feels that through counseling, maybe people can benefit from her unfortunate life experiences. This is a part of her that she can never get rid of. Rather than sulking in her unfortunate situation, she has turned a bad experience into a positive thing. Her writing is flooded with emotion concerning the field of counseling. Every paper that she wrote discussed counseling. Although Jill doesn't write publicly about her family situation, it appears as if her writing is reflective of her personal rhetorical context.

As John continued to help her work on the college essay drafts, he could not fail to recognize what was happening to him simultaneously in his personal project, a site where he was coming to terms for the first time in his life with his father's influence on his personal and professional decisions. His final reflective essay notes:

Emotion, whether happy or sad, has been the key that has inspired and motivated me throughout the course of this year. Emotion is what drove me to choose my personal project topic about my dad, and the emotion of curiosity is what drove me to study the personal context of high school students. A form of emotion has been the driving force in everything that I have ever been involved in regardless of the task. Without emotion I would never be motivated to either choose or not to choose to perform a task.

He continues:

On the other hand, re-vision is equally important to my writing, as is emotion. Although emotion serves to motivate me to write, re-vision allows me to present my true emotions and ideas on paper. Through re-vision, emotion becomes evident across my writings and allows the reader to try and tap inside of my mind. . . . Only through re-vision does my emotion seep through onto paper and make any sense . . . re-vision is not only an important element in my writing, it is also important in my daily life. Through re-vision I have become a better baseball player, orator, debater, etc . . . my [personal] project contained a fusion of tones which is similar to my personal context.

Writing, therefore, does more than provide functional communication, or so John concluded by the end of the course. Through exposure to Jill's work and following the details of his own writing, he could say with assurance that "our life experiences construct us and thus our writing. I couldn't escape who I was, even in writing." He even began to revisit many of the writing projects from prior courses in his major and determined that, although at the time it seemed like he was just "completing the requirement," emotional investment in the topic was a regular motivation for him to complete the work successfully. Like Stacey, John had begun an internal discovery about writing that was reinforced through the intersubjective experience of the community tutorial.

These personal connections, whereby the college students gradually saw themselves more fully as writers through their interactions with the high school students, became a consistent theme for those completing the community tutorial project. Often the college mentors felt frustrated and dissatisfied about their lack of success with particular students because, as I discussed earlier, the case study site was far from perfect. Some students would come unprepared for the small group sessions or scribble down their assignment just minutes before the college students arrived. It was clearly evident that some students were just going through the motions. In contrast, others in the same group would not only be prepared, but ready to contribute the type of constructive response so helpful to their peers' writing success.

A notable hallmark, then, of the community tutorial project is the frequency with which the college students discover through their small group and individual interactions that self-expression is one of writing's most important features, more important even than getting an assignment done. One college student, Kiran, learned this lesson by watching what some high school students were able to accomplish with journals, a form of personal writing that she acknowledged had never interested her. In the middle of the tutorial project, however, when a personal situation turned into a crisis, she quickly refashioned her personal project from an analytical discussion of current political events to a personal journal. In this new approach, she actually imitated what she saw many of her high school students doing—a model that finally provided her with "an opportunity to take care of myself for a change."

Several advantages exist for the high school students as well, including their growing understanding of the importance of revision and specificity in writing, although certainly the most obvious was interaction with slightly older students who provided them with individual attention and served as reminders that college is a possibility. At first I thought this project might also lead to an experiment with after–school tutoring for high school students who needed extra help with writing. Bringing college students into the immediate classroom environment was essential, however, because I soon learned that after–school programs never reach some of the students who stand to benefit the most. They never take the opportunity or perhaps are not able to stay after school even if they need and want the help.

Beth, in particular, illustrates this reality. She introduced herself on the first day by simply saying there wasn't anything special about her and she didn't do anything after school. Of course, this contrasted vividly with many students who had cited involvement in clubs or sports teams or spoke about special academic interests. As a result of her involvement with the community tutorial, Beth began to develop a close bond with one of the college students, never failed to complete her work, and passed English class for the first time all year at the end of that particular marking period. She learned to write about her own experiences in a college essay; in fact, she learned to value those experiences. Beth's college mentor describes what happened:

> [i]t became my goal to get Beth to expand on her ideas and study the improvements of her drafts. My case study was now based on a student who originally had no interest in the project and ironically was becoming one of the most enthusiastic participants. The next time we went to [the high school], I seemed to have a growing relationship with the students, especially Beth. . . . For one of her assignments, she wrote about her friend, Ronny, who had been shot. Though her essay was only about a half a page, I could grasp how intensely this had affected her life. Working from this feeling, I urged her to expand on her ideas and tried to explain to her that simply telling a story wasn't nearly as effective as conveying her emotions. Beth not only listened to my suggestions, but proceeded to turn in her next draft with great improvements. . . . The fact that I was obviously paying her the most attention seemed to spark an interest in this girl that was never touched.

Many high school students were personally and academically affected by this tutorial project, but even if Beth had been our only success, the experience would have been worth it. Quite simply, if our project had been conducted after school, we never would have reached her.

Of course, this project was not without its problems, ones that we continue to address. For example, it is not entirely possible to tell in advance how college students who seem like enthusiastic volunteers for the project will participate within the dynamics of an unfamiliar high school setting. After all, these are third-year college students from a variety of majors, not student teachers. One young woman, although extremely interested when she signed up for the project, became very withdrawn as the experience unfolded. She interacted in a reserved manner with the high school students yet described herself as actively engaged with them. Even though I brought this behavior to her attention and suggested alternatives, the student remained introverted. I now take even more time to describe the high school project before my students volunteer, even enacting some possible scenarios through role playing. On the one hand, I do not want to predetermine my students' reactions before they have a chance to engage in the tutorials; on the other hand, I try to ensure that the college students achieve some comfort level with what they can expect.

Occasionally the college students need to work at giving more feedback to the high school students, and frequently the high school students come to class unprepared with the assigned writing. The informal chat sessions we have when driving back and forth to the high school allow me to make suggestions and field questions as the tutorials proceed. We also use email extensively to keep in touch about various activities the college students want to try. Additionally, the high school teacher surveys the reactions from the high school students after each tutorial. She and I then discuss those reactions so that I can give appropriate feedback to my students. They, in turn, often email the high school teacher for suggestions and input. If there are specific issues about group activities or behavior, we can begin to address them before the next tutorial. Even though each week the optimum interaction may not be reached, these problems help create the exact kind of life situation I believe my students need to experience in order to put their problem–solving and literacy skills into action.

Contemporary views of literacy development sometimes make broad claims about the interdependency between academic (not to mention social and economic) success and reading and writing development. As Walters (1990) suggests, "The reputed consequences and promised blessings of literacy are legion" (p. 174). Harvey Graff (1987), however, avoids choosing between conceptual dichotomies that privilege literacy over illiteracy. He notes that human history did not unfold in a linear movement from illiteracy to literacy, but that human developments allowed rather "a deep process of reciprocal interaction" between the oral and the literate "as literacy gradually spread and gained in acceptance and influence" (p. 25). For Graff literacy is a basis or a foundation, "not an end or conclusion . . . *a technology or set of techniques for communications and for decoding and reproducing written or printed materials*: it cannot be taken as anything more or less" (p. 19; emphasis in original).

The community tutorial project illustrates a particular technique or set of skills, an approach to literacy instruction in which knowledge is "embodied in a doing, a knowledge in which what is made is not separated from the making of it" (Brandt, 1990, p. 193). Language, after all, has many possible results. It can serve to communicate information and feelings. It can serve to represent and describe both message sender and recipient. Additionally, it can create a deep, reciprocal engagement with action itself:

> Becoming literate is not learning how to handle language divorced
> from action but coming to understand the action that written lan-
> guage relates to, coming to realize that written discourse is about
> what people do with it and that what appears before you on the
> page has everything in the world to do with what you're supposed
> to be doing. (Brandt, 1990, p. 192)

Critical literacy skills gained through the community tutorial project,
then, emerge from a concrete situation that calls on students to do something that will help someone else and to engage in cooperative partnerships, at the same time that it creates the possibility for enhanced self-
knowledge and a discovery of their own abilities as writers.

The simple performance of writing activities would not be
enough for my students to arrive at this deeper understanding of writing's possibilities. It takes the interactive, communal effort and the internal reflections of the entire course, as suggested by Bruner (1996):

> Achieving skill and accumulating knowledge are not enough. The
> learner can be helped to achieve full mastery by reflecting as well
> upon how she is going about her job and how her approach can be
> improved. (p. 64)

Through community tutorials students engage in a dialectical and social
act (see LeFevre, 1987), and the result is a heightened sense of their own
literacy power. They discover their own capacities as writers through
practiced interaction with other writers. This is an action–charged enterprise, one that asks students to construct individual goals, enact verbal
and written group collaboration, problem solve in real-life situations,
reflect on the application of their knowledge, and, ultimately, understand what it takes to be a writer.

APPENDIX

- Course Syllabus
- Personal Project Assignment
- Case Study Assignment

The Act of Writing as a Creative Process

Think about the moment when the flow of human creativity results in a unique invention: Thomas Edison turns on his light bulb. Georgia O'Keefe sets her paintbrush to canvas. Gutenberg releases his printed page. Langston Hughes composes "A Dream Deferred." Microchips. Opera. Poetry. Jumpshots. The list of human inventions turned out through the creative process goes on and on. And included, believe it or not, are your own written inventions: college essays, final exams, personal journals. How does the idea of a creative process apply to the act of writing? Do our creative ideas simply emerge like sparks of inspiration, or do they incubate as a variety of thoughts, experiences, feelings over a period of time? **What can we learn about our writing, its strengths and its weaknesses, by looking at our own process of invention?** This is the question we will pursue together this semester and in a variety of ways:

- reading what others have to say about how the creative process works from Aristotle to Mozart to Anne LaMott and writing about what they say in a reader's notebook and through short essays.
- investigating your own creative process through a semester-long personal project combined with progress accounts.
- developing your own research on the subject through a case study of an individual writer or an ethnographic study of a group of writers.
- reflecting on the connection between process, invention, and the writing self through a final, culminating essay.

Our course builds on many of the principles and practices introduced in your previous required writing classes: it believes that the act of writing is social and thus asks for various forms of **collaboration** (discussion, group brainstorming, peer response, and so on); it believes that **process and product** are equally important to the act of writing and thus allows incubation time for developing ideas, drafting, revising, and editing; it believes that the act of **writing can be used to learn and to communicate** and thus asks for different types of writing in various settings, including journals, annotations, polished essays, and so on. In a very important sense, however, this advanced course is different because of the way it expects students to engage in an inquiry about the specific feature of writing itself, examining the relationship between the general principles of a specific feature of writing and its particular application to your own writing and that of others.

Purchases

1. Looseleaf paper for a reader's notebook and process journal.
2. A pocket-style portfolio folder
3. Textbooks available at the SUB:
    Elbow, Peter *Writing Without Teachers*
    LaMott, Anne *Bird by Bird*
    Ghislen, Brewster, ed. *The Creative Process*
    Murray, Donald *The Craft of Revision*
4. Additional essays on reserve:
    These include selections from Aristotle, Janet Emig, Jack Selzer, among others.

Requirements

1. Attendance. No more than three absences allowed.
2. Engaged Participation.
3. Reading: as listed on the schedule, in the order listed, on time, and in full. Bring required readings to class.
4. Writing:
    *   informal responses to readings in a reading journal: for each assigned reading in the first part of the course, write at least a one-page response in which you comment on what the reading meant to you, why you agreed or disagreed with it, or how you related to it personally. Bring these entries to class, prepared to share them.
    *   four short essays (3 pages each) in response to readings; word-processed. These will grow naturally out of your reading journal entries and will be assigned in class.
    *   one long-term personal project; genre, length, and topic to be determined. You will not necessarily share this with anyone in class, but on a regular basis you will submit progress accounts of what you are writing and how.
    *   one research essay, either a case study or ethnography (10 pages); wordprocessed.
    *   one culminating reflective essay (5 pages); wordprocessed.
5. Collaborative teams for research project, meeting during class and outside of class and making regular team reports to the class.
6. An e-mail account. Go to Machinery Hall immediately and secure an account. We will share addresses and communicate accordingly on a regular basis.

Special Feature

The case study or ethnographic approach to research is particularly applicable to those students majoring in management, human development, or education. Anyone who plans a career working directly with people in some capacity will undoubtedly have to report on that work in written fashion, often using the case study genre. I have been able to set up a special case study/ethnographic site for interested researchers at a local high school in an 11th grade English class. Between four and six students can select to participate in a community tutorial project at the high school, mentoring high school students on their writing projects in small group settings and turning that experience into the research project for our course.

Assessment

There are deadlines on the course schedule for all reading and writing assignments. All writing assignments, even wordprocessed ones, are considered "works in progress" and will receive commentary and "as is" grades. Any writing project can be rewritten and resubmitted at any time. The final portfolio will include all final, finished products of the major assignments.

Final grade determination:	attendance, participation, teams	25%
	reader's notebook, process journal	25%
	final portfolio	50%
	(4 short essays, research project, and final essay)	

Personal Project and Progress Reports: Instructions

The personal project asks that you begin now to develop a written piece on a personal topic of importance to you. Unlike the other kings of writing you will do in our course, this particular piece will not necessarily be shared with others during the first half of the class unless you decide you want to share it. It can be a new kind of writing for you, something you have never tried before, or it can be an extension of some writing you are already engaged in, perhaps something for another class. It can be something you've always wanted to take the time to do but haven't. **For now, the importance of this project is not the topic or the form that you choose, but in what you discover and describe about your work as a writer while you do it.** First, however, you need to choose a topic and then write at least twice a week for about 20-30 minutes at a time. Here are some possible topic choices:

- take up a current events topic that has great personal interest for you. Begin reading about it on a weekly basis in daily newspapers, weekly newsmagazines, or relevant books. Then write about your response to the topic on a weekly basis, perhaps in journal entries, incorporating your feelings about the topic itself with the information you are gaining through reading and observing.
- write a detailed description of the place where you come from or currently reside. Spend time each week describing and analyzing a different characteristic of this place. Who lives there and why? What kind of things are going on there? What experiences have you had there? and so on.
- write the story of your life so far, a memoir if you like.

- write about an important personal or persons in your life, and choose a different perspective to write about every week: physical, mental, spiritual, emotions, etc.
- write about your relationship to various aspects of human life. Choose a difference aspect each week: food, travel, children, race, religion, family, shelter, and so on.
- write detailed descriptions of your dreams and discuss what they mean to you.
- write about what is happening in our class. Keep a class journal where you cover your reactions to the people and discussions going on during our class.
- keep a journal about another class, describing and analyzing what is happening there and what you think of it.
- choose one or two interesting books that you have always wanted to read and write about your reactions to the reading.
- choose a topic you have always been interested in and begin researching it, developing a set of notes about your reading and a set of written reactions about what you think of the research as you do it.
- choose a topic of your own.

Progress Reports—What will you actually turn in?

Once you've chosen your topic, begin writing at least twice a week. Then, I will ask that you complete and turn in progress reports of what you're doing. In other words, in at least one full page, explain the details of what and how you are writing. In essence, you will watch yourself as a writer, as if you're taking snapshots of yourself as you write, by answering the following questions:

- What are you writing about? and why?
- How much are you writing, for how long, and when?
- Under what conditions are you writing?
- Who do you have in mind as you write?
- Is your writing changing? Are you revising as you go? How and why?
- What rhetorical choices are you making about your writing? and why?

Each time you turn in a report, you will be updating me on the nature of your project.

Case Study Project

The project that you will spend a considerable amount of time on this semester, maybe the most amount of time, will be the case study. A proposal describing your plans for this project is due on February 6th.

This is a preliminary description of the project. We'll continue to talk about it as the time for your proposal nears.

Your case study will look at a specific case of writing in the "real" world, and that, by the way, includes this University. **You will do case study research in order to find out if the theory about the creative process that we have read and discussed actually applies in a real writing situation, to what extent, and why.** Search out a specific discourse community, or a member of a specific discourse community, one that you have access to or can get access to. You will observe and/or collect specific examples of writing and information about writing and writers, then present some of the most salient examples of this data and interpret it in a reasonable and informed manner. You will draw conclusions from the date rather than begin with conclusions.

Possible groups: writers in a workplace you are familiar with/have access to
                                 writers in another class that you are taking
                                 writers in the department you are studying with
                                 writers in a high school setting

Evidence of the writing process represented by the group you choose can come from three possible sources (there could be more): (1) direct observation, (2) from what the writer says, and (3) inferred from products. The key in presenting and using any evidence in your paper is to present as much, as varied, and as specific evidence as possible. Avoid generalizations from data that you do not include. Present specific examples of evidence, like direct quotations, notes taken during writing process, selections and snippets from real texts.

You need to pick a case study project that allows you to observe, interview, collect samples, and possibly survey.

Suppose you choose the high school case study site?

1. You will make five trips to the 11th grade English class there: working with students in small groups, helping them with a writing project that is much like your long-term personal project, observing the way they write and how their writing changes, interviewing them about writing, and so on. Your collaborative team will be the other students who travel to the high school, and as a team you can decide on many of the case study methods.
2. You will make the five trips during regularly scheduled class time on Feb. 13, Feb. 27, March 5, March 19, March 26.
3. You will have an opportunity to meet the teacher of the high school class ahead of time.
4. You will have access to the assignments that the high school teacher gives her class.

Suppose you do not choose the high school site?

1. You will then use the five "project days" on the syllabus schedule to do the necessary field work for your case study project.
2. You will form collaborative teams based on similarity of project sites.

REFERENCES

Aristotle. (1991). *On rhetoric: A theory of civic discourse* (G. A. Kennedy, trans.). New York: Oxford University Press.

Brandt, D. (1990). Literacy and knowledge. In A. Lunsford, H. Moglen, & J. Slevin (Eds.), *The right to literacy* (pp. 189-196). New York: Modern Language Association.

Bruner, J. (1960). *The process of education.* Cambridge: Harvard University Press.

Bruner, J. (1996). *The culture of education.* Cambridge: Harvard University Press.

Dewey, J. (1916). *Democracy and education.* New York: Macmillan.

Elbow, P. (1973). *Writing without teachers.* New York: Oxford University Press.

Emig, J. (1971). *Composing processes of twelfth graders.* Urbana: IL: NCTE.

Graff, H. (1987). *The labyrinths of literacy.* London: Falmer Press.

Lamott, A. (1994). *Bird by bird.* New York: Pantheon Books.

LeFevre, K. B. (1987). *Invention as a social act.* Carbondale: Southern Illinois University Press.

U.S. Department of Education. (1993). *Reaching the goals: Adult literacy and lifelong learning.* Washington, DC: U.S.Government Printing Office.

Walters, K. (1990). Language, logic, and literacy. In A. Lunsford, H. Moglen, & J. Slevin (Eds.), *The right to literacy* (pp. 174-188). New York: Modern Language Association.

8

Community Literacy and Literature—Another Missing Theory

Anita Helle
Oregon State University

In recent years, the term *community literacy* has come to stand for a project-based orientation toward education in a variety of community settings. According to Peck, Flower, and Higgins (1995), who have theorized this emerging movement, community literacy projects share some broadly defined goals and practices. Typically, they arise from a commitment to literacy as a form of action and reflection, and they assume a context or contexts in which knowledge acquires collective purpose and significance. In most community literacy projects, such contexts or "sites" of action develop in partnerships between universities, schools, and nonacademic community agencies or groups. Typically, too, they directly or indirectly address patterns of exclusion or injustice. Within these settings, problem solving, dialogue, and negotiation are crucial tools for critical literacy. Expected outcomes may range from tapping into lost and excluded sites of knowledge in the community, to developing new or alternative forms of "literate action" (Peck et al., p. 199).

As Peck, Flower, and Higgins (1995) have observed, the possibilities of "literate action" in community settings often depend more on bridging gaps than assuming built-in continuities: the "vision [of community literacy] centers on building productive intercultural relationships in which equity is established through mutual learning and transactional practices of writing and dialogue" (p. 203). Until recently, many, if not most, community literacy projects have developed through credit-bearing courses in composition and in writing centers; thus, they have bridged gaps between the official composition curriculum and what Gere (1994) aptly describes as composition's "extracurriculum" (p. 75), that storehouse of ways in which people use writing to accomplish what they deem necessary to their lives. In fact, community literacy and service projects could be said to perform these constructive and critical roles by, among other things, opening up *differences between* more traditional models of academic literacy and and more action-oriented traditions of education such as those represented by the legacies of John Dewey and settlement house projects (Long & Flower, 1994). For example, in the relationship between Carnegie Mellon University's service learning courses and the Pittsburgh Community Center, student tutors assist parents and at-risk teens in troubled homes and neighborhoods to develop negotiation and survival skills. In Herzberg's (1994) composition courses at Bentley College, students visit a homeless shelter, work as tutors, read from literacy narratives, and write about them. But as Herzberg cannily points out, in his stories of students who attempt the "easy A" by adopting an easy attitude toward "epiphanies" and sentiments, students who do community service learning composition courses do not necessarily transform their ideas about *culture*. There is no obvious way by which community service learning can automatically lead to the goals that community literacy proposes unless students question traditional academic attitudes. Indeed, community literacy projects come closest to meeting their social goals when they work on the presentation of literacy and literate traditions from both ends, from the perspective of what it means to "do" academic work in English, as well as what it means to serve the community.

In the narrative that follows, I propose that community literacy projects should include an exploration of the dynamic tensions between literacy and literature. Cultural studies proponents (Berube, 1998; Eagleton, 1983; Scholes, 1989) make the argument that there exists something akin to an "extracurriculum" of composition on the margins of the Arnoldian "literate" tradition, an extracurriculum of popular genres that have not typically been the subject of literary criticism. This extracurriculum also offers opportunities for theory, practice, and research in terms of critical literacy goals. As the field of community literacy develops, the terrain of such research and practice may be found in the unsettled canons of American literature, in the blurring of distinctions between "local color" and national significance, and in themes that emphasize the regional as well as the global. It may also be found in the day-to-day decisions teachers make about the appeal of the curriculum, textbooks, materials, and assignments to students in the climate of educational reform, where much is thrown open to question. The materials may include not only the voices and stories that may be lost or neglected in the official literature curriculum; they include community resources lost or neglected by educational bureaucracies, such as the contribution of regional and professional writing to community memory, and the role of community arts organizations that give official and unofficial support to cultural literacy projects in the community.

In *Rewriting English*, Batsleer, Davies, O'Rourke, and Weedon (1985) remind us that in the discourse of literacy crisis in the 1980s, literature and the disciplinary structure of English seemed to have nothing to do with public concerns:

> In education, everyone is concerned about literacy. By no means everyone is concerned about literature. We're all expected to be literate. We're certainly not expected to be "literary." Literacy is basic; people need it in order to do practically everything else. Literature isn't: most people get along quite nicely without it, most of the time. (p. 14)

In the 1990s, the climate in public education has changed. Conditions are often more chaotic as states respond to national standards. Curricular decisions are frequently informed by challenges to disciplinary authority (Giroux, 1995). There are high stakes to educational reform, and the literature experts are no longer in charge. Manifestations of these conflicts include more self-conscious questioning about the place of literature in the "new literacy" curriculum (Willinsky 1990), and by the potential for more fluid movement among disciplinary branches of English, including literature, composition, and "basic" skills (Berube, 1998). In the following case study, the application of the vision and methodology of community literacy to a literature project can be seen as continuing the current emphasis on broadening English studies, while augmenting critical approaches to redefining reading and writing in schools (Willinsky, 1990).

RESITUATING LITERATURE IN CONTEXTS OF POPULAR AND DOMESTIC LITERACY

Several years ago, in response to the crisis of public confidence in higher education of the 1990s, the land grant institution where I teach added extension education as a third mission after teaching and research. My colleagues in rhetoric and myself began to think about graduate programs in literature, rhetoric, English education, and what had been termed "community outreach" as parts of a complementary whole in literacy studies rather than as a set of fragmented programs. A high percentage of our English majors sought master's level degrees at our institution in order to teach in secondary or community colleges. Yet, for a number of participants in our program, the journey from traditional English major (read "literature major") to English teacher was fraught with confusion about disciplinary norms and their relevance to the more democratic contexts of public school practice. The immediate goal of reorganizing our graduate programs was to ease the transition between English major and English teacher, informing conventional methods of teacher training with thinking about cultural and critical literacy.

Questions about cultural literacy and its possible relevance to the work of English in public schools and community settings was an immediate and pressing issue for both program faculty and students. Trend's (1992, 1995) important work on the subject of pedagogy, culture, and community-based education makes an important argument about a parallel between the "great divide" between orality and literacy and the "great divide" between professional writers, artists, and teachers, an argument to which I have often returned because it helped me to see that some of the best opportunities for prying open the politics of literacy lay nearest at hand. In Oregon school reform, literature and literacy crises have recently swirled around the place of literature in the school curriculum. The battle is over whose stories are going to be told, and whether the state sees the student reader and writer primarily as a consumer or producer in the arts.

Trend (1992), who is best known as an advocate for critical literacy in art and media education, argues for making more explicit the linkages among literary theory, cultural theory, and pedagogy. By redirecting teachers away from instruction strategies and routines based on predetermined content, to a focus on how literature, literacy, and the arts can be resituated in local and domestic contexts of use, "public" literacies may also change. In the interests of shattering literacy dichotomies, Trend renders a different "fit" between literature and literacy, one that values both the pragmatic and aesthetic features of communication. In this perspective, the pedagogies of advanced, cultural literacy and so-called "basic skills" general education in reading and writing can both be seen as forms of cultural production:

> The pedagogical dimension of cultural work refers to the process of creating symbolic representations and practices with which they are engaged. This includes a particular concern with the analysis of textual, aural, and visual representations and how such representations are organized and regulated. . . . It also addresses how various people engage such representations in the practice of comprehension and significance. . . . Pedagogy in this sense represents . . . a project of possibility. (p. ix)

Lest this appear to be a heady beginning, let me hasten to say that the kinds of projects teachers and citizens encouraged us to take up through extension education projects in public schools in Oregon were anything but abstract, even when they were profoundly conflictual. Teachers wanted us to help them meet new standards, to write letters in support of more literature in the state school curriculum, and to provide them with more diverse opportunities for identifying and representing literature in ways that would make it important to their students. Given these insistent needs, the publication and dissemination of a new regional literature anthology which had been edited, published, and promoted by a progressive teacher's association (and NCTE affiliate) in our state readily became the occasion for our first major literature and literacy project in 1995.

The Oregon Literature Series (1992-95), consisting of six volumes (one each of nonfiction prose, poetry, autobiography, short fiction, letters and diaries, and folklore), is arguably the most ambitious ever undertaken by a citizen group.[1] From the beginning, the publication of this six-volume anthology had many of the hallmarks of what Willinsky (1990) has used to define a popular literacy event. The "active sociality" (p. 174) of the project was foregrounded throughout its prepublication phases through public input from allied citizen groups—librarians, professional writers, and community arts organizations. Each volume of the series had been noticed and reviewed in local newspapers and small presses and had inspired public readings and celebrations. The general editorial preface, written by one long-time member of Oregon's educational and professional writing community, George Venn, addressed an audience presumed to be suspicious of traditional school canons but

---

[1]Similar state regional anthologies, but on a lesser scale, have been created in Maine, Minnesota, Vermont, and Tennessee, typically with some help from teacher groups.

unwilling to give up on the demands of cultural literacy. The preface forecasted a future in which citizens and school children alike would have a working knowledge of regional literature once unavailable to them, just as the literature of colonized people had once been overshadowed by the literature of colonized nations. The scale of presentation was set to maximize inclusion and diversity, encompassing 150 years of state history and representing over 500 writers who had been born in Oregon or lived in the state for a time, through oral transcriptions as well as traditional genres. The fact that the copyright to this cultural treasury was held by a 700-member teacher's organization rather than by a commercial publishing company made it anything but the traditional textbook. By the time the last volume appeared, the scope and quality of the series had gained national recognition,[2] but it was by no means obvious what its fate would be in public schools.

Events surrounding the reception and dissemination of the regional literature anthology in schools had the earmarks of a popular literacy movement in another way: the idea of using the series in schools was a point of resistance to a new, official version of the state school reform and statewide selection of textbooks to match reform goals. One widespread complaint we heard among teachers was that the new statewide curriculum offered an impoverished version of literacy in all content areas, including literature. In the waves of outcome-based education sweeping the state, several drafts of the new statewide English curriculum neglected literature and writing as content areas and included only impoverished notions of literacy in general education/vocational categories. Meanwhile, it appeared that some of the same reactionary forces that were contributing to an impoverished vision of literacy in the state curriculum were also contributing to a backlash against long-standing funding for programs that had provided support for visiting artists and resident professional writers and writing programs in schools. For a while, it appeared that all publicly funded writers-in-the-schools special projects would go the way of all defunded education "frills." Both English teachers and writers in the community found long-standing common interests in a literature curriculum to promote public knowledge of culture and community driven toward the margin. As controversy and debate over the new state curriculum in English swirled around the fate of literature, the regional literature anthology appeared to be a resource for an alternative literature curriculum—a rallying point in the struggle against increasingly tedious versions of "school English" and a potential source of alliance among teachers and authors represented in the series.

---

[2]The series was recognized as a National Endowment for the Arts demonstration project in 1993 and was the winner of the NCTE Multicultural Award in 1995.

The inaugural event in what became a year-long project with teachers (all levels from secondary through college) and writers from around the state was a public conference on university grounds but open to citizens and community arts groups. The purpose of the conference was to explore some of the controversies and contestations of literature and literacy in the context of school reform. Because the Oregon Literature Series and its potential use in schools was one of the main topics of discussion, the conference was organized around themes of literature, culture, and community identity. There were lectures and group workshops on parallels between regional literature and postcolonial identity, regional literature and multicultural diversity, and regional literature and ethnographies of culture.

As a result of the conference, one group of teachers formed an electronic forum to share ideas on teaching from the literature series as a supplement to state-mandated textbooks; another group of teacher-researchers, whom we followed for over a year, joined with authors represented in the series to co-create an alternative curriculum for the series to be piloted in schools and other community-based education programs. These consisted of five teams of teacher-writer pairs in rural and urban settings. I administered the project as a representative of the university, but my co-organizers included the president of the teacher's organization and a community arts coordinator from a local arts association. At the end of the project, teachers submitted portfolios of work and presented at another round of conferences sponsored by the NCTE local affiliate. Graduate students from the literacy program worked with some of the teams, helping us to gather information and conduct follow-up interviews when the project was completed. In addition to the university's goal of encouraging literature majors to see themselves as literacy workers in the community, our goals were to mobilize community education groups to join with public school teachers in providing models of literature and literacy instruction and to stimulate public conversation regarding the ongoing place of literature in the school reform curriculum.

A crucial dimension of the year-long project was its collaborative structure and methodology, which was inspired to a great extent by the Carnegie-Mellon project. Although we were working within the terrain most obviously associated with literature and cultural studies, the community literacy model provided approaches to shared inquiry which seemed essential if we were to avoid reinstating some of the old dichotomies and historical antagonisms between literature and literacy. To this end, we took the position that the literature series might best be understood as a symbolic representation of community and culture—a representation of "Oregon" and "Oregonians," whatever that might mean. We further assumed that the cocreation of a new or alternative curriculum could be conceived performatively as a style of "literate action" (Peck, p. 199). Following the social-epistemic orientation of other community literacy projects, we determined that our collaborative partnerships between university researchers, public school teachers, and representatives of community art associations and writer's groups would be grounded in the "lure to connect across boundaries of culture and consciousness" (Peck, p. 209).

This was not the usual method of curriculum development. We did not begin primarily with cognitive structures of disciplines, or with state-prescribed mastery outcomes. Rather, much of the work of the project took place through what I later came to think of as "bridging conversations" (Peck, p. 205), that is, negotiation of differing interests. Whereas the teachers' association wanted the series to be purchased by the schools, the interests of arts groups and writers' organizations were that published authors would be seated at the table when it came time to determine how their work was being used. In the next section, I describe resonance and dissonance among these interests.

BRIDGING LITERATURE AND LITERACY: CRITICAL DISSONANCE AND COLLABORATIVE RESONANCE

"Collaborative resonance" is used by pedagogy theorists to describe the "intensity of co-labour of learning communities" and the heightened consciousness of difference between expectations and outcomes (Cochran-Smith, 1991, p. 282). Although such resonance, with its interplay of conflict and difference, might be taken as a feature of many, if not most, collaborative endeavors, we became especially interested in what happens when expectations about literature and literacy collide in the selection of materials for teaching and methods of instruction. The next subsections are meant to suggest both "sites of conflict" and "sites of intention," with the community literacy model of literate action operating as both theme and mode of discovery.

Authors and Teachers

Griffith (1988) has observed that the traditional discourses of English privilege literature over writing, and, therefore, the profession of authorship has higher standing than the profession of teaching. Because the relationship between the roles and functions of professional authors and (typically) unpublished public school teachers was one of the hierarchies

that this project was, at least in part, attempting to unsettle, it is not surprising that some of the residual tensions in these cultural roles would
be visible through collaboration. Collaboration was set up to challenge
this arrangement by making sure that the author was given a say in how
his or her work would be taught—something that typically *does not* happen in schools—and the teacher was given a say in constructing an alternative to the official curriculum. But this does not mean the dialogue
between authors and teachers was always democratic. Divisions within
the politics of literary authorship and the politics of school instruction
often were reinstated in other forms.

A number of these dilemmas surfaced as the co-created curriculum began to challenge the (assumed) seamless continuity of a rational-
ized, bureaucratized "state" curriculum. Problems were particularly
likely to erupt where collaboration was interpreted to mean "fusion"
rather than dialogue. This was the case when one teacher, who seemed
otherwise amenable to the terms of the project, ran up against one
author's very firm insistence on the place of literature as a privileged
type or use of language. For the teacher, what was important was finding poetry that would be at least congruent with the unit other teachers
in her school would be teaching on the Western experience. Her frustration developed around the poet's refusal to help her find or interpret
"cowboy" poetry as the genre most fitting to that unit. "He doesn't get
it," the teacher told me. "I am committed to using the literature to develop a theme already decided by my humanities team." Ironically, the
poet's complaints sounded remarkably similar on the surface. He complained the teacher "didn't get it"; what was important was for students
to "have an experience with language, to see what the language of poetry can do," and for that, he thought, they just needed exposure to the
"best poems" regardless of theme. The teacher's desire to conform to a
preset plan is not the point of this retelling. Rather, the underlying irony
of the situation—one of the collaborative projects that did not work—is
that the teacher and writer were working at cross-purposes in their
underlying models of the relationship between literature and literacy. In
the teacher's view, the pedagogical function of literature instruction was
to transmit a model based on the (presumably homogeneous) norms of
vernacular, shared, public history. For the poet, the private experience
with language was the ultimate test of literacy gains.

In other cases of collaboration between published writers and
teachers, the knotty divisions between them seemed to loosen through
the process of negotiating difference. In one exceptionally productive
team, a white male teacher and African-American male poet and war
veteran worked together to find a history of common differences around
memories of war, heroism, and masculinity in urban neighborhoods.

They were lucky in that the poem they began with, Harold Johnson's "The Names of Summer: A War Memory" (Venn & Hardt, 1992), provided a discursive context through its emphasis on the transactional power of naming. The poem contrasts comic book renderings of war and heroism with the speaker's experience "meeting the face of the enemy" on home turf—a truckload of Japanese American ballplayers from a nearby internment camp were regularly brought to the summer baseball lot. They became his teammates, even as he learned elsewhere to "other" the enemy. In recognition of the all those who make up the tragedy of human community in the arena of war, the speaker in the poem assumes a public and commemorative identity, even as he is reporting on his experience. Recognizing the ironies of human survival and the need for healing in times of violence, the speaker recites names of the living and the dead as he rounds the bases after a last hit of the summer:

> "Well, this is the last Sunday, Hallie," and school started
> and other seasons washed over that summer.
> But now here come the names . . . Genesis,
> Exodus, Leviticus,
> Inaba, Nakasone, Yamaguchi,
> Watanabe, Morita, Kitagawa,
> Shimura, Fujitani, Matsushita . . . (p. 222)

The portfolio that developed through this collaboration provided a particularly rich texture of buried connections between literature and literacy. Among other things, it included:

- ideas for helping students understand the social function of naming to create community and identity;
- response-based suggestions for eliciting contrasts between public and private functions of naming: what it means to remember names, to repeat them, and to repeat them in changing contexts; and
- extensions of reading regional names into national and global contexts of names, events, and commemorations, especially on themes of social healing.

Transforming Literacy Dichotomies: Formal and Functional, Culture and Kitsch

A concern some of the participants and organizers when we undertook this project was that the emphasis on "local" and "regional" might simply reinforce banalities and stereotypes. Typically, however, this did not happen. The emphasis on the relationship between literacy and literature in social and community contexts tended instead to reinforce the idea of literacy as a multiple and multifaceted event that is not easily encompassed in singular categories of identity. The literacy lessons developed by the five collaborative teams accommodated a variety of topics, from critical thinking and values education to multidisciplinary and cross-media projects. If anything, it is the range and possibility of this curricular invention that deserve pointed emphasis:

• In one rural school community, where surrounding open spaces were being annexed to provide for nearby suburbs, a teacher and poet developed a unit on what happens when one space disappears and is replaced by another—for example, when a marshland turns into a shopping mall. A visiting poet demonstrated how "field poems" based on observation and description could be used to "map" the pattern and detail of that movement. Students developed their own "maps" of land use change at a nearby slough, using two different "languages" of description—in one case, the language of biology (with the help of a university researcher), and in another case, the language of lyrical description, modeled on the example of the poems. One disciplinary language was used to reveal what might be missing in another.

• In another rural community, where a number of students and their families had been migrant workers, students read and discussed a short story about the harvesting of peppermint fields by Craig Lesley, a widely published Oregon writer who, like the character in his story, had been injured by a peppermint mower on the job. As the author visited with the class, students began to ask questions about the difference between the language the author was familiar with from working in the peppermint fields and the language he used in his fiction. This discussion led students to develop their own lexicons of the different languages and registers of language that could be used in school, at home, and at work.

• The anthology selections provided a rich repertoire of references to visual and material culture in the region—houses, food, popular icons, memorabilia, and other objects of everyday use. A number of these became occasions for student ethnographic projects that explored relationships between material and social history. In what eventually became a signature piece from the project, a typical writing assignment involved collecting and comparing various representations of barns, rendered not only through literature but through other media such as photography, television, advertising, and folklore.

One of the principal objections to projects that link literacy and literature is that they necessarily displace aesthetic concerns in favor of a broader, functional definition of literacy (Pearson, 1994; Willinsky, 1990). Although this is a valid concern, especially when market forces give added emphasis to literature as a social commodity and—as in the case of early drafts of the Oregon common curriculum goals—define the role of the citizen in relation to the arts primarily as a consumer, we found the presence of professional writers in the classroom, working alongside the teacher, disrupts the usual economies of production and consumption to a certain extent. For one thing, the notion of "voice," which serves at best as a metaphor or emblem of style in traditional literature instruction, assumes an embodied history and presence when professional writers visit classrooms to read and talk about their work. Furthermore, we found that teachers and writers did not seem torn "between" emphasizing stylistic features or literary conventions and cultural context because the relationship between the literary and the social was already established on common ground; the texts frequently provided the opportunities for familiar reference, even as they complicated familiar stereotypes. When the economies of reading as consumption and writing as production were disrupted, we found that cruder oppositions between "functional literacy," defined in terms of the power of decoding, association, and identification skills, and "articulate literacy," which has by contrast been linked to a "wider set of interpretive skills" (Sussman, 1989, pp. 10-11), also tends to break down.

What we did hear on occasion from published authors in the series was the concern that the conditions of work in the classroom— schedule disruptions, availability of texts, opportunities teachers had to prepare students in advance—might contribute to a banality or "dumming down" of the works taught in schools. This was a complaint which is related to the privatization of literature and reading, but it is also part of the broader problem of identifying literature with culture and kitsch with everyday life and ordinary working conditions. Kitsch as it one literacy theorist, Sussman (1989) defines it, promotes and is grounded in nostalgia, resolution, cohesion, and simplified formulae; literature that is culturally valued, on the other hand, assumes the value of leisure: it promotes complexity, nuance, and relies on history and on the differential play of language.

Another way the project helped to break down dichotomies between kitsch and culture was that it forced writers, teachers, and students to reconsider the role of memory and cultural preservation and its meaning in their lives. One writer came up with a strategy for moving students beyond a nostalgia-based notion of literature and writing by contrasting ways in which language and writing simultaneously not only help us to remember and preserve but to alter memories of self and community by showing what is missing. In this collaborative project, poet and teacher arranged to prepare students for the poet's visit to class by first helping them organize and develop double-entry notebooks for their own memories of neighborhood and community life. After several weeks of reading and writing from the Oregon Literature Series, making memory books, and collecting other community memorabilia, the poet visited the classroom. He introduced his own work from his own notebook of writing about "spots in time." The theme of the lesson was the role of memory as a "means of reflecting upon something you might like to come back to." The memory theme extended to collective memory and action research when a few of the Asian American students in the class discovered the Issei (first-generation Japanese) poetry represented in the literature series and appearing in print for the first time. Students were surprised and interested that this writing had been a missing part of their own constructions of community memory. Their discovery led to some oral histories of voices missing from communities and further to writing about histories and memories that had never been told. The ability of students to move quickly beyond a banal celebration of community life depended on drawing on first-hand experience with the ways in which their own writing transforms memory. The image of the poet as a figure who performs occult mastery of remembrance was also demystified by the poet's performances of revisions as memories he "comes back to" and changes.

English Majors and English Teachers

Benefiting directly from the opportunity to create curriculum before their authority and identity as teachers became fixed in professional-managerial models, students in the literacy program gained sophistication and authority in their role as beginning teachers through the collaborative process. For them, the journey from the "English major," in which they were primarily consumers of text, to English teacher, in which they were expected to be agents and actors, was enhanced by the opportunity to envision teaching and to observe these enactments of relation between the literary and the social. To be sure, some students in the teacher training program have objected to a more open model of curricular change and process, preferring the security of the textbook and the state curricular goals. But for many, if not most students, plagued with questions of authority in the beginning stages of constructing a teacher identity, the lessons of collaborative development, of curriculum negotiated between writers and teachers, appeared to contribute to a more sophisticated understanding of the relationship between literary theory and literacy practice. One student, reflecting on the use of the literature series in her classroom (she called it our "untextbook") commented that an ethnographic approach to teaching through the culture or "whole way of life" (Williams, 1977) of community enabled her to define teacher authority differently:

> What I tried to do with this project is help the students learn something about how making something of their lives in their neighborhoods and communities was like doing something with what we read. They used the [fiction anthology] to look for ways that others before them had solved problems they encountered every day. They also looked for recognizable "landmarks" in their lives, and we turned this idea of references to familiar landmarks into talking about cultural messages given and received. I pretty much turned the students loose to discover what references they already recognized in a story because the writer was working with material already somewhat familiar to them; then, we "retold" all the old stories and myths of community—stories about vacant lots and sandholes and bike paths, discovering in most cases the differences between myths and realities of community. . . . I was [initially] nervous about my authority, about [whether I would be] seen as the "teacher" when I wasn't the primary "interpreter." What I discovered was another way of looking at the teacher's role. I felt that if I could convince the students that they were experts, at some level, in aspects of local culture and the life of their communities, that my "expert" role was also satisfied.

OUTCOMES AND CONCLUSIONS: COMMUNITY LITERATURE AND LITERACY IN THE BROADER PERSPECTIVE

The literature series project had a significant institutional impact on the sense of our direction as a program that connects rhetoric and literacy studies to teacher training. It also had a social impact. Inasmuch as the forms of "literate action" I describe foreground the power of textuality, they may appear to lack the radical aims of addressing overt material injustice which serve as the critical elements of some community literacy projects. However, I propose that because literature *is* a social institution, a critical element of this study consists in providing a *different mode of access* through what Williams (1977) describes as the culture or "way of life" of community. Among program faculty, collaborators, and students—outside and within the university—at least four discernable outcomes have resulted from applying the vision and methods of community literacy to literature projects:

1. We now teach more literature about literacy in our graduate rhetoric coursework.
2. We have developed new community-based projects in popular and vernacular literacies.
3. A second generation of projects has developed as a result of the work of graduate students in our program.
4. We have formed new partnerships and shared information with programs at other schools and universities.

In graduate teaching seminars, as well as in a required literacy studies course (WR 495/595 Literacy, Composition, and Literature), confronting the gap between literature and literacy instruction is a clear goal. Beginning with a study of how of how modernity and modernism construct literate subjectivity around cultural dividing lines, students examine tensions between literature and literacy as a problem, issue, and idea. Students may read theoretical texts such as Foucault's (1979) *Discipline and Punish*, Berlin's (1996) *Rhetorics, Poetics, and Cultures*, and Thomas McLaughlin's (1996) *Street Smarts: Listening to the Vernacular.* Students also analyze literacy myths and literacy narratives in autobiographies, memoirs, and narratives of socialization, colonization, and empire by professional writers and educators such as Richard Rodriguez, Mike Rose, Lisa Delpit, Jamaica Kincaid, Linda Brodkey, bell hooks, Victor Villaneuva, and Jane Tompkins.

Eldred and Mortensen (1992), among others, have identified the literature about literacy with narrative that takes relationships of language, culture, and schooling as a dominant theme and motif. As part of these seminars and coursework, I add the requirement that students develop narrative histories of literacy based on interviews with other subjects, examining the relationship of literate subjectivity to motifs of home, schooling, nation, gender, class, and ethnicity. Literacy narratives drawn from literature of the region, as well as from locally published writers, bring an additional frame to the study of literacy for students preparing to teach or tutor in community literacy settings.

The understandings we have gathered about intersections of literature and literacy in social, cultural, historical, and political contexts have helped us toward a number of future undertakings. One spin-off from our initial project has been to extend the understanding of contemporary literature from its regional contexts to mass markets genres. The study of literacy narratives in "teen zines" allows us to do this. "Teen Zines" are mass-produced magazines in tabloid which represent subjects that are of critical interest to teenagers. Some, including rap magazines and sci-fi zines for teens, are commercial pulp industries in themselves; another category of teen zines are those written by and for teenagers through community not-for-profit agencies that have direct or indirect links to public education programs. These include "zines" such as *LA Youth, YO! Youth Outlook* (both California based), *New Expression* (Chicago), and *New Youth Connections* (New York City). In the latter category, one is likely to find issues that explore a wide range of youthful identity themes, from "cruising" teenage romances to gangland episodes and family violence. McLaughlin (1996) has helped us see ways in which literature by "teen zine" writers is and is not like the voices represented in the regional literacy series project and in some of the teen writing that responded to this project. McLaughlin (1996) argues that, like regional writing, teen zine texts subreference themselves in relation to the communities they establish by citing familiar names, places, common references to community styles, and attitudes.

According to McLaughlin (1996), teen zines also contain a great deal of authentically critical writing about culture and community through the stories they tell of lives that do not fit in, and they offer a critical vocabulary for understanding the social forces that produce subcultural styles. In practice, they may or may not also include a critical literacy component. Once students in my classes have the opportunity to become familiar with the idiom of teen zines by reading a number of the stories, autobiographies, poems, articles, and letters they print, I ask them to identify those moments when the vernacular text may resist ease of interpretation through simplified formulae. Like the Oregon Literature Series project, the study of teen zines helps to move students who intend to teach toward a better understanding of the vernacular literacies they will meet in the field.

Also of importance, teachers and students who have worked in our community extension projects on literature and literacy have gone on to implement institutional change through the development of school programs that redefine relationships between literature, literacy, and cultural stratification. For example, in an alternative education program developed by one of our former students, "disengaged" teens are invited to the learning process "through literature and through an intense and rigorous writing process focused on the personal narrative essay."[3] Students are invited to write narratives in a number of typical teen zine genres and on typical teen-zine topics: They are invited to write narratives entitled "My Past Struggles and My Future;" "Snapshots: My

---

[3] I am grateful to Sheila Shafer for permitting these citations from her program description at Corvallis High School and for allowing me the opportunity to attend and observe her classes.

Personal Album," which includes portraits of parents, guardians, favorite hangouts, and descriptions of best and worst writing experiences; and narratives on problems familiar to teens in the community. The literature studied is multicultural and includes work from Sandra Cisneros, Toni Bambara, Annie Dillard, Junot Diaz, Alice Hoffman, Abraham Rodriguez, J.S.L. Morris, Tom Romero, Barbara Kingsolver, Toni Morrison, and a host of student writers. The program also models the presence of artists and educators working together to support literacy development: Artists frequently visit the class, not only to model styles of personal narrative but also the role of literature and the arts in defining the public sphere. Following the example of Tim Rollins and the Art and Knowledge Workshop in the South Bronx in New York City (Willinsky, 1990), the social studies component of the program is focused on the theme of the "Artist as Social Critic." Local artists and writers visit the classroom to demonstrate "socially acceptable, even socially applauded ways to 'protest' against social institutions and traditions." The brochure for the program notes that "Students are given an opportunity to examine ways in which the artist, writer, film maker, painter, musician has traditionally pointed out [the need for] changes in the status quo that would better serve the needs of the human community" (Shafer, 1997). In the long-range plan for the program, the program director proposes that student writing and the issues it presents be published in the classroom's own teen zine.

What we underestimated when we began to use community literacy to rethink the structure of English were the number of opportunities that might be presented for collaborative partnerships and information sharing with programs similarly interested in relationships between literacy and literature. In the past year, one of our partners has been the Lannan Foundation, whose archive of video interviews and readings by well-known living poets and writers from across the country is an important resource for community literacy projects of this kind. Because the tapes often feature poets and writers talking about the relationship of the writer to social responsibility, our students, who are now developing their own community literacy and literature projects in high schools and community colleges, can draw on the testimonies of professional writers to help their students define community issues and projects that matter to them. Another important resource are programs and publications sponsored by the Teachers and Writers Collaborative Group, which has recently proposed a national "Writing Across the Country" Network ("WriteNet") to connect and promote organizations and projects that share the belief that professional writers make a unique contribution to the teaching of writing and literature. The WriteNet website would give a broader perspective to the rich texture of community literacy and literature projects in local settings by identifying common issues that arise in teacher-writer collaborations, writer-in-the-schools programs, administrative and funding issues, problems of using literature to tap issues of teen and student life, and curricular ideas.

Because community literacy and community service projects are a national phenomenon,[4] it is also fitting to conclude by noting that such projects may be seen in their broadest perspective through questions they raise about our disciplinary structures. We are certainly not alone in raising such questions. Watters and Ford (1995) remind us in their introduction to *Writing for Change: A Community Reader* that writing and reading about community issues in nonacademic contexts is "radical in the true sense of the word" because students return to the roots of the discipline and to the practical concerns of Aristotle and Quintillian (p. xii). One might add, as well, that in Aristotle and Quintillian's era, the multiple splits between rhetoric and literature, culture and consumption, were not what they are today. Nonetheless, one has only to log on to the Community Literacy Network Newsletter, begun by Elenore Long and Linda Flower (1995), to recognize that much of the work of community literacy going on throughout the country holds significant promise for raising questions about cultural and critical literacy, as well as the future work of the profession.

Working on community literacy and literature projects is an inevitably contradictory business in a society divided about its educational priorities. Yet in just a few years, the Community Literacy Network has published hundreds of "pencil portraits" in cyberspace; their increasing variety indicates that we are not alone in redefining and adapting community literacy constructs to meet current needs. Originating primarily in credit-bearing courses in composition programs and writing centers, community literacy has only recently served as a rubric for projects that could stretch to include literature and creative writing. Talarico's (1995) *Spreading the Word: Poetry and the Survival of Community in America*, a narrative of his experience serving as poet-in-residence for the City of Rochester, New York and its community centers; Marissa Januzzi's service learning course on narrative and hunger at the University of Utah; the Teachers and Writers Collaborative website; and our ongoing work on literature and literacy in Oregon are examples of new and recovered connections among the work of artists, professional writers, and teachers through community literacy projects. By assuring that community literacy as a concept and emerging tradition takes a multifaceted view, literature and literacy projects keep us aware

---

[4]I recognize potential differences between community service as weak volunteerism and community literacy's emphasis on social change.

that, in the long view, critical literacy must be grounded not only in "basic" skills—whatever that may mean—but in transformative knowledge of the relationships among culture, pedagogy, and history.

ACKNOWLEDGMENTS

Thanks to colleagues Lisa Ede, Kay Stephens (co-organizer of the Oregon Literature Series project), and Ann Staley (Northwest Writing Institute), as well as to the Oregon Arts Commission, the Oregon Council of Teachers of English, and the Oregon Committee for the Humanities, all of whom supported the Oregon Literature Series project.

REFERENCES

Batsleer, J., Davies, T., O'Rourke, R., & Weedon, C. (1985). *Rewriting English: Cultural politics of gender and class*. London: Methuen.

Berlin, J. (1996). *Rhetoric, poetics, and cultures*. Urbana, IL: NCTE.

Berube, M. (1998). *The employment of English: Theory, jobs, and the future of English studies*. New York: New York University Press.

Cochran-Smith, M. (1991). Learning to teach against the grain. *Harvard Educational Review, 61*(3), 279-310.

Eagleton, T. (1983). *Literary theory: An introduction*. Minneapolis: University of Minnesota Press.

Eldred, J.C., & Mortensen, P. (1992). Reading literacy narratives. *College English, 54*(5), 533-547

Emig, J. (1990). Our missing theory. In C. Moran & E.F. Penfield (Eds.), *Conversations: Critical theory and the teaching of literature* (pp. 77-96). Urbana, IL: NCTE.

Flower, L. (1996). Negotiating the meaning of difference. *Written Communication, 13*(1), 44-92.

Foucault, M. (1979). *Discipline and punish: The birth of the prison*. New York: Vintage Press.

Gere, A.R. (1994). Kitchen tables and rented rooms: The extracurriculum of composition. *College Composition and Communication, 45*(1), 75-91.

Giroux, H. (1995). Academics as public intellectuals. *Minnesota Review, 41-42*, 310-323.

Griffith, P. (1988). The discourses of English teaching. *English Education, 89*, 191-205.

Herzberg, B. (1994). Community service and critical teaching. *College Composition and Communication, 45*(3), 307-319.

Long, E., & Flower, L. (1995). *Community literacy network newsletter.* Internet. Pittsburgh: Community Literacy Center. Available: km39+@andrew.cmu.edu.

McLaughlin, T. (1996). *Street smarts and cultural theory: Listening to the vernacular.* Milwaukee: University of Wisconsin Press.

Pearson, P.D. (1994). Integrated language arts: Sources of controversy and consensus. In M. Moran, J. Smith, & L.C. Wilkinson (Eds.), *Integrated language arts: Controversy to consensus* (pp. 11-31). Boston, MA: Allyn & Bacon.

Peck, W.C., Flower, L., & Higgins, L. (1995). Community literacy. *College Composition and Communication, 46*(2), 199-221.

Scholes, R. (1989). *Textual power: Literacy theory and the teaching of English.* New Haven, CT: Yale University Press.

Shafer, S. (1997). *Fresh start program profile.* Corvallis, OR: Corvallis School District.

Sussman, H.S. (1989). *High resolution: Critical theory and the problem of literacy.* New York: Oxford University Press.

Talararico, R. (1995). *Spreading the word: Poetry and the survival of community in America.* Durham, NC: Duke University Press.

Trend, D. (1992). *Cultural pedagogy: Art/education/politics.* New York: Begin and Garvey.

Trend, D. (1995). *The crisis of meaning.* Minneapolis: University of Minesota Press.

Venn, G., & Hardt, U.H. (1992-1995). *The Oregon literature series* (6 vols.). Corvallis: Oregon State University Press.

Watters, A., & Ford, M. (1995). *Writing for change: A community reader.* New York: Prentice Hall.

Williams, R. (1977). *Marxism and literature.* New York: Oxford University Press.

Willinsky, J. (1990). *The new literacy: Redefining reading and writing in the schools.* New York: Routledge.

9

Poetry, Community, and the Vision of Hospitality: Writing for Life in a Women's Shelter

Rosemary Winslow
The Catholic University of America

> Art makes for a community of feeling, or what good is it? . . .
> Without poetry, there is no society. . . . The Bible puts it better:
> Where there is no vision, the people perish.
> —Louis Simpson (cited in Moran, 1997, p. 49)

Guided by the vision of hospitality—a poiesis of community—Bethany Center for Women is unusual among shelters for the homeless. The vision of welcoming the stranger with dignity is evident in the shelter design, from the refusal to refer to people as "clients" to the ample public and private physical spaces. The church, the shelter, and the poetry group I lead there aim to implement the vision of hospitality in making a community that recognizes and supports difference and individual identity—that welcomes the stranger into its midst as a gift it needs to grow. The vision itself, as well the experience in making community and working for social justice, is one that has rich implications for language and community studies. Here, I explore one area—Simpson's claim in the epigraph that poetry is necessary for community, that common feeling and vision are essential ground, that poetry, in its broad sense, is envisioning and making structures of possibility that community and the individuals they comprise need in order to be vital.

Bethany Center is a community within a community connected to other communities. Located in a wing of Luther Place Memorial Church five blocks from the White House in the heart of Washington, DC, and 10 blocks from where I live, it is a community of women within a church community, which is itself at an intersection of business, government, and residential communities. Twenty years ago, Luther Place was faced with a crisis in which it found itself surrounded by increasing street crime and numbers of homeless people and had to decide whether it was to close its doors or continue by doing something about the situation that threatened its existence. In the 1960s, the location was concentrated with civil rights and antiwar activist offices. Benjamin Spock had his headquarters across the street, and Roberta Flack organized a coffee house in the church dining hall. By the early 1970s the area was overtaken by drug trafficking and prostitution. Church members had to clear the lawns of hundreds of condoms and needles on Sunday mornings. An increasingly large number of people without homes had congregated in the area, and dozens lived amid the crime, sleeping on the church lawns and steps at night. Luther Place's response was to gather around the vision of hospitality, an ancient tradition of welcoming strangers into the home for safety, rest, and replenishment.

POETRY WRITING, COMMUNITY, AND LITERACY

Poetry cannot be separated from social and cultural contexts, or from the immediate community context in which it is read and written. In this study, poetry was read and written in the context of hospitality as a practice of building community. As a vision rooted in identity narratives and emerging through time from conscious selection and ordering of diversity into wholeness, it is a way of making community creatively—a poiesis of community. What does this poiesis of community have to do with the study of literacy? I am interested in exploring how a vision of hospitable community advances literacy work, what poetry contributes to community, and in what ways it is a lifeblood to individual and group. As a vision of the stranger, the other, as gift, hospitality is a poiesis literacy increasingly needs. Recent research suggests that the capacity to make a resource of difference and to envision future possibilities is foundational to community and a community's literacy (Peck,

Flower, & Higgins, 1995). It is also a means for deepening and enriching the individual life. Heath (1996) has shown some ways in which imaginative writing is chosen over other genres by some people at some times in their lives: "These writers do not see or need writing that is gate-opening within institutions as the only—or even the most important—writing for them. Instead they see their writing as soul-opening at particular periods in their lives" (p. 231).

Yet there has been little research on what poetry means to people in their lives and what it does for them. In her closing remarks to *Composition in the Twenty-First Century: Crisis and Change*, a volume of essays in which prominent scholars envision the future of the field, Bloom, Daiker, and White (1996) laments that there are two "conspicuous gaps" in the book: one is "the slight concern with the liberatory and textual power of creative writing," and the other is "the indifference to the economics of these various versions [the book's essays] of disciplinary and consequent social reform" (p. 276). To study writing in a homeless shelter is to inquire into these gaps. It is also to study how poetry writing is "soul-opening," a foundation for community literacy, and a kind of literacy that is, means, and does much more than this.

By way of making a start into this inquiry, I examine what poetry was, meant, and accomplished for five women who were regular participants for all or most of five months in a writing group at Bethany Center. As a shelter, the community must continually remake itself as people enter and leave. As women in crisis, displaced from their homes and communities, indeed from much of their former lives, they must in some way remake or renew themselves. In order to understand how literature enables self and community change, I first summarize the hospitality vision in this community context and then draw from a phenomenological theory of literature that views literary acts as deriving from human need and transforming consciousness and reality. These two background sections are used to explore what happened in the writing group at the shelter. From this examination, we have a view of how poetry enables renewal in personal and community life. Although five women is a small number, and five months not long, the fact that the five were actively engaged in using literature for such renewal yields some insight into poetry as essential to survival and to renewal of self and community.

THE VISION OF HOSPITALITY

The vision of hospitality is expressed in Biblical narratives, in lengthy passages in Leviticus, and in terse mandates such as "love the stranger."

In Matthew 25, Jesus reminds his followers of the mandates, enjoining them to help those in need—to give food to the hungry, drink to the thirsty, a place of lodging to the stranger. In 1968, after the burning of one of the streets bordering the church in the riots that ensued from Martin Luther King, Jr.'s' assassination, the church was mindful of Matthew 25 and opened its doors to residents who were without food and shelter. For the next five years, the church periodically took in refugees from El Salvador and other countries. But in 1973, the congregation was mobilized to act with sustained commitment to the situation on the streets. A new pastor arrived in 1970 and brought to the church the ideas in Father Henri Nouwen's (1971) book, *The New Hospitality*. Nouwen retrieved and reinterpreted for contemporary times the ancient tradition, linking the Matthew text to Jesus' revitalization of a much older mandated practice. It is necessary to summarize the main ideas of the hospitality vision as it provides the basis for the community's identity and poesis.

The hospitality tradition was more widespread than the Hebrew people, occurring among the Greek populations and throughout much of Africa, where it survives today. It was both a way for travellers to receive essential assistance and a way that people identified themselves. A people would think of themselves as ones who extended hospitality to strangers, and this meant that they recognized the value, dignity, and fellowship of all human beings. Citizens of Kenya today regard themselves as people of hospitality—it is who they say they are. They speak of and value this identity, which goes back thousands of years (Kibaba, forthcoming). In some other countries such as Zimbabwe, populations are divided over the value of the ancient identity because the rule and practice of hospitality permitted easy colonization. The practice of hospitality allows untroubled border crossing but carries a risk. Outsiders are invited in, but they may be thieves or murderers (or colonizers in modern times). On the other hand, the stranger could be a god or a messenger of a god, whose presence might bring a gift to the host. Thus the practice impels an ethos of trust and hope that overcomes fear through action. It also establishes an instability of hierarchy through mutual recognition of human dignity and reciprocity of gift giving. Because the stranger is a human being in need, the host is bound to give the gifts of food, shelter, rest, and replenishment for the continued journey. The guest does not have to give anything; he does not even have to reveal his name or identity. Difference is assumed, valued, and left intact. In Homer's *Odyssey*, for example, the hosting peoples gave the traveller food and clothing, told stories about who they were, and equipped him for the next part of the journey. The traveller did not have to reciprocate with stories, did not even have to reveal his name, but could if he chose.

The encounter with the stranger entailed fear on both sides. In the land of the Cyclops, which Homer called the land of the lawless, the host inverted the hospitality rules, going so far as to eat his guests instead of feeding them. In the Greek language, a single word—xenos—serves to denote both host and guest.

In the Biblical tradition, emphasis falls on the potential for gifts from God or prophets and protection of the powerless and dispossessed. In the Genesis story in which Abraham and Sarah host two strangers who turn out to be messengers of God, the promise of a son is the return gift for a night of shelter. In a story in I Kings 17, a poor widow offers hospitality to the prophet Elijah. Although she has food only for one meal, she invites him to share it with her and her son. The result is that she becomes the recipient of daily, miraculous replenishment of flour and oil as long the prophet sojourns with her. When hosting the stranger turns into benefit for the host, he becomes the guest. Contemporary hospitality vision and practice continue this idea of the host becoming the guest in virtue of the gifts received from the stranger-guest, who thus has a double identity role of host. Among the gifts the homeless guests confer are the opportunity to confront spiritual and moral pride—thinking oneself is better and more worthy than another human being. Day to day, the vision is translated into small acts that reflect an awareness of individual identity and value, empathy, and attempting to know oneself and the other in increasing depth and complexity. It encourages both host and guest to become learners together. Contact is an opportunity for self-transformation. The vision and practice oppose mass thinking about homeless people as unworthy, as having caused their own situation and being deserving of it. It also opposes a body of research and way of thinking that, although perhaps necessary in some way, categorizes and labels homeless people as objects instead of individuals. In recent years, researchers have begun to recognize that understanding the homeless and the causes of homelessness proceeds more accurately from histories of individuals than from classifying characteristics (Golden, 1992; Liebow, 1993; Snow & Anderson, 1993).

THE NATURE OF POETRY AND THE TRANSFORMATION OF SELF AND COMMUNITY

In *The Fictive and the Imaginary: Charting Literary Anthropology*, Iser (1993) discusses two kinds of acts, the fictive and the literary, whose existence argues as evidence that the literary is a primary human need and contributor to social and cultural life. I explore some major aspects of Iser's theory in order to illuminate how the nature of poetry is such that it is much more than a mere expression of feeling or imagined scenes, that it may explain changes in self and world perspectives and the transfer of changes into life.

Iser distinguishes literature from the merely fictive or the merely imaginative by showing how it is the "paradigmatic interplay" of these two acts of consciousness, "the result of their being freed from immediate pragmatic needs" (p. xiv). He travels beyond definitions of literature as mimesis, or fiction, or the imaginative by characterizing it as a "triadic relationship among the real, the fictive, and the imaginary." "The real" is "minimally defined" as "determinacy"—set meanings in the form of conventional schemata and systems. What we take for "the real" are ideas about it. The imaginary disrupts the real and exposes it as constructed when it "assumes an appearance of reality in the way in which it intrudes into and acts upon a given world," causing "the determinacy of reality [to be] exceeded." The fictive in turn operates to give form to the imaginary, a form that is a selection and an indeterminate recombination of the real (p. 3). The fictive act is intentional and boundary crossing, a deliberate making of a textual world out of selected parts of the actual world:

> every literary text contains a selection from a variety of social, historical, cultural, and literary systems that exist as referential fields outside the text. The selection is itself a stepping beyond boundaries, in that the elements selected are lifted out of the systems in which they fulfill their specific function. . . . The elements are differently weighted than when they had their places in their respective systems. Deletion, extension, weighting—these are all basic "ways of world-making," as Nelson Goodman has outlined. (p. 4)

Both the writer's creation of the text's world and the reader's re-creation of it require the breaking apart of various schemata and systems and the forming of a new, possible, set of relations among them using the parts selected. The act of selection, being paradigmatic, is responsible for setting up the text as a place for play, a place where new possibilities can form and be acted out. The act of combination, being syntagmatic, is responsible for sequencing the selected parts into meaningful re-formations. Combination also "makes every word dialogic because of intratextual boundary crossing" (p. 228). As parts of different schemata that were previously kept separate are selected and thrust into the play of re-creation, the voices arising from those schemata are also opened to reworking through dialogic interaction in the textual space.

Thus, the reading of poems and the writing of one's own poems opens up to view and inquiry the ideas of the orders of reality, exposing them as constructions—as *made,* and hence to the potential of being remade. Writing poems engages the imagination in envisioning new possible forms by putting parts of the real into play in new patterns. It is the writer who must find a new position with respect to the real, but she controls the selection and ordering, defining for herself new relationships, new possible identities that she can play out in the text. Iser writes that the "lyrical self" arises as "the point of intersection among the schemata that are drawn into the poem from various forms of extratextual discourse" (p. 9). Style arises from voice, the "individual delineation" of these other forms of discourse, which the voice goes beyond by "stepping over" (p. 10) their borders to bring only parts of them out into the text (selection) and to combine the parts in new ways (combination). Old orders are broken down by selection, and new possibilities of relating to what is intersected (combined) are formed. The voice, if recognizably individual, goes beyond the intersected forms into a new form of discourse that presents a perspective which is a new dialogue among old and new versions of reality. As ideas of orders of reality break down, and writers begin to establish new patterns of organization for their relations to the world and forms, identifiable styles and more structured poems emerge.

This breaking up and remaking of self and reality is one reason why the literary is essential to human flourishing. Individuals draw on the envisioned potential structures for renewal, and so do social institutions. Because of the literary's detachment from pragmatic needs, potentialities can be played out without practical consequences. The fictive act provides a medium for the imaginary act to play out potentialities in an "appearance" of reality, giving a lifelike, coherent shape and place for such play that the imaginary act does not otherwise have (e.g., in dream or reverie). The fictive act enables decomposing of existing schemata, but drives beyond these to recompose what was decomposed. In order to find a place from which to speak, the self must find a point of intersection—a point of view, a stance—within the selected and recombined parts and discourses of reality.

A second reason for the need for the literary is that it fulfills primary human drives. Iser argues that the drive to see ourselves face to face beyond what we can presently see and know is a primary human drive, which the existence of literature demonstrates. But this search to know the self is doubled-edged: it is fruitful, and endless. The more the self is revealed, the more it is also revealed to be ever partially concealed, ever complex, never completely definable. The literary enables the playing out of another part of the self without losing sight of or suppressing other parts. Iser calls this attempt to see two faces of ourselves simultaneously "doubling"—a kind of "splitting of consciousness" that "is a basic human requirement" (p. 246). We can make another face without relinquishing a previous view of ourselves, thus revealing ourselves, our identities, as infinitely potential within consciousness. The literary also satisfies another, opposing drive—to bring closure toward a determinate knowing of ourselves, to compose the dissonant, seemingly oppositional and conflictual into one fabric, one vision, one whole. Although we seek to find our other faces and to know the self as ultimately unknowable in its entirety, we also can only tolerate such interminable knowing temporarily. Inevitably we seek the determinate meanings of closure, and literature satisfies this need as well by bringing a new and more coherent, but more expansive, structure to the sense of the self.

A third reason that the literary advances human flourishing is that it prepares individuals for deeper and more complex interpersonal relating. The revelation of the complex and partly hidden nature of the self is a positive value in a society or community that supports individuality and difference. Literature enacts the instability of roles and the complexity of self. It requires sustained open attention to exploring alternative points of view and reminds us that this exploration is never, finally finished; it is always open to revision. By exposing the boundaries of schemata and selves and going beyond them, literature makes apparent the unknown territory beyond boundaries. But because literature is anchored in the real, it draws new lines of relation, filling in what it exposes as unknown with a new "stabilization of the external world" (p. 301); as it decomposes old orders of reality, it recomposes new orders of reality. For Iser, literature's great advantage is that it is not immediately pragmatic, allowing us to step out of ourselves with the safety of not losing ourselves; in play, we can interpret ourselves as we need to, unfolding ourselves without fear. As the new stabilizations are the structures from which the coherent voice, a second self, speaks, a new arrangement of interpersonal relations can be made. For readers, as they must enter the worlds and points of view created by another, horizons are expanded and sustained, and empathic listening is practiced. Literature provides a place for the stranger to become more known to self and other, but carries with it the awareness that such knowing is ever in progress—it is never full and final. This inexhaustible creative potentiality extends interminably the entrance of the stranger through the community's door, conferring the gifts of the individual's (guest/writer) resources on the community (host/reader). The community as host, for the writer to explore self and to put itself in the position of empathic listening in order to understand other points of view, benefits through the contribution of more points of view to its dialogue. In turn, such a community is more capable of sustaining a place of safety for the further unfolding of the individual and the community's vision of openness to learning. These are necessary conditions for critical literacy, for community literacy, and for any nonoppressive dialectical dialogue.

Literary activity is thus not mere superfluous play; rather, it enables the conditions needed in a community for individual search and unfolding to flourish. When one remains within the boundaries of the existent practical discourses one knows—the fictive without the imaginary—one is limited to repetition of the already constructed. Iser writes that the real world needs this world of possibilities because the actual world is created from the array of possibles in a process of self-unfolding. Because the world, and selves, are always more than

> one limited possibility of themselves . . . continual self-unfolding has to be sustained by playing out the plenum of possibilities through a constant alternation of composing and decomposing fabricated worlds. As there is no way to grasp how this alternation operates, the playing out can be enacted only in its potentially innumerable variations in order for it to be perceived as it happens. (pp. 235, 236)

Intellectual "grasping," in other words, is insufficient for sustaining vitality, the necessary change of living systems. It is literary activity that advances envisioning into unfolding and renewal.

POETRY AT BETHANY CENTER

If Iser is right about the need of human beings to engage in literary acts, that it brings about changed views of reality and self, and that these are necessary to self-unfolding in ways that change relations to others and the world, then we would expect to see evidence of what he describes. The five women who wrote regularly moved through three stages: breaking down ideas of reality, beginning to envision and speak in new voices, and developing a characteristic, individually recognizable style and structure. I summarize the evidence of these stages and follow with what the women said in a group conversation had impelled the changes.

Ideas of Order: Fiction and Reality

The learning in the first few weeks might be characterized, for all of us, by a dawning awareness of the strength of cultural ideas about reality and the extent to which they can be exposed as partly fictional. Present ideas inhibited trust, which it turned out needed to be built before literary work could advance. In my journal, I recorded my own fear of what might happen in this new situation, and in reviewing it realized my recorded observations of others often indicated a tentative trust, the face of a deeper fear of me and the situation as manifested by alternating participation and pulling back. For all of the women, there was eagerness one week, then some reason not to be part of the group the next. There was worry I might not want to return, and worry about what a college professor would think. I too was concerned whether anything positive would happen and worried that the writing might take them into areas they were not ready to look at—that real damage might be done. We were all to some extent in new worlds, and our images of reality from prior experience carried over. I knew something in general—something about women in the middle of deep pain and life change. They knew something of professors, knowledge of them from the other side of desks, things heard, stereotypes. But none of us knew each other, and none of us had been in this kind of writing situation before. Although I thought I knew what students in classrooms needed to learn (even though I am not so sure now), I was not sure what I had to offer here, except a few poems each week and an opportunity to write, to share the writing orally, and to see what the writing looked like in typescript. Focus on the hospitality vision of trust, openminded attention to difference, of making and receiving gifts (everyone's resources and actions), and of trying to see the individuality and value of the others and oneself guided my choices of activities and the group interaction. Literary writing advanced these aspects because it was detached from pragmatic needs, enabling everyone's ideas to be accepted as theirs without a push toward specific or immediate pragmatic goals.

Although trust was built in part through hospitable practice in the group sessions, it was helped along by the selection of readings and the very attempt at writing. To forward the decomposing and nullifying of then-held ideas about reality, but staying far away from our own specific situations and spheres of action, I selected poems that clearly reconstructed conventional ways of thinking—Charles Simic's "Tapestry," Rita Dove's "Horse and Tree," and several from Lucille Clifton's Book of Light—poems that envisioned the poet's relation to the globe or to nature. After reading aloud and the women's offered comments, I suggested they first write a poem in which they used an object in the world as a metaphor. Then we moved to writing a poem about the whole world and followed it with a collaborative poem on the same subject. A few scattered words and phrases gleamed with the beautiful or the unusual, but mostly the result of these, perhaps misguided, exercises was an array of conventional images—the world as a nice, safe, wonderful place to be—expressed in sometimes grand language. I was amazed.

No hint of pain. I wondered how women in such distress could write these things, and I wondered why they did.

All of them thought this was what poetry was supposed to be, and probably that this was what I wanted. Most everyone mentioned that they thought poetry was supposed to rhyme, and only one, Denise,who brought down a notebook filled with poems in perfect, but very regular, iambic pentameter rhymed couplets, could produce much in the way of rhymed lines. None of the poems I brought had many rhymed lines, and they wondered about this. And they all thought poetry had to be strictly original. In these ideas, they were not much different from my college students. How they were different was that when they wrote the first collaborative poem in the second week, and another in the fourth week, they all insisted that their sentences be theirs, not combined with any one else's. Some insisted on separate verse paragraphs.

And they are different in this way: they more readily dropped their ideas about poetry when a topic or frame for fictionalizing their actual experience of the world occurred to them. The moment at which this happened for those present during the second week was after reading Lucille Clifton's "The Earth Is a Living Being," writing a collaborative poem, and then reading her poem "Sixty," a celebration of the strength of women who helped the poet climb to that age. As unsatisfactory as the collaborative poem may have been as a poem, and as tension-filled a moment as it was, it perhaps brought them together as women at that moment who were about to write a poem about women in their lives. They were engrossed as they wrote their individual poems. Iris, who became a regular, started before I was even half-way through the reading. When they finished, they read what they had made, each one offering a piece of her life that recorded a felt connection to another person. One was about a grandmother, another about a friend, others about deceased or estranged husbands, children, lovers. Tears streamed down some faces. Nobody said anything—there was just long attentive listening. Good things were happening in the poems, during the writing, and during the oral reading. Each one was speaking to a lost loved one: the images of the happy world were gone. The earnest longing showed in the intensity of their bodies and the words of the poems. The topic of writing about a specific person had opened poetry onto the actual world and provided an imagined structure for talking to someone actually absent but present and alive in the mind and life of each.

While all the writers who joined the group later went through a period of "getting real," those who were present that second week did it faster and never went back. To them, poetry was imagined talk, a way of envisioning a solution to a real problem that could not be, or was thought to be incapable of being, resolved except through poetry.

Exploring Poetry's Voice: The Challenge to Envision and Speak

In the poem about the grandmother written that second week was the seed of the next set of writing activities. At the very end of the remembrance, the poet, Denise, turned directly to her grandmother to say, "Grandma, I love you so." As the session ended, I suggested poems can be a conversation, someone talking to someone else. They liked the idea, and they arrived the next week with ideas about addresses. Some wanted to write actual letters, and some wanted to send them. Some had already written and brought poems that were letters to people they knew. Denise's was titled "An Evening at Home"; it expressed and explained her feelings for her parents, and she declared that she was not going to send it, observing, "you can say more things in a poem," meaning more than in a letter intended to be sent. Aurora followed with a rejoinder that she was going to send hers. It was the first of many to her 2-year-old son—she had lost custody of him through her difficulties—a controlling husband and her rapidly progressing multiple sclerosis.

The third week, I brought in two poems that showed poetry as talk. Both were by Langston Hughes—"Mother to Son" and "When Sue Wears Red." I asked them to notice how the two poems had a different rhythm and feel, especially how the lines in the first ended with phrase ends, and the second was syncopated by its line breaks at mid-phrase. As soon as the women discovered they could envision other voices for themselves and had one way to control the emotional feel and power of the voice, they began to speak in ways and to say things that went beyond their accustomed social roles and restrictions. They began to write avidly, asking for "homework," cheerfully aware of the irony of that term. They wanted more "challenge," a term they later used as an alternative to "homework." They were also learning how to structure poetry, without my saying much beyond pointing out certain things in the example poems and doing a few exercises to teach the power of lineation. The group discussion of example poems and each other's poems was enough to continue the deepening of their understanding about how poems worked. The world's knowledge and details were brought into contact by writing poems about adages and about ordinary places—the city bus, the post office, the shelter at night. We read Adrienne Rich's poem, "Letter to Myself," and poems celebrating the body. When we wrote about hands, Denise and Aurora wrote about their fear of losing the use of theirs. Their poems turn at the end toward a loving embrace of the limbs that were failing them. They had discovered another benefit of poetry—the challenge to envision an altered perspective when reality cannot itself be altered. And they had begun know poetry as a place to work out the structure for those new perspectives.

In the group, they found people who would listen and respond to their new envisionings—what they saw themselves to be, past, present, and future. They were learning to speak a side of themselves they did not even know existed. As importantly, they were learning to listen with acceptance to different points of view, and they were learning to put themselves inside of others' points of view in order to understand. They began to speak of and value how different they each were, when previously, for some who spoke openly of this learning, they had devalued and distrusted difference. They began to speak of their poems as gifts they offered each other and received from each other. They said they were gifts of themselves. They spoke of never having had such close friendships with anyone. Two spoke of husbands who had isolated them from their friends. All had parents or friends who continually disparaged them and wanted them to be different than they were. Deeper empathy was clearly emerging out of the growing capacity to explore their own selves and positions while also being able to set these aside temporarily in order to enter the perspectives of others. Each discovered how different from the others' her experience was, yet how beneath that difference lay an area of commonality, not in images and ideas and histories, but in feeling. In other words, the more each differentiated herself in her poems, the stronger their sense of connection grew. The more the self became known, the more the capacity to listen to and understand others increased. And although the poems still often spoke to absent others, they found poetry's voice, which speaks sometimes in a structure to specific people but always knows its real audience is a community of understanding readers.

Style and Structure: Recomposing Selves and Worlds

By the eighth week, the weeks of experimenting with voices, stylistic features, subjects, and structures bore fruit in distinctive styles and framed structures. The discovery that poetry could contain ideas they found conflicting and hold them together in a satisfying, resolving structure became the most important feature—and use—of the medium. Their full awareness of this emerged at the same time as the emergence of individual style and poems structured to present and resolve conflict. This poem by Aurora, written in the eighth week, shows this development and characteristic features her poems would have from then on:

> I remember
> The dogs barking and licking my legs
> The tears falling when it was time for bed
> I remember

> The ruler smacking my hand
> Your voice singing lullabies
>   I remember
> The smell of gas on Byrd Street
> The taste of cherry lollipops, How Sweet
>   I remember
> You
> I remember

The poem is addressed to her mother, with whom she could barely stand to speak even on the phone. The discovery of another way to view her childhood and speak about and to her mother gave her another role, for both herself and her mother, to place next to the view and voice she already had. The poetic envisioning of other possibilities assisted an eventual reconciliation, a transferral into practical discourse that also happened for all the others. After this poem, Aurora wrote many poems about taking her feelings back under her control, whereas before she felt she had given them away or put them in the power of others. The voice was strong and self-unfolding. One poem, addressed to her ex-husband, ends with this clear assertion of present change and future hope:

> My heart will come out of this
> I see the truth
> My heart stopped being yours, and became mine
> I am so glad, now that I see.

The previous self and its roles did not disappear, but there was another assertive self alongside it, so to speak, positioned at the intersections of conflicting experience and controlling the selection and combination of details. Her discovery that she could use repetition, punctuation, line breaks, and spaces flexibly and powerfully gave her a new way of structuring her reality that included tension, drama, and feeling in a coherent format. She always used concrete detail and conversation to bring the real world into a new structure, one of her own making and under her control. The style and structure enabled and signaled this control.

Denise, who had been attempting for four months to write in something other than rhymed iambic pentameter because, as she said, it interfered with getting at what she wanted to say, expressed her sense of two selves in a series of poems about her previous view of herself and her new one. Just as the tight prosodic and rhyme structure of her poems had kept her locked in a mode of presenting a surface over substance, she realized she had presented a surface self, which she called a "facade." Under it, through writing poems, she discovered a real self that hurt, was confused, less strong and "together" than she had imagined. What she had thought was real was seen to be a fictional version of herself she had made up. The real person was there in the truth that had emerged in the writing, hard as nails—even harder than the person she had imagined herself be—for looking straight at the truth of one's life takes great strength. She eventually saw that this strong side was as true as the weaker side she felt she had covered over with a facade. She credited the group's responses to the feelings she was portraying in the poems with giving her the encouragement she needed to look beyond her "surface." What was "surface" were the old schemata and her old style, which kept her locked in the same way of thinking and being; the group helped to support her frightening move out of her locked position.

Donna joined the group in the fifth week and spoke frequently of her amazement that each person's style was different. It was a new idea for her that people were allowed to be different and that this was not only okay it was good. Donna wrote many poems about past, but unresolved conflicts in which people had pressured her to conform. One poem detailed an embarrassing and maddening experience framed with a fire and ice contrast. It began, "I'm on fire in the third grade," and ended with "Frozen again." Like Denise, she wrote dozens of poems that spoke out of previously suppressed feelings and thoughts, reconfiguring her position within past and present circumstances. The experience of reading her writing in the group was especially powerful for her, as if she herself had "thawed," let more of herself emerge, and found that her experience, her own history, was valued. She spoke and wrote about this, and also about how the ability to put her experience into a structure gave order to chaos. From this awareness and sense of control, she found hope and strength to go on—change was indeed possible.

For Iris, finding a style and structure meant moving from brief, quickly composed scenes with sharp details to longer poems written over longer and longer periods of time in which her sharp sense of telling detail drove home a new awareness. In the beginning weeks, she wrote short poems of 4 to 10 lines, in simple but direct and strong language. I did not know this until a private interview conducted at the end of the project, but looking back I can see that her ars poetica expressed her awareness of a new way of being in the world. These two poems record the new ability to be patient with herself that she had learned from poetry—a task did not have to completed in one sitting. Ideas can come, change can come, and the unexpected can be a source of delight.

> A blank sheet of paper
> Sits in front of me
> Awaiting my written idea
> Staring at me
> As if to say.
> "I'm empty, fill me in"

Be patient with me
For soon you will not be empty.

The Art of Writing a Poem

When you write a poem, remember
Sometimes you draw a blank
Inspiration comes from somewhere
Let somewhere come to you
Just wait for the right moment
Keep paper and pen nearby
Just write what somewhere dictates
And let the poem be the surprise

Although the writing itself taught her to tolerate the tension of waiting for closure, so did the others' poems and the supportive environment of the group. During the first weeks of the group she typically cried when she listened to others read their poems, but this dissipated and was replaced by pleasure. In an interview at the end of the spring, she said the writing had taught her to tolerate not finishing a task in few minutes. She had been able to start filling out job applications as a result. She said she had also "come out my shell"—the image of a self emerging into a more a participatory mode. Her developing close connection to others in the group was marked by continual experimentation with the devices she saw others using, incorporated without losing her own distinctive style. In this poem, she borrows Aurora's manner of omitting punctuation and Denise's experimentation with near rhymes. Yet, the voice and structure remain quite firmly hers. Written at the end of the spring, it also exhibits her theme of learning patience and her new way of recording insights about scenes in long poems.

Lincoln Memorial
The monument has so many steps
It's hot so I take it slow
Each step is tedious
But each step is one step closer
To what I want to see
I watch the other tourists
Their cameras around their necks
They're running up and down the steps
And chatting as they run
A vendor nearby is busy
His line is long and slow
I see impatience in their eyes
And see the vendor
Serenely handling each one

With patience and care

It's hot today
I'll join his line
And think about what I've seen
And pray for tolerance
For all mankind

Beatrice joined the group in the fourth week. She was 16-years-old and had recently arrived in the United States from a war-torn African country. In the first weeks she wrote stiff poems, letters to the Pope, her parents, her country, and her boyfriend that expressed pure unconflicted love and devotion in the conventional language of a dutiful young woman. By the fourth week, she was beginning to find structures for her ideas, and a voice and occasional images that were powerful and original, yet grounded in the everyday. Like the others, she moved away from previous ideas about what poetry was, what her family and other figures in her life represented, and what her place was in the world. Also, like the others, before the end of the spring she was writing in increasingly controlled structures and language that explored and envisioned the nature of life and her stance toward it. The insights are keen for a 16-year-old, and the set of experiences is truer to felt life—less imagined than in earlier poems, although more fictionalized. In this, her last poem, she records the orientation of the early poems' unquestioning acceptance and breaks open into questioning that stance.

The Just
Mr. Benjamin calls every child
in the yard and invites them to
join him to church each Sunday
and promise to have a good time.
The service is very nice as he said
and we drove home feeling really happy
about the day.
Mr. Benjamin is sick, he is hospitalized,
he is dead, he is buried and forgotten.
And now Margaret, she graduated high
school three years ago. She is working
hard to support her mother, brothers,
sister and daughter.
Margaret goes fishing, she falls into
the river, she drowns, she is missing,
she is dead, she is buried and
soon to be forgotten about.
Holy Lord, do the just leave our
sinful world so fast and easily?

Is it because they might change
from their good ways and be
sinners or because they are
just too pure for the world?
Please Lord, tell me for I am
very eager to know why.

A New Place

In order to understand better how these five women viewed their experience of writing poetry in the group, I interviewed them privately and as a group. The group interview was a 1-1/2 hour dialogue in which I presented three questions: What do you or don't you like about poetry? Do you think poetry can change anything? What has the group done for you? With the first question I hoped to get at what the women thought poetry was. The second question arose when Iris mentioned that the group was a "catalyst" for writing. I asked the third question in order to try to distinguish the effects of the writing itself from the effects of the group.

The responses revealed that a close community of writers within the larger shelter community had developed, characterized by closer friendship than any of them had ever known before. Writing had opened up new areas of the self, which found empathic response, which further drove self-unfolding and the vision of a hopeful future. All of them spoke of valuing the ability to make sense of chaos, to sort out confusion, to give a visible concrete shape to experience and thoughts, to reveal what they "didn't know was there." Other reasons they gave for liking poetry were that it was a "release valve," a term that echoed through the conversation. It was "fun," a "challenge," the "achievement of something to be proud of," and an avenue of "hope." These responses consider the human drives to express emotion in safe ways, to do satisfying and valued work, to attempt and master the difficult, and to see a future. Iser (1993) considers all these to be drives that poetry satisfies. The women were quite aware that poetry was not the mere expression of feeling, but the reshaping of experience in new forms, the envisioning of new possibilities in a medium detached from pragmatic needs. The control and mastery of one's world was expressed by several. Iris thought of it as realignment: "If you can write a poem, or draw a picture about something—a dog, a cat, life, death, marriage, courtship—it gives direction to what was up, sideways, down." Donna talked about self-unfolding: "My art [poetry and drawing] reveals what people are becoming and is extremely important. We are finding out who we are. We are dealing with our conscious being." Denise emphasized composing new forms for experience and the safety from pragmatic needs the literary allows: "It's not so much putting feelings on paper, but making sense of at least one of the 17 things charging around in your head. And new things come out—-go out to the person you're writing to—fear, love—and come back to you. You can get past the fear of saying something to a person. . . . You can see the words and sounds. They are comfort, encouragement. You can see things won't always be this way."

The sense of control to shape by making was supported by participation in the group. Denise continued her comment by elaborating on the sense of being able to keep on living by seeing that the "impossible" was possible: "Donna didn't think she could write, and she has done some of the most stunning poems—more powerful because she didn't know she could. Achieving the poems gives us strength to go on." Donna offered that the group's acceptance of everything she wrote was an important factor in her ability to discover and envision new areas of herself: she had experienced criticism (the subject of many of her poems) as a "block to creativity." In the group "nothing is criticized, because it is one human being putting down what that human being feels, and other human beings care what that is. There is no fear about what you put down." This is a good summary of poetic envisioning and of the hospitable community's valued giving and receiving of the gifts of individual selves. Iris, too, came close to the hospitality vision in the shelter when she called the group a "catalyst," a "spark plug for creativity," and a "time and place for the opportunity to write."

The group indeed provided a place and a time for them to unfold the vision of "welcoming the stranger." When I asked whether they thought poetry could change society, they did not want to engage the question. What they knew, and what mattered, was that poetry had changed them. Denise began, offering an example of how poetry makes new envisioning concrete, and how it then transfers into practical discourse. On Mother's Day she had been able to call her mother because she was free of "pain" after putting it "down on paper, where you can ask yourself how it feels and looks, and release it." She thought people were afraid to risk, and poetry gives you that courage "to take a chance, to see the past, the present, the future . . . to follow the person that comes out in poetry . . . is a chance for one person to express themselves. It changes the person. Whether it changes culture is irrelevant. That another person has a chance to read it and feel it is important." Denise had used poetry for practical ends in another way the previous week. She had written two poems addressed to her therapist following a session in which she felt she wasn't being listened to and was being asked why she felt the way she did. Denise had taken this for nonacceptance of herself, but did not know how or whether she could say directly what she was feeling and thinking. The poems helped her sort out what to say, and although she had not intended to give them to the therapist, she did, effecting a satisfactory resolution. Others had similar stories to tell of giving poems they had not intended to send to friends and relatives, with an aim for change in the relationship. Sometimes change occurred, sometimes it did not, but the women always felt it had been a good move because they had not remained silent. They had risked doing something.

The group was the one place where she and the others said they could write whatever was inside without anyone questioning them about why they said what they did. Denise expressed the importance of this acceptance for women in their situation. From writing, "I learned a lot of things about myself, some of them good, some of them bad, but it was easier on my psyche. I could turn the negatives around—I could look at it—and I learned I didn't have to like everything. What I feel can't be wrong, because I feel it. Some of us have never had the opportunity to express ourselves. We've been slapped, beaten, [etc.]. Nobody can say it's wrong because it's yours." Writing, as a place to think without interruption from others and to be listened to in the same way was, tied to growth. "Having been in this room, we've learned we can grow. . . . I don't think I've grown as much in other groups as I have in this group because I was writing sincerely what I wanted to say without being interrupted, without anyone asking me a question about—'why would you say that?' Writing poetry is an opportunity to say whatever you wanted to say. . . . The uninterrupted flow of thought has been so important." Within the shelter community, this community of writers had the opportunity to deepen their understanding of hospitality through daily practice as they wrote and shared their poems during and outside of the group time. Although the shelter organizers and staff have carried forth the vision for some time, the transient nature of the community means that there is a wide range of understanding and commitment to it. As a poesis, it can only unfold from the accumulation of small actions of the individual members of the community. Poetry gave them a place and a medium for bringing the vision to life. The women understood it this way. Throughout the conversation they called their poems "gifts"— "Reading poems was our offering."

From Poetry to Life

Because all five women saw themselves on the edge of survival, poetry writing was "writing for life"—an activity that helped them survive that day, that week, the horrors of the past, and the collapse of their former lives. The presence of poetry writing itself stimulated interest and involvement in other literacy work. By the third week, hope in the future was expressed by the women asking for tutors to help them and others in the shelter work toward graduate equivalency degrees. The shelter staff found tutors for those who wanted them. Filling out applications for jobs, medical aid, and social security was less fearsome. Some sought out books to read, and discussions about them started among residents. Some sought out information on financial assistance for college. My presence as a college professor and their own discovery that they could write helped them believe they could do things they previously considered beyond their capabilities. Those who had college and advanced degrees emphasized the pleasure and creative potential of learning, something they said they had not experienced in academic settings. Pleasure and creativity may be especially poignant for those who have difficulty envisioning an improved future.

I have focused on the learning of new, open, and empathic modes of interpersonal relating. I noted two important reasons this learning is vital to community building and community literacy. First, these modes of relating are essential if the community is to sustain itself through conflict and adversity and work with other communities. They assist the movement past current schemata and modes of thinking and acting into creative problem solving. Second, the process of dialectic dialogue within a community and community literacy's "search for an alternative discourse" depends on the acceptance of differing views and the opening up of these into creative envisioning of new solutions. Without trust and the voices and resources of everyone, a community's life and discourse are endangered—possibilities for problem solving remain hidden, and repression of opinions and oppression of the different may result.

I have also focused on the ways poetry enables new modes of relating. In poetry, self and community vision unfold into new possible structures that are tentative, indeterminate, and unstable. Creative breaking down and building up of new structures keep schemata of self and world open, complex, and vitally related to "the real." Poetry's fictive medium provides a place for remaking one's understanding of the past by structuring a new position and potential self that are anchored in "the real." Although the expression of feeling and use of the imagination are important, in poetry these are advanced into new ways of seeing and ordering. This is poetry's nature, and it is the one that leads out of the past into the trust and hope for the future.

Poetry brought these women to a new view of themselves as capable writers who could act in the world. At the end of the spring I was called out of town on a family emergency. While I was away, they went to an open mike reading at a local bookstore and read their poems. There they met a sixth grade teacher from the city schools who invited them to visit his class. They read their poems, talked about homelessness, and wrote with the students. Since then one has become a spokesperson for the homeless and has found work as a paralegal. Two others have moved out of the shelter into their own residences. The other two are hampered from being self-sufficient because of severe medical conditions.

Of course, poetry writing does not resolve everything. For these women though, it was an important avenue for change and resolution. Human beings are complex, a truth poetry reminds us of. And so are the causes of homelessness and its solutions. The vision of hospitality led to what is now widespread practice—the concept of a "continuum of care." The term surfaced first at Luther Place, emerging from the hospitality vision as replenishing supplies and equipping the guest for his continued journey (Winslow, 1996). The definition and movement to implement is a poesis—a making of community that is an unfolding of vision into articulate form. As the vision unfolded through work with the homeless and spread its praxis through government and social service agencies in Washington, so the vision operated on an individual level as well. The practice of writing poetry provided the means and medium for some individuals to unfold the vision in their own lives, enabling new ways of being and participating in community in practical and literate action.

This poem, written as the lead poem in a 96-page collection from the five months of writing at Bethany Center, embodies a collaboratively composed vision of poetry writing and the shelter community, with the poetry group as its "heart." In it, the poets have set themselves within the the church's metaphor for the shelter—the urban oasis in the urban desert—but transform it according to their own experience of writing poetry. Unlike the composing of the early collaborative poems, this one flowed out in a single voice as words and phrases were contributed back and forth with palpable joy. Individual styles and sentences were relinquished into a seamless common voice and vision. It composes the feeling and vision the five women had come to share.

Heart of the Oasis

Soft warm blood—
The kind of passionate flow
      that makes us all human
The rush of living pumping
The experience of toes
    squishing through mud
    pumping to a rhythm

The ocean is rough, the waves are
                        merciless. Upon it a little ship
trying to survive. Struggling for the

peace it can find
in a soft landing
on the shores of an island

Loved.
Protected.
Encouraged.
Strengthened.
A place of solitude, discovered
at last.
Not an illusion.

In the midst of
the unjust, unfeeling
waves of the city

—Poets at Bethany Women's Center

ACKNOWLEDGMENTS

I would like to thank the residents and staff of Bethany Women's Center for the opportunity to work among them as a volunteer and for their support of the project. Jeannie Hunter, director of the center, was especially helpful in arranging my visits and providing materials, equipment, and a space to meet. The many women who participated in the writing group sessions taught me much about generosity, courage, and strength. I owe most to the five women, named pseudonymously, for the privilege of knowing them and reading their work, for permission to use their writing and interview statements, and for making this study possible.

REFERENCES

Bloom, L.Z., Daiker, D.A., and White, E.M. (Eds). (1996). *Composition in the twenty-first century: Crisis and change.* Carbondale and Edwardsville: Southern Illinois University Press.

Golden, S. (1992). *The women outside: Meanings and myths of homelessness.* Berkeley: University of California State Press.

Heath, S.B. (1996). Work, class, and categories: Dilemmas of identity. In L.Z. Bloom, D.A. Daiker, & E.M. White (Eds.), *Composition in the twenty-first century: Crisis and change* (pp. 226-242). Carbondale and Edwardsville: Southern Illinois University Press.

Iser, W. (1993). *The fictive and the imaginary: Charting literary anthropology.* Baltimore and London: The Johns Hopkins University Press.

Kibaba, M. (forthcoming). Ethnicity, nationhood, and civil society. In G. McLean (Ed.), *Civil society and social reconstruction: Who belongs?* Washington, DC: Council for Research on Philosophy and Values.

Liebow, E. (1993). *Tell them who I am: The lives of homeless women.* New York: The Free Press.

Moran, R. (1997). An interview with Louis Simpson. In *Five points* (Vol. 1, pp. 45-63). Atlanta: Georgia State University Press.

Nouwen, H. (1971). *The new hospitality.* New York: Doubleday.

Peck, W.C., Flower, L., & Higgins, L. (1995). Community literacy. *College English, 46,* 199-222.

Snow, D.A., & Anderson, L. (1993). *Down on their luck: A study of homeless street people.* Berkeley: University of California Press.

Winslow, R. (1996). *Between two circles: "Host" as metaphor in two civil groups languages of inclusion and exclusion.* Paper presented at the Council for Research in Philosophy and Values, Washington, DC.

——10——

Applying Critical Literacy Theory to the Experience of a Nursing Home Writing Group

Elizabeth Oates Schuster
Eastern Michigan University

This chapter provides an account of an ethnographic research study that explored the transformative function of writing in the lives of persons living in a nursing home. For three years I studied a nursing home writing group, individual writers, and their family members. Nursing homes are places where various factors such as ageism and extreme physical and mental frailty create barriers to freedom of expression. Most people living in a nursing home have reached or come very close to total dependence on others (Shield, 1988). In this kind of setting, opportunities to be expressive and to maintain one's autonomy are limited. I wanted to find out in what ways participation in a writing group provided residents with the means to find and express their voices.

An article by Supiano, Ozminkowski, Campbell, and Lapidos (1989) had a particular relevance to my study. The article explored the transformative function writing played in the lives of residents who participated in several nursing home writing groups. The following is the authors' interpretation of the changes experienced by the residents:

> Before participating in the writing groups, few residents had much experience with writing and fewer still considered themselves writers. Findings from the writing group indicated that participants came to view themselves as writers. On completion of the group, significantly more participants were writing and using writing as a vehicle for problem resolution. In addition, participants were enabled to relate feelings and ideas to other residents, and life experiences and memories to both residents and staff. Residents actively engaged in meaningful roles as writers, empowered by the expression of their creative individuality. (p. 388)

After reading the Supiano et al. (1989) article, and participating in a pilot study that involved my observation and cofacilitation of nursing home writing groups, I began to see how critical literacy theories might help to explain what was happening in the writing sessions. I felt that more was occurring in such projects than met the eye. Perhaps, by applying critical literacy theories to the experiences of a nursing home writing group, a new and deeper understanding of the function writing played in the lives of older writers could be accomplished. As a result of my initial explorations, questions about the experiences of nursing home writing groups began to emerge and guided my research:

- In what ways do the residents in a nursing home use writing to make sense of their pasts and present lives?
- In what way does writing negotiate and transform relationships between the writer and staff, the writer and family, the writer with other writers and residents, and the writer with himself or herself?
- Are members of a nursing home writing group able to, through reflection and dialogue, begin to perceive their lives and their places in the world differently?
- What does it mean to be a writer? By becoming a writer does the person begin to feel any differently about herself or himself?
- In what ways does writing function as a vehicle for interpreting the social world, in this case, a nursing home setting?

The study determined that writers living in a nursing home used their writings to negotiate and connect with their inner and outer worlds and to make sense of their past and present lives. Writing also provided the opportunity to express strong feelings and to give voice to individuals who, due to ageism and institutionalization, often found themselves to be disenfranchised from society. The writers used their writings to convey to future generations important life lessons, wisdom, and guidance. The writings were used as a means of reaching out to family, staff, and other residents. And, writing was like a mirror as it provided a self-reflection for the writer to ponder as well as a window for the reader to peer into the inner world of the writer. Finally, the writers had a sense that their voices were being heard and that their writing and the response to their writings provided a reason for being alive.

The balance of the chapter consists of an overview on the critical literacy theories and concepts that guided my study, and a discussion of the research and findings. It is divided into the following sections: a review of the literature on critical literacy, the process of writing, older adult literacy, and literacy in the context of a nursing home; my approach to research; a description of the social context for the study; an account of the writing group and of one of the writing group sessions; a summary of the findings as they relate to the earlier research questions; and future research considerations.

THEORIES ON CRITICAL LITERACY

In the past, theorists maintained that literacy had a significant impact on the social and economic growth of societies throughout the world. Graff (1987) maintained that by erroneously attributing such capabilities to literacy, by *overvaluing* it, "we remove it from its sociocultural context" (p. 18). Significant attention was given to the numbers of people who can read, the masses who could fill out a form—the quantitative aspects of literacy. Yet, until recently, very little attention was paid to the *consequences* of its use.

The outcome of any literacy process is an indicator of how literacy should be "qualified." One end may be for individuals to become "literate, autonomous, critical, constructive people, capable of translating ideas into action, individually or collectively" (Graff, 1987, p. 38). If this is indeed the goal, then it would be very much in synchrony with the thinking of critical pedagogists such as Giroux (1988), Friere (1989), and others who underscored the *usefulness* of literacy.

Friere (1989) defined literacy as "a process of becoming self-critical about the historically constructed nature of one's experience" (p.

153). Here, literacy is employed not only as a way to understand the context of written texts, but as a means for understanding the self and for assessing and reconstructing one's relationship with society. It is also understood as a way of sharing experiences in a way that emphasizes caring for one another (Britton, 1982; Giroux, 1988; Willinsky, 1990). Reconstruction includes "social reconstruction" of one's world in a way that provides meaning and expression of one's own needs. In this way, people are no longer a part of Friere's "culture of silence" (Giroux, 1988). Their voices are finally heard.

The New Literacy

The concept of "new literacy," (Willinsky, 1990), although conceived with the needs of children and young adults in mind, is relevant to the experiences of the older adult learner. Here, literacy is perceived as a social process that expands the students' range of meaning and connection. Students become meaning makers as they find their own voice and create a community. By editing, publishing, and distributing their writings to the community, their works become public and "part of the daily web of meaning in which we find ourselves" (p. 16).

Literacy connects the inner meaning with the meaning the public brings to the process, and in doing so, creates a "web of meaning" (Britton, 1970, p. 248). In this way, it encourages a greater engagement with one's world. Willinsky (1990) summed up this interactive nature of literacy when he wrote, "New Literacy rhetoric is full of individuality and personal integrity of meaning, while at the same time it extols the intersubjectivity of response, the supportive environment of the workshop, and the public reach of writing" (p. 205).

During the course of my study I, too, became aware of the possibilities of how writing might be used to create a community. The writings functioned as a catalyst for *creating* a social world, a community of words. By becoming writers and by participating in the writing group, some of the residents of the nursing home found a way to take control of their lives and to build a community within the institutional walls. The community, rather than being dependent on a diverse population playing out a complexity of roles, relied instead on the writings to bond its members. The key role players were the writers and the key group was the writing group. The experience of the nursing home writers illustrates how critical literacy concepts may be applied to the experiences of the older adult learner in a way that will benefit an understanding of the underlying dynamics at play. A "community of discourse" (Willinsky, 1991, p. 182) is found not only within the institutional walls of a school, but within the institutional walls of a nursing home.

THE PROCESS OF WRITING: THE ACT OF MEANING-MAKING

A number of scholars (Beach, 1990; Britton, 1970; Brooke, 1991; Greene, 1988; McGinley & Madigan, 1991; Willinsky, 1990, 1991) perceived writing as a process of evolving meaning. Brooke wrote that writing was an "act of discovery, reflection, and critical thought" (p. 116). Written language, from the viewpoint of critical literacy theorists, may be understood as "a vehicle through which certain values, attitudes, beliefs, and standards of personal and community life are valorized and constructed" (McGinley & Madigan, 1991, p. 5). Therefore, writing may be perceived as a means of "making sense of the world" (Greene, 1982, p. 79) and may be used as a vehicle to carry the person, who late in life is attempting to make sense of it all, to a place where the meaning of life can be constructed and reflected on.

The actual act of writing may help the individual to organize the vast number of life experiences, and in doing so, make them memorable and understandable (Britton, Burgess, Martin, McLeod, & Rosen, 1975). And throughout the writing process the writer, by articulating "a feeling, thought, or attitude more clearly" (Martin, 1975, p. 35), changes. Transformation of the self is an example of how writing is "one aspect of identity negotiation, one way that people can negotiate how they view themselves and how they want others to view them within the complex interactions of contemporary society" (Brooke, 1991, p. 6).

In a writing group or class, the writing process is a collaborative one. The student writer does not face the task of making meaning alone, but meaning is made through a collaborative effort between the student and teacher-facilitator (Britton, 1982). In the nursing home writing group, Alison, the facilitator, played an important role as a partner in meaning making. She supplied the topic of the week for the writing group, and when the writers read their work the following week, she offered comments on both the structure ("See how that rhymes?") and/or on the quality ("I have never heard the term 'sunflake' before . . . [she reads a part of the poem aloud] when the sun light hits the snowflake . . . [and then to the group] now that is beautiful!"). Also, the writers frequently related to what their colleagues wrote, and it was common for a lively conversation among many members to ensue. In this way, the writing connected lives and connected the writers with the world.

PERSPECTIVES ON OLDER ADULT LITERACY

Before reviewing the literature on older adult literacy, I first consider why and how literacy may play a very important role to the person who is moving through the final stages of life. I found that while there are few studies that explore the transformative function writing plays in the lives of young children and how literacy is used as a vehicle for change (McGinley & Kamberelis, 1991), there are even fewer that address the effects literacy has on the lives of older adults, particularly those living in institutional settings (Fisher, 1990). Yet, many of the concepts developed by critical pedagogists and critical literacy theorists may be readily applied as a way of better understanding the experiences of the members of the nursing home writing group.

For example, the making of meaning of one's life is a critical aspect of late adult development. According to the psychologist Erickson, persons in late life may struggle with the issues of generativity versus stagnation and ego integrity versus despair. The generativity crisis involves finding a way to guide the next generation, a way to leave something of one's self behind (Atchley, 1997). Productivity and creativity are major themes at this stage of the person's life. The creative act of writing assists the person in breaking out of a state of stagnation by providing the means to leave tangible and lasting proof that one did exist and that one's life made a difference. Also, the written document extends guidance and direction to future generations years, decades, and even generations after the writer's death.

Ego integrity involves the person seeing his or her life as having meaning and accepting him- or herself as is, with all the blemishes. Persons who reach this stage of integrity feel that they have done the best they could do under the circumstances and life is complete. Individuals who experience despair reject life and feel like failures (Atchley, 1997; Kaufman, 1986). Writing is like a window into the soul and offers to the writer and her or his family an opportunity to view an innermost world. It was not uncommon for a nursing home writer to use his or her writing as a means to come to grips with feelings of despair, grief, sorrow, and loss, as well as to celebrate and express love, joy and happiness. The revisiting of important life events is an attempt to make sense of how these life experiences shape who one is and how one perceives him- or herself. Working out the despair by getting it down on paper, sharing it with the community of writers and family, and knowing that his or her voice was heard, relieved the burden of pain and assisted in the achievement of ego integrity.

Other Thoughts on Late Life Development and Writing

Gutmann (1987) wrote, "Later life development does not show itself so vividly, as in earlier adulthood—instead, it may cause no more than the quiet ripening of selected mental and spiritual capacities, or a gradual shift in appetites, interests, and occupations" (p. 28). The "gradual" and "subtle" characteristics of late life development may be due to the adaptive strategy known as *continuity* (Atchley, 1989) whereby "middle-aged and older adults attempt to preserve and maintain existing internal and external structures . . . by using continuity (i.e., applying familiar strategies in familiar arenas of life" (p. 183). Optimum continuity means that "the individual sees the pace and degree of change to be in line with personal preferences and social demands and well within her or his coping capacity" (p. 185).

The perception of writing as a process that assists in identity formation may aid in the understanding of how writing may help the older adult to achieve optimum continuity: "Writing becomes meaningful for individuals when it supports their attempts to be certain kinds of people in their world" (Brooke, 1991, p. 10). Brooke also noted:

> The central tension in identity formation is a tension between social and internal understandings of the self. In any given context, a person's bearing, past, and behaviors imply that the person is a given sort of individual, but this implied identity may or may not correspond with the person's internally felt sense of self. The problem of identity formation, thus, is how to deal with this ever present distance between implied and felt identity. (p. 12)

It is apparent that the processes of "optimum continuity" and identity negotiation have a great deal in common in regard to an older individuals' primary goal, which seems to be the "fit" between the internal sense of self and how one is perceived by the social world. If this is the case, then the process of writing may not only facilitate the older persons' efforts involving identity negotiation (Brooke, 1991) but may play a integral role in their attempt to achieve optimal continuity.

The Function of Literacy and the Older Adult

A review of research on older adult literacy conducted since the late 1970s revealed that only a few studies had been conducted in this area and that scholars were struggling to identify and determine how literacy functions in the lives of the older person. Most of the research has concentrated on reading rather than reading and writing, or writing as a single topic. In many instances, researchers drew on surveys of the general population for data (Rigg & Kazemek, 1983).

In 1979, *Educational Gerontology* devoted an entire issue to older adult literacy. A review of the contents revealed an interesting array of articles on topics ranging from the affective aspects of literacy (such as enhancement of life through reading; Gentile & McMillan, 1979; Lovelace, 1979; Wilson, 1979) to reader ability and reading strategy-oriented issues, including text learning capabilities (Glynn & Muth, 1979; Haase, Robinson, & Beach, 1979) and use of cue systems with older adults (DeSanti, 1979). Two general overview pieces discussed the primary problems confronting older readers: the illiteracy rate (Lumsden, 1979) and the lack of curriculum materials directed to the needs of older adult learners (Kingston, 1979).

Other researchers (Lovelace, 1979; Watson, Robinson, Chippendale, Nickolaus, & Jenkins 1979; Wilson 1979; Wolf, 1980) found that the function of literacy in older persons' lives moved beyond functional competency. In each instance, older adults noted how reading and writing activities helped them to stay involved and socially engaged, to build social contacts, and to contend with the challenges aging presents. In this way, the researchers began to discover the transformative function of literacy in the lives of older adults. Literacy was perceived as a means of reconstructing one's relationship with the world. In this context, writing and reading were also understood as a way of sharing experiences in a way that emphasizes caring for one another (Britton, 1982; Giroux, 1988; Willinsky, 1990).

In the early 1980s, Courtenay, Stevenson, and Suhart (1982) began to address the more quantitative aspects of older adult literacy. The emphasis of this research efforts was on functional aspects and competencies such as filling out forms and applications, rather than on how reading and writing functions in the lives of older adults. The study was a survey of the measurements used to determine the level of functional literacy among older adult populations. The survey revealed that a satisfactory description of older adult functional literacy did not exist and that older adults compared poorly to younger adults in regard to their *ability* to meet basic literacy demands placed on them by society such as reading forms and rudimentary communication skills. Finally, they decried the lack of measurement tools created specifically with the needs of older learners in mind. In their conclusion directed to educational gerontologists, Courteney et al. suggested that consideration be given to the *meaning* of functional literacy (not necessarily from the older adult's perspective, but from the researcher's point of view). They asked: "Is it reading? Is it the ability to communicate and compute at a basic level?

Or should one define literacy as affective–motivation, perseverance, and dependability?" (p. 350).

The Transformational Function of Literacy

In 1983, Rigg and Kazemeck reviewed research on the literacy needs of the older adult. More specifically, they looked at the mature adult's reading behaviors, interests, and habits. The findings noted that for too long educators have assumed that older adults must be brought up to par with a younger, more educated population and that, in the eyes of many researchers, the older adult is "incompetent, inadequate, and in the need of 'fixing up' by some professionals" (p. 419). However, the researchers believed their colleagues' biases were unconscious and revealed a lack of thought and examination of what is actually occurring as the older adult goes about his or her daily routine.

Rigg and Kazemeck (1983) had discovered a small but welcomed counter movement to the studies of the past. Rather than basing their assumptions about the older learner on a comparison between the experiences of the elementary student and the older adult, scholars were "reading, writing, speaking, and listening to elders in nursing homes, retirement centers, senior centers, and other institutions" (pp. 419–420). Instead of practicing "assumptive thinking" about the literacy needs of older adults, the researchers went to the source (the older person) for their information.

PAST STUDIES ON THE FUNCTION OF LITERACY IN THE NURSING HOME CONTEXT

It is ironic that at the reflective stage of late life development, when a person is assessing the meaning of life and attempting to realize optimal continuity, little opportunity is provided for dialogue and exploration. This is particularly true when one is placed into a nursing home, an environment akin to Friere's (1989) "culture of silence" (p. 97), a condition that suggests "a structure of mutism in the face of overwhelming force of limit situations" (p. 97). Too often, on institutionalization, a person's voice ceases to be heard due to the minimal or nonexistent means available to express oneself.

Nursing Homes as Communication-Impaired Environments

An article on nursing homes as "communication-impaired environments" (Kaakinen, 1992, p. 260) represented the only recent account on this topic. The study focused on communication through oral language. Fifty-three per cent of the 72 residents from eight similar nursing homes who took part in the role-playing type interviews said they talked less since entering the home. A few referred to implicit and explicit "rules" about talking including do not talk loud, do not gossip, do not argue, do not talk during rest period, do not talk after 10 o'clock at night, do not cuss, and do not discourage others. The following were behavior rules to live by: "1) do not complain; 2) do not talk with the opposite sex and if you do keep it to formalities only; 3) do not talk about loneliness and dying; and, 4) do not talk too much" (p. 261).

According to Kaakinen (1992), the perceived rule about "taboo" topics can be changed by establishing small discussion groups, including memorial groups. For example, in the writing group I studied, the facilitator enhanced the writing process by sharing the memorial writings with family members, and, in one instance, by making them a part of the funeral service. In doing so, the writers' feelings and emotions were acknowledged as was their relationship with the deceased.

In conclusion, Kaakinen (1992) advised nursing home staff to create programs that foster interpersonal communication and encourage conversation. One of the keys to success is a group leader who is skilled in small group activities. Alison, the writing group facilitator, was a wonderful example of a dynamic, effective leader. She skillfully led each group, giving heartfelt praise and asking questions that usually spurred additional comments, and she always maintained eye contact and touched the writer who was talking. In doing so, she provided a safe environment where writers could come to explore their past, present, and future lives without fear of reproach. Instead, the opposite would occur and writers would bask in the glow of Alison's love and joy of sharing lived worlds.

Literacy in the Nursing Home

It is important to reflect on "the different manners in which language operates to define ourselves and the situation of schooling, family, friendship, and other valuable institutions [and] . . . how literacy operates in different settings" (Willinsky, 1990, pp. 234-235). Even though Willinsky was referring to the school environment and extending our thinking about possibilities beyond the classroom walls, I believe his words have a special meaning for those who work with persons living in another kind of institution, the nursing home.

Only a handful of scholars (Fisher, 1990; Koch, 1977; Lovelace, 1979) have delved into the ways in which literacy functions in the context of the nursing home. Fisher's qualitative study was initiated in response to Kasworm and Medina's (1989) call for research that countered the movement in assumptive thinking by observing older adults in their own domain and interviewing them on their literacy experiences. Fisher found that for residents the primary purpose of writing was correspondence to stay in touch with family and friends through letters, thank-you notes, and greeting cards. Other writing activities included writing in a log and writing for the nursing home newspaper. Here, the research began to touch on what ways literacy may be functioning as a way of making meaning in the resident's life, and yet it failed to apply the current understanding of how literacy functions in the life experiences of the writers. Fischer mentioned only in what way literacy serves as an important communication link, but *why* is it important? How does the process play itself out? How are other's lives touched by the writer's writing?

Even though Lovelace's (1979) work was titled *Reading Activities to Enhance the Lives of Nursing Home Patients*, the author chose to focus not on the ways literacy might enhance the lives of the residents but, instead, devoted most of the article to the problems encountered by staff when attempting to offer a reading activity. After reviewing the list of concerns, including a detailed table on disabilities, I came to the conclusion that these issues could be identified as problems for staff when attempting to conduct *any type* of activity. In particular, the arguments around sensory and memory loss as barriers to effective programming (Lovelace, 1979) were weak and led me to question the author's knowledge of the aging process. Rather than addressing the possibilities, the deficits were emphasized. This deficit approach to aging was apparent while reviewing a number of the articles on older adult literacy. I was often struck by the lack of sensitivity and understanding regarding aging, including dangerous stereotyping and biases that are unfounded in actual experience.

Koch's Poetry Workshop

In contrast to most of the other studies on older adult literacy, Koch (1977), a professor of English, wrote a vivid account of his experiences leading a poetry writing workshop for six months in a nursing home. In his account, he conveyed a concern for the writers and a desire to learn about what it was like to live in a nursing home and to be so old and yet to have survived.

It was in the mid-1970s when Koch decided to offer a poetry workshop in a nursing home. The result is an intriguing account of his experiences which includes a compilation of the writers' poetry. Prior to his involvement with this workshop, Koch wrote a book, *Rose, Where Did You Get That Red?* (1973), which described his experiences teaching poetry workshops in a public school in New York City. The reasoning behind his decision to offer a similar experience to much older writers is revealing:

> The idea to teach old and ill people to write poetry had come to me as a result of an interesting hour I spent working with poetry at the Jewish Old Age Home, in Providence, Rhode Island, and as a result of other hours, much less happy ones, I had spent as a visitor in nursing homes where nothing of that kind was going on. I wanted to see what could be done. I saw, even in their very difficult circumstances, possibilities for poetry—in the lives of old people looked back on, in the time they had now to do that, and to think and with a detachment hardly possible to them before. If, in the blankness and emptiness of a nursing home, they could write poetry, it would be a good thing—a serious thing for them to work at, something worth doing well and that engaged their abilities and their thoughts and feelings. (pp. 4-5)

Apparently, Koch sensed the lack of any opportunity for residents to fulfill their need for self-expression and to have a voice. Additionally, the older individual's need to remain actively engaged in his or her life, to remain connected with the self and to the world is a force that Koch meant to capture.

Koch (1977) placed the older adult writers' poetry in the foreground. The reader is provided with an example of a writing, followed by Koch's comments as to the topic, the structure, the writer's past, and how prior experiences played a role in the conceptualization of the poem. His method was to read a few poems as inspiration to the writers and then take dictation, as many of the writers were not physically capable of writing down their poems. This section on dictation had particular relevance to my own work:

> After the poetry idea was presented, the students, in most cases, dictated their poems to us. Dictation, necessary because of physical disability, such as muscular and visual difficulties, was helpful to students whose limited education would have caused them worries about the correctness of their writing—spelling, grammar, and so on. Speaking their poems made it much easier, especially at the start, but I think, too, throughout the workshop. My students in general felt easier and more relaxed about talking than about writing, had command of more words and had more chance to say things musically, humorously, colorfully, and movingly. (Koch, 1977, p. 32)

I confess that I had not considered in any great depth the reasons, other than physical and mental limitations, behind why a resident might want their work dictated. It is natural to be more comfortable speaking one's thoughts than to get them down on paper. The residents I worked with had similar educational backgrounds, and some voiced a lack of confidence with their writing skills. While conducting the study of how writing changes a person, I noted that perhaps one of the most revealing findings was the meanings the writers brought to the term "writer" and how, by becoming a writer, residents gained prestige and recognition. To be a writer and to take on this completely new and foreign role, when most others were falling by the wayside, gave the writing program an added uniqueness.

Also observed by Koch (1977) was the great value the writers placed in having their works read aloud and shared. "Reading the poems aloud was important for the students' pleasure and continuing interest in poetry, and also for their learning more about it" (p. 39), and later, "Writing poems, they discovered them and made them into art. They were richer for that, and so . . . were those who heard their poems and read them" (p. 57).

In a chapter on writing as a process, Murray (1980) also noted the importance of reading aloud one's work. However, the reasoning for doing so is a little different than Koch's:

> When students read their papers aloud they hear the voices of their classmates without the interference of mechanical problems, misspellings, and poor penmanship. . . . It is equally important for the writer to hear his or her own voice. Our voices often tell us a great deal about the subject. The piece of writing speaks with its own voice of its own concerns, direction, meaning. The student writer hears that voice from the piece convey intensity, drive, energy, and more—anger, pleasure, happiness, sadness, caring, frustration, understanding, . The meaning of a piece of writing comes from what it says *and* how it says it. (p.15; emphasis in original)

When one of the writers in the nursing home writing group read her sad and heart wrenching account of The Great Depression, her words were filled with pain and anger. She was choked with tears while reading her account. Nellie (another writer) began to cry as she told of almost losing her home. Lorraine left. She said she could not stand it when people cried. She said some of the people just want attention.

This is yet another example in which thinking about concepts originally conceived with the younger learner in mind may be used to better understand the experience of the older writer. In fact, in this instance, the sharing of one's work may be even more important, as the older person's time and ability to make sense of the world and to find meaning in the life already lived for the most part, is, unlike most younger writers, limited. To receive acknowledgment for one's writing in later life may mean the same as receiving acknowledgment for the value and meaning of one's life.

Critical Literacy Concepts Applied to the Older Adult Experience

Koch's experience is the rare example of taking an idea that originated in a public classroom to a very different setting, the nursing home (Koch, 1977). It illustrates the possibilities for programs and thinking developed with the younger learner in mind to be used effectively with persons at the other end of the age spectrum. And, Koch felt certain that positive change occurred due to the residents' participation in the poetry workshop. He wrote:

> Our students did accomplish things. I am not sure that helped them to adjust to life in the nursing home. Rather, I think, it slightly changed the conditions of that life, which was better. I don't think I would like to adjust to a life without imagination or accomplishment, and I don't believe my students wanted to either. It is in that sense, perhaps, that it can best be understood why it is better to teach poetry writing as an art than to teach it—well, not really teach it but use it—as some form of distracting or consoling therapy. As therapy it may help someone to be a busy old person, but as art and accomplishment it can help him to be fully alive. (p. 44)

The last line may be the answer to my discomfort when I read the other articles on older adult literacy. Often, the authors wrote about writing as a means of providing distraction, leisure, and busyness, and the writer as a recipient/victim of goodwill, rather than of the potential writing holds for immersing the writer into life, for remaining fully in the world, fully alive.

In conclusion, the function of literacy in the lives of older adults as a research topic has not enjoyed the level of attention it deserves. It is apparent from a review of the literature that, to date, little thought has been given to how the processes of writing and reading may affect the older persons' relation with him- or herself and the world. Several unanswered questions regarding the transformative function of writing occurred to me as I wrote this chapter: How does writing assist the older person in negotiating the late stages of life? How does becoming a writer influence the older person's sense of self and identity? How does writing and reading help the older adult to stay connected to his or her world? And, why is it important to be concerned with these and other related issues in the later years of life? In many ways, these questions are reflective of the primary research questions noted in the introduction. In particular, they relate to the ways in which members of a nursing home writing group perceive and interpret their world, the negotiation of relationships, and the use of writing to make sense of past and present lives.

AN ETHNOGRAPHIC APPROACH TO RESEARCH

The goal of ethnographic research, according to various researchers (e.g., Agar, 1980, 1986; Eisner, 1991; Glaser & Strauss, 1967; Hammersley & Atkinson, 1983; Smith & Kornblum, 1989; Van Maanen, 1988; Wolcott, 1991), is not only to describe the world as observed, but to find out and explain how members of groups interpret their world. I felt that the methodological approaches I employed in the study must provide an opportunity to explore the ways writing functions in the lives of older persons living in a nursing home. I wanted to understand what was going on in the writing group, in the minds of the writers, and in the minds of those whose lives were touched by their writings.

A triangulation process for this study is evidenced by the collection of multiple data sources: the writers' written products, observational fieldnotes, transcriptions of the interviews, and other forms of documentation provided by staff persons consisting of materials on the nursing home and other relevant readings. The research process included collecting information through participant observation of the writing group. For the first half of the session, I observed the facilitator's interactions with the group as the stories written the previous week were read and discussed. During the second half of the one hour session I functioned as a participant by volunteering to take dictation from individuals who were unable to write on their own.

Throughout the three years of the study I also conducted in-depth interviews with six writers, six family members (one family member per writer), the writing group facilitator, the activities director, and other key staff persons. The selection of the writers and family members I interviewed was based on the writers' relationships with family members (how often they interacted with one another and the family member's interest in the writing and the writing process) and the level of their writing activity.

Analysis of Information

Analysis was an ongoing process that began prior to entering the field as the relevance of various theories were considered and as themes and new theories emerged during the collection of information. The theories on the transformative function of writing (e.g., Beach, 1990; Britton, 1970; Brooke, 1991; Greene, 1988; McGinley & Madigan, 1991; Willinsky, 1990, 1991), older adult development (e.g., Atchley, 1989, 1991; Gutmann, 1987; Kaufman, 1986; McClusky, 1974), as well as existing knowledge on life in nursing home settings (e.g., Brody, 1985; Gubrium, 1975; Johnson & Grant, 1985; Kaakinen, 1992; Kane & Kane, 1982; Kidder, 1993; Savishinsky, 1991; Shield, 1988; Supiano et al., 1989, Vladeck, 1980), guided what I chose to pay attention to, the way I described situations, and my interpretations of the findings.

My familiarity with the current thinking on the transformative function of writing motivated me to pay greater attention to, among other things, relationships, the writers' remarks on their feelings and concerns, their conception of their world, and the families' comments on how the writings affected their understanding of their older relatives' experiences while living in the nursing home. The research on late life development clarified the stages of older adult growth. The issues of the need to contribute, to achieve integrity over despair, to find some thread of continuity which, in turn, leads to a sense of identity, all informed my interpretations on how writing may be used as a tool to age successfully and to achieve various levels of older adult development. Finally, the readings on life in nursing homes, along with my personal experiences, sensitized me to the "realities" of institutional living and the experiences of the very old and frail. This knowledge, in turn, heightened my awareness and understanding of the environment I worked in and the world the writers functioned in each and every day.

Analysis of the gathered information began during the formulation and clarification of problems and issues to be studied and continued right on through the report writing process. Informal analysis took place as I wrote notes in the field; as hunches were generated on emerging themes, ideas, and topics; and through discussion with colleagues and fellow researchers. Formally, analysis started to take shape in the forming of analytic notes and memoranda, as I thickened fieldnotes and began to consider emergent concepts and themes.

THE SOCIAL CONTEXT

The social context for my research, the Evan Nursing Home, was a 215 bed licensed nursing home located in a midwestern town of about 10,000 people. The nursing home employed approximately 200 staff persons. It was designed in a wheel shape with the nursing station in what the staff called "the centrum," or the center of the wheel. The home was located on the ground floor and was attached to a community hospital. The residents' rooms were located in the wings that extended out from the center.

THE WRITING GROUP

The Evan Nursing Home writing group originated in 1987 through a grant that funded a series of nursing home enrichment projects in sites throughout the county. Approximately 20 writers attended the group (average age, 88 years) and met once a week for one hour. The writing took place in a dining room, off the centrum. Eight foot long tables were set up in a large U shape. Two to three writers in wheelchairs sat at one table. Alison, the writing group facilitator and an occupational therapist, had a podium with a microphone situated in the center of the U. She did not stand behind the podium. Instead, she took the microphone off the stand and walked to the center with the microphone wire trailing behind. The extension for the microphone made it possible to reach the writers when they read their works or if they wanted to join in the discussion.

A session began with Alison passing out the "published" versions of the writers' work from the previous week. Each writer was asked to read her or his story or poem and then Alison led the group in discussion. After the writings were read, and time permitting, Alison referred the group to the writing idea on the last page of the handout and reminded the writers that they could write on any topic they chose. Most of the writers who were able to write on their own usually left at this point to write in their rooms. Those who needed help were assisted by Alison and other volunteers. The writer dictated a story and the volunteer took great pains to record it as it was spoken with minor editing. Alison took the handwritten pieces home, typed them on her personal computer, made enough copies for each member of the group, and distributed them at the next session.

The following represents a thematic account of what occurred one summer day as the writing group considered topics such as hobbies, family and spousal relationships, and the significant contributions a volunteer made to life in the nursing home. The section also includes accounts on renewing old friendships and of my experience as a recorder of stories. Taking dictation is like a dance between the writer and the recorder, each one searching for the meaning in the words, the right way to express a thought. During this process we each learned a great deal about each other and about ourselves.

A Hot Day in July

One day in July, the writing group session began with every one singing a rousing version of "Happy Birthday" to Joe, one of the beloved volunteers. Lorraine, who earlier had passed a birthday card around for everyone to sign, led the singing. Her strong, deep voice, made considerably louder by the microphone, reverberated throughout the dining room. There was cake and party decorations and most of the writers were in a festive mood.

Once things settled down, Gwen read a story about her "most beloved hobby," carpentry:

My Most Beloved Hobby

I had many different hobbies in my life, but one that stands out most is "carpentry." We had an attached garage on our lovely home in which we had a wonderful workbench. It had a large vice at one end–peg-boards on the wall holding all kinds of tools, including hammers, saws, all sized nails, screws and a special miter saw. I made picture frames, shelves, little fancy kinds to decorate my kitchen corners, even a couple of large patio frames for the door, covered with plastic to keep out the winter chill. It was fun. I look at my aged wrinkled hands now and I can hardly believe how much they have accomplished in the past. Nice memories.

This was one of the many times a writer's past surprised me. I enjoyed imagining Gwen, in earlier years, working in her garage, creating, and so strong and full of life. Each time I learned something new about the writers through their writings, I saw them with fresh eyes.

Next, Esther read a poem full of love for one of the volunteers:

My Friend Avis

I have a dear friend Avis.
I love her very much.
I hope that we'll be friends
And always stay in touch.

She plays the organ especially fine
Which touches my heart with great divine.
For all that she does and has to say
I am thankful for her whenever I pray.

After Esther completed the reading, Alison, as she often did, gave positive feedback and support. "The poem rhymes and has a wonderful rhythm. You must have worked long and hard on that. Too bad Avis is not here to hear it. She is working in the front office today, but I know she will read it soon." Esther literally beamed with pleasure at Alison's words of praise.

Following Esther's piece, Alison read a tribute Sadie wrote to her son who had died of cancer the previous week, which was also about her strained relationship with her husband.

Aspects of Love

My love was not as strong as my husband's. I always feel guilty about this but he was a good man. I only realize now just how good he was, but I went along with his thoughts and did what he most wanted. He passed away early in life.

We had 4 sons. They didn't seem to be his life; he always seemed to want his freedom. My boys educated themselves and they are doing very good, have their own families and homes. We are a close-knit family. My boys have deep love for one another.

I just lost my second son with cancer. How we miss him and how we mourn him. His wife is holding up pretty well.

After Alison read the story, one of the writers asked where Sadie was. Alison said, "She's up north with her family and that's a good place for her to be right now." Gwen said, "She used to be my roommate. I went to see her to cheer her up." Alison responded, "Yes, you and she share a common experience with the loss of your children."

Joe, a volunteer, remembered a song that included the line Sadie had put into her story, "I only realize now just how good he was." Joe began to sing the song and many of the writers rocked back and forth in their chairs, nodding their heads. Even though the topic was a somber one, the writers were smiling and enthusiastically applauded Joe when he was done. The talk of the death of a child while celebrating Joe's birthday created a bittersweet feeling.

Alison brought the discussion about Sadie's loss of her child and the comments about her husband to a deeper level when she concluded the conversation about Sadie's story with, "Sadie felt guilty about her feelings about her husband. Her children didn't seem to be a part of his life. But she took care of them and I would hope that Sadie won't feel guilty. By writing this, maybe she will feel better."

Miranda's story was read next and it, too, was about a less-than-perfect marital relationship and the effects of the strain on the children. Miranda reclined in a large Lazy-Boy-type chair on wheels. It was cushioned and she lay almost flat on its surface. Her long shoulder-length hair, streaked with gray, hung down loosely. She had a soft voice with a lovely, rolling southern accent. Miranda came from Tennessee and had raised seven children on her own while nursing a sick husband. She asked Alison if she would read her story. Before she began to read Alison said to Miranda, "I gave it the title, Hush. I hope you think it's all right."

Hush

Lots of times they'd start to argue with him
And I told them, "Don't waste your time. Leave him alone."
They thought I was awful.
I'd make them hush.
I didn't argue with him and I wouldn't let them.
They'd have a solid racket goin' all the time
If you'd let them alone.

He'd get up and remember something we said
In talking the day before.
Might be me, might be the kids said something.

I'd tell him to hush. We didn't mean nothing by it.
He'd hush when I told him to.

The kids knowed I meant to hush when I told 'em to hush,
So he didn't have nobody to argue with.

I stayed in control.
That's the only way we could have any peace.

After he died I told 'em all,
They hushed when I told them to hush.

That's the way it was.

Alison asked Miranda if she wanted to say anything about the writing. Miranda replied, "No, that's all I wanted to say." Many times the writers felt that their stories had said all they wanted to convey, and they did not feel any need to discuss their writings further. This was often the case when the writings were deeply personal.

Hazel began to read her story titled, "To Obey?":

To Obey?

The word of obey is a terrible "thing." If you are really in love, "obey" is not included in the marriage. You are always concerned whether the deal would please the other or not. You would never consider to act or so something you know would hurt or disappoint someone else. You would always wonder would the other be hurt or disappointed in your action. To hurt someone else besides yourself is really a bad action—not only to yourself but the other one as well.

"Does anyone want to comment on obeying?" Alison asked, "And how it did or did not work for you?"

"It didn't work for me," Edie said.

"It didn't work for you?" Alison responded.

"No, it didn't work for my *husband*!"

The group broke up into laughter, and Gwen said, "It never bothered me one bit, we loved each other so much." Alison said, "I think that's what Hazel was saying, if you are really in love, obeying isn't important." She added, referring to the loose theme of marital relationships, "Notice how when each one of us talks about something similar, it comes out in a particular style, when something is meaningful to us."

As the session reached closure, Alison drew the group's attention to a letter Edith's granddaughter wrote to her father. It was published in the local newspaper on Father's Day. Edith was so proud of her granddaughter and of her son, and she wanted to share her happiness with the group. In the tribute, Edith's granddaughter expressed how her father (Edith's son) had lovingly and successfully guided her through childhood and young adulthood. Gwen said, "My dad was that type of person. When he said 'No!' he meant he loved us very much."

As the group disbanded, some going to exercise class, others returning to their rooms, Alison said, "Edna wrote last week about her father saying, 'No' to card playing but she did it [played cards] anyway. This brought to mind the generation gap and you can write about this or something for Joe [for his birthday] or anything else you want to write. We didn't have time to write today but if you'd like to write something during the week we will pick it up or if anyone has anything they would like to write today, I will visit your room in the afternoon." With that, the writers went on their way and another session came to a close.

Renewing Old Acquaintances

Many of the writing group members came from the same towns and, in some instances, as in the case of Avis and Evelyn, they were related. It was often through the writing group that members discovered these connections. The discovery often led to looks of joyful surprise and then, typically, discussion ensued that interwove common memories into a shared story.

An example of a shared story evolved one day when Evelyn read a story about baseball:

Baseball

Oh yes, I played baseball with my brother.
We played in our yard so my mother could watch us.
The neighbors children–6 or 7 boys and girls–played with us.
But our folks didn't like to have us mess up the lawns for the bases.
We made a lotta holes in the lawn, I'll tell ya.
I can see them holes now. We probably ruined the lawn.
Them were the good days.

There was much laughter as Evelyn read this story. Many of the members obviously related to getting into trouble for tearing up the lawn while having a good time.

Emily, who was Evelyn's neighbor when they were children, next read her writing on baseball, and it was so remarkably similar to Evelyn's story that Alison asked Evelyn after Emily was finished, " Did you know Emily when you were neighbors? Did you play in each other's yards?"

Evelyn responded that they had each written about the same neighborhood games even though they were not aware that was what the other was writing. Alison exclaimed, "I didn't know you were writing about the same games!" From there, Evelyn and Emily struck up a conversation about the games and the rest of the group either listened or offered their memories, creating a group shared story about neighborhood baseball.

On another day Gwen wrote about her joy in discovering a friend whom she had not seen for at least 30 years:

Renewed Friendship

Viola–I met her in 1926 as she was introduced to me in the neighborhood when I arrived in Perrystown. We were good friends for many years, and she watched over my son, who was 2 years old at the time, while I went shopping. Viola and I played golf many times together.

As we later moved to Perrystown, I lost contact with Viola. Can you believe, we met here! I never saw her again until we both became patients here in this home 2 years ago. We were in Bible class one day when I saw her and we met.

What a wonderful meeting. I see her often, her room is near mine in G Wing.

Taking Dictation and Getting It Right

Every other session provided the opportunity for the writers who were not able to write on their own to dictate their stories to volunteers. One day, I looked around the room and saw Jennie anxiously turning her head, this way and that, waiting for someone to come and listen to her story. I pulled a chair up next to her and right away Jennie blurted out, "I am 87 years old!" She took me by surprise as normally there is some kind of introductory remark like, "Hello, Jennie, what are you interested in writing today?" But it was not unlike Jennie to get right into her writing. She did not often have something to say, but when she did, she wanted to get it down and get it down immediately.

Jennie was short and pudgy in build. She had bird-like eyes that peered out from behind her glasses. Her gray, wispy hair was cut short and often mussed and her speech was very rapid, like a firing machine gun. Her voice was raspy, sometimes making it difficult to hear her. Therefore, the dictation session with Jennie went quickly, and I had a difficult time keeping up with her repeated barrage of words.

"I am 87 years old!" Jennie almost yelled.

"Okay," I said, trying to get situated before she fired another round. "I'm going to write that down, okay?"

"I ask people if they can guess my age . . . "[she paused for me to write down what she was saying].

"Uh-huh," I mumble as I furiously recorded her words.

". . . and they tell me that they think I am 70!" she laughed.

"They think you're 70? That's great. Why do you think that is?" I responded, smiling because Jennie was smiling and her good humor was catching.

"Well, I don't look that old. Can I tell you about my granddaughter?" It was typical of Jennie to leap from one topic to the next. She spoke very abruptly and paused after every few words for me to get her story down. It was important to both of us that I get it down right.

"Sure," I said, and nodded my head.

"She lives in California."

"Okay, let me, let's see . . . She lives in California," I was trying to keep up with her dictation and continuously checked back to make sure I had it right.

"She writes to tell me what . . ."

"What does she tell you?" I asked.

". . . that she's playing golf." Jennie was speaking very rapidly, as though we were in a race with time. By the end of the dictating session I felt out of breath.

"She's playing golf?" I was not sure I heard her correctly. Her words all bumped into one another and I had to keep checking to make certain I had the right words.

"Uh-huh," Jennie nodded.

"Hang on a minute," I said as I wrote the words down. "Is she a pretty good golfer?"

"Yes, my other daughter . . ."

"This is your daughter or granddaughter?"

"Other granddaughter . . ." By now, Jennie was a little frustrated. She wanted to get her story down and she was becoming impatient with my questions.

"Granddaughter," I said with renewed determination.

" . . . lives in Columbia."

"Oh, well that's not as far away as California!" We both cracked up with laughter. "[The town's names] end with the same letters and that's about it."

"Yeah, she teaches in Glenville."

"What does she teach?"

"Eighth grade."

"Eighth grade?" I realized I must have sounded like a parrot to Jennie but I was having a hard time hearing her. Her voice was soft and there was a lot of background noise, other persons dictating and staff coming in to transport writers to their rooms or other activities.

"Do you want me to read what we have so far?" (Once a writer had a few lines on the paper I asked if she or he would like hear the work in progress.)

"Yes," Jennie excitedly responded.

I read what she had dictated. We chuckled together again when I read the part about people misjudging her age.

"That's great," Jennie said. She asked me to repeat one part and confirmed that I had it right. Now she was ready to go on, but first had to ponder what she wanted to say next. "Let me think for a moment."

"Sure."

"My daughter lives in Oakland." By this time, Jennie was getting tired and confused. Her voiced was somewhat slurred and she was not able to keep her train of thought going, often forgetting where she was at mid-sentence. I began to think to myself that it was about time to wrap it up.

"Oakland!" I exclaimed. "My husband works in Oakland on Meyer Road.

"What's his name?" Jennie inquired, with little interest.

"Well, his name is Curtis Schuster, he runs a nursery up there."

"Oh yeah, yeah," nodded Jennie, politely.

I determined that I needed to encourage Jennie to reach closure, as she was fading fast. "So far you have, 'My daughter lives in Oakland.'"

"She usually comes to see me once a week."

"I imagine you look forward to that visit."

"Yes," Jennie nodded her head in affirmation, "she does my washing."

"She does your washing?" I was often writing while I was listening so I frequently needed to ask her to repeat her answers.

"Yes." I noticed how Jennie's answers were becoming shorter and her voice was losing its enthusiasm.

"So she takes it and brings it back?"

"Yes, she brings me clean clothes."

"What do you do when she comes for a visit?"

Jennie shifted in her chair and answered, "We talk about things . . . about what we've been doing."

"Talk about what you have been doing?" I repeated.

"Yeah . . . and about how she's been playing golf."

"Oh, she plays golf, too?' I asked

"No, not that one." Again I felt Jennie was tiring, and it was apparent she was becoming confused.

"This sounds good! Do you want me to read it again?" Jennie wanted to hear her story again so I read it one more time. She nodded her head and smiled as I read.

"Yes, that sounds good."

"All right, great. Thank you, Jennie," I said as I touched her arm and looked into her eyes. "We will make sure we get this printed up."

The following is Jennie's story as it appeared in the handout the following week:

My Family

I am 87 years old.
I ask people to guess my age
And they tell me they think I am 70!

My granddaughter lives in California.
She writes to me and tells me about playing golf.

My other granddaughter lives in Columbia.
She teaches in Glenville.

My daughter lives in Oakland.
She usually comes and sees me once a week.

She does my washing and she brings my clean clothes.
When she comes we talk about what we've been doing.

This exchange with Jennie demonstrates how the dictation/writing process was often a combined effort of writer and volunteer recorder. Often, those who could not write were the ones who had multiple physical and mental dysfunctions. They were often medicated. Medication can cause confusion as well as drowsiness and fatigue. In these instances, the volunteer took on an additional responsibility of guiding the writing process. This mutual effort demanded the volunteer's utmost attention and pulled out of the writer stories that may not have been told otherwise. There simply were not many people who had the time (or who would take the time) to listen much less write the resident's words down on paper. The exchange, then, was a social exercise in that the writer was engaged in verbal conversation with the volunteer. In addition, the words the writer spoke were carefully placed onto paper and then typed and read. This extra care with the writer's words added another meaningful dimension to their stories. The writer knew that the volunteer felt the words were very important and valuable.

The meaningfulness of the writing was enhanced and extended when the story was read the following week to the group. The writer's colleagues acknowledged the oral reading with nods of heads and often added their own recollections/interpretations of similar or the same events either verbally or in writing. At this point, the story left the writer and became the property of the whole. Many stories were posted in the centrum and numerous others read and shared in the memory. Thus, the story went from unspoken thought to verbal expression and to written word, as the volunteers recorded their thoughts, to an oral reading with the group and ensuing verbal discussion and dialogue, and finally to communal reading as visitors and staff read the displayed written pieces. Most residents in nursing homes are lucky if even one person sits down to partially listen to his or her story. The writing group provided a deeper, multilayered, and more meaningful way of communicating and connecting with one's peers, family, and community. This process confirmed to the writer that her words, and therefore her life, held value and was worthy of the public's attention.

The following section represents the findings of the 3-year study. It is divided into themes as they relate to the original research questions listed in the introduction. Themes in this section include making sense of the past and present, the transformation of relationships, perceptions of the writers' place in the world, and, writing as a vehicle for interpreting the social world.

TRANSFORMING WORLDS THROUGH WRITING

The persons whose lives I studied and came to know over a 3-year time span were, for the most part, very old. In our society this means that little was expected of them. Old age is a time of rest, reflection, and letting go. We do not see the old-old and frail very often as we go about our daily routines. They are not found in the local grocery store, the service club meetings, the gas station. We sometimes see a very old person at church or at the doctor's office. For the most part, the old-old and frail spend their days at home or in a nursing home. Either way, they are not often part of their community's daily events. So, when a very old one takes it upon herself to become visible again (or to maintain her visibility), to express herself, when she dares to reach her hand out rather than wait for one to reach out for her, what happens?

For the writers I studied at the Evans Nursing Home, writing was a way of negotiating their inner and outer worlds—worlds fraught with change and loss, joy and regret. Writing connected them with their worlds, helped them to make sense of the past, and made certain they would not be forgotten. In some instances writing provided the rare opportunity for the residents to make a statement or to express strong feelings of fear, anger, love, hope, and pain.

Writing also left a permanent record, a piece of that individual for those left behind to hold onto and to cherish. In Myerhoff's (1978) book, *Number Our Days*, one of Jacob's (a character in the book) strongest desires was shared by many of the older Jews Myerhoff interviewed and by the writers I had the honor to know—the need and desire to be remembered. Like the older writers I studied, Myerhoff's participants were disappointed when they learned that she would not use their real names in her book. "Everyone wanted to leave a personal statement, wanted to be identified with an enduring record, some indication of what happened to them, what they believed, that they had been here" (p. 36).

Making Sense of The Past and Present

While observing the writing group and interviewing the individual writers, I was struck by the way in which the residents used writing as a means of coming to peace with their past and as a way to cope with present circumstances. Lenora, a member of the writing group, wrote, "I think about the past and how it's helped me to do what I am able to do today." Perhaps the leaps between past and present did not seem as great to the older writers as they would to their younger counterparts.

Emma, another writer, wrote a story called *Time*, in which she expressed her consternation over how fast time goes by as one grows older. "When I was young I thought summer would never come as time went so slow. Now the days pass quickly and the seasons are shorter as time goes fast." In this context, in which time moves quickly and deliberately, the space between decades grows shorter and connections between eras are easily made.

In the writing group, Alison and the writers maneuvered gracefully through what often seemed like a mine field of difficult and heart-wrenching topics. Often, humor was employed as a means of coping with the pain that sometimes erupted as members remembered and discussed memories laced with grief and emotion. For example, when Alison introduced the topic of The Great Depression, many of the writers conveyed vivid stories and recollections of this devastating time in their lives. It was a communal grieving as shared memories emerged. As discussion ensued, the writers struggled, often with great intensity and emotion, to confront their painful pasts and to come to some kind of resolution. Getting it down on paper, out in the open for others to read and respond to, may have assisted in the healing process and allowed the writers to move forward and come to a place of peace.

The writers strove to understand and cope with their present lives through remembrances of past experiences and the lessons and strengths they bore. Sometimes, their recollections opened old wounds and caused fresh grief to surface. Other times, the stories evoked laughter and joy. In all cases, there was a sense of the communal experience among the writers, and among the writers and the persons who read and listened to their work. It was when I interviewed the individual writers and their family members that I began to realize how deeply many of the lives of the writers' relatives were touched by the writings and the extent to which relationships between the writer and their family members, the writer and other writers, and the writer and staff and volunteers, were transformed by the writings.

The Transformation of Relationships

While observing the writing group I began to notice how the writings often were an attempt by the writers to relate to one another, to staff, to family, and the community beyond the walls of the nursing home. The writers wrote poems or stories about a staff person, they created Christmas calendars and cards—which featured their writings—as gifts to relatives and friends, and their writings were posted on the centrum for all to read. However, it was not until I spoke to the individual writers and their family members that I began to realize how it was not only the group facilitators and the writers who were making the effort to use the writings as a means of relating. I discovered that family members were taking it upon themselves to make the writings part of their lives by including poems in marriage ceremonies, reading aloud stories written by a grandparent at family reunions, and creating an album or a journal of a writer's work to share with family and friends.

It was a member of a younger generation, Megan, a granddaughter of one of the writers (Esther), who opened my eyes to new ways of perceiving the function writing played in the lives of the writers, and how writing was a means by which family members might gain a better understanding of their relative's experience in the nursing home. Her insights provided some of the most important findings of the study. Megan saw the writings as documentation of Esther's adjustment to her new life in the nursing home. At first, Esther's writing focused on her husband, her family, and her personal history. As she became more accustomed to her new life, the writings were more about the nursing home, the staff, and activities in which Esther was involved. Finally, as Esther became more comfortable with writing she began to try her hand at poetry and to think of herself as a writer.

Megan had conceptualized an evolutionary model based on her perceptions of her grandmother's transformation as documented in the writings. The writings provided the family and the writer with a look into how a loved one was adjusting and coping, not only in the broader sense outlined earlier but on a day-to-day basis. In this way, the writers communicated to their relatives that they had made, or were on the process of making, the transition and they were going to be all right. In the case of Esther's family, this awareness brought relief, and the guilt they felt for placing her in the nursing home was somewhat lessened.

As the writers shared their stories they discovered communal memories. In doing so, they created a bond forged by shared pasts. However, the writers were not satisfied to stay focused on the past and present but insisted, with a strong sense of purpose, on reaching out to future generations with words filled with hope, strength, advice, and good common sense—wisdom so greatly needed in these troubled times. Staff persons and volunteers were the recipients of some of the writers' words of praise, and the residents' acknowledgment of the staff's efforts resulted in the expression of feelings of gratitude from both sides. The writings helped the writers and their families to come in contact with their inner world of joy and sorrow and assisted in the resolution of pain and grief, but also provided families with a window in which to peer through and acquire the knowledge that their loved ones were all right, that they were making the transition from their home to the nursing home successfully.

At times, the function of writing was transformed from a window into a mirror of family relationships. The mirror reflected the family's desire to be involved with the writer and whether they valued the writer and his or her writing. Here, family members, especially the younger generations, began to perceive the oldest members of their families as more full, complete, and accomplished. The young ones began to relate to the old ones in ways they never had before. They had something in common. Sadly, writing also mirrored a darker image, when the family was detached from the writer and riddled with a past full of unresolved pain and grief.

The writers' stories helped to build a bridge that spanned time and space between the writer and his or her past and present worlds, often creating connections with memories and people from their pasts. They provided a permanent historical record, one that was used and referred to not only by the family members but by the writers themselves when their memory began to dim. Finally, the writings often surprised loved ones and friends, by dropping a voice from the past into their laps unexpectedly, seeking to rekindle the warmth only a close friendship based on years of shared struggle and joy can create.

Perceptions of the Writer's Place in the World

Identity is one factor that influences a person's sense of place in the world. An individual's identity is not stable, but instead is "created and recreated" over a lifetime. As the person negotiates through life, layers of experience upon experience shape the ever-transforming and elusive structure known as identity. Aging, then, may be conceived as a:

> continual creation of the self through the ongoing interpretation of past experience, structural factors, and current context . . . and identity is built around themes . . . as past experiences are symbolically connected with one another to have meaning for a particular individual. (Kaufman, 1986, p. 151)

When a resident moves into a nursing home he or she struggles to maintain his or her identity. The process includes reflection and interpretation of past experiences and current context (Kaufman, 1986). For many, a move from one's home to a nursing home causes an abrupt shift in identity as the individual seeks to find a way to fit within the new context. The resident still has his or her past experiences and themes to rely on for a sense of inner continuity, but the new external institutionalized world, fraught with regimented routine and threat to individuation and privacy, creates discord. The result may be a sense of discontinuity. Add to this the multiple role losses, or a significant decline in the opportunity to play a role the resident experiences when leaving behind his or her life in the community, plus the unwelcomed acquisition of the role of "resident," and it is not too difficult to see how identity and sense of self is often found floating in a nether world.

Under these circumstances, any process that might enhance the ability of the resident to regain some control and reestablish identity must be perceived as being invaluable. When the writers composed a written piece, it was the themes of their lives they were writing about. When they read and shared their writings with one another, staff, volunteers, family, and friends, they were recreating identity, grasping, in some cases, onto some semblance of the person they thought they were and testing and exploring the person they had become.

The writers' individual identities formed a group identity as they shared painful and joyful memories, grieved over the loss of a fellow writer, discussed historical events and trivial but mutually cherished moments, and grappled with the increasingly astounding antics of the world outside their windows. Each writer had his or her interpretation of the stories and poems, but through dialogue the group created a communal meaning. One writer told a story about crime in Chicago, and the writers discussed current problems caused by increasing violence in the world. Another writer wrote about bridges, and the group responded by sharing stories about all of the bridges they had crossed or watched being built. This way, each contributed new images to the group's memories and experiences. The present reshaped the past and the group grew closer, the bond stronger, when a writer could say, "This is not *my* memory or *your* memory, but this is *our* memory." So, part of each individual's identity was that of writing group member, and part of the writing group's identity was made up of each individual's identity. Shared memories, shared current living experiences, and the writers' shared hopes and dreams for themselves, their families, and future generations created a bond made of words.

Another way in which the writers' places in the world changed was through the creation of a community made first of a bond of words, and then through initiatives taken to move their writings out into the community. This act of "turning the tables," so to speak, with the residents becoming the initiators of communication was unusual, to say the least. Typically, the resident of a nursing home is the beneficiary and in the receiver position of various goodwill efforts made by staff persons, family, volunteers, and church and service groups. Through the distribution of their writings to the inner and outer communities (inner, meaning the nursing home, and outer, meaning the rest of the world) the writers were in control and empowered by being the initiators of the interaction. They had complete autonomy when deciding what to write about, and they had the opportunity to enhance their individuality through written expression. It may be argued, then, that through writing the resident created a more homelike setting—a community within a community.

Perhaps one of the most intriguing aspects of the writing group was how the writing process itself provided the residents with a means to reciprocate. Too often, persons who have become very frail and old are perceived by society as being unproductive, and worse, unnecessary. Sadly, the older adult, yielding to the pressure of both internal and external forces, begins to assume the role of passive receiver—a role that is characterized by increased dependency. The writing group countered these forces by first establishing a community of writers. Through their participation in this community, the residents had a new role to play, not as residents but as writers. As their efforts as writers became recognized and distributed beyond the walls of the nursing home, their identities shifted to an even greater extent as their audience responded to their effort to connect. Typically, nursing home residents assume roles that are diminished in power and their purpose in life is questioned (both by the older individual and society). The writers, on the other hand, were empowered by succeeding in their efforts to build a new skill and ability, taking on new and vital identities that were valued by staff, family, and society, and taking control of one small, but significant, portion of their lives.

On Becoming a Writer

One compelling reason for a resident to refuse to try the writing group was that he or she did not think of him- or herself as a writer. A writer was someone who wrote prose or poetry, whose work was published. Most of the persons who participated in the writing group had little or no experience composing stories or poetry prior to coming to the nursing home. Their inexperience sometimes caused them to approach the group with feelings of trepidation, peppered with anxiety. When Esther first came to the nursing home, she was not at all confident of her writing abilities. She was afraid to read her stories aloud to the group, and when she did, her voice was soft and quavering. The transition from non-writer to writer happened for Esther when others started showing interest in her work and when her work was published and distributed to other writers and her family.

Esther also began to think of herself as a writer when she began to work on stories in her room, asking Megan, her granddaughter, and less often, Gwen, a fellow writer, to assist in the editing process. The most prolific writers took their writings back to their rooms to edit, often producing several drafts before a final one was deemed "good enough." Lenora called this "playing" with her work. These writers had to their advantage the ability to write on their own, with no need for assistance, and they were not encumbered by any significant mental decline, including major sensory loss.

At times the writers expressed amazement at their own work and the positive and welcoming reception their writings received from the other writers, family, staff persons, and visitors to the nursing home who could read their posted compositions on the centrum walls and in the showcase next to the activity room. Gwen once told me that when others read her work, "It makes me feel not so helpless. . . . Writing makes you feel like you're here for some purpose." Priscilla more or less echoed Gwen's sentiments when she said the following about people reading her writing on the centrum wall: "Sometimes you get the feeling that it [recognition of her writing] makes you feel necessary." The intrinsic value of writing went beyond recognition from the outside world. Inside, writers felt pride, a new-found confidence, a sense of purpose, and perhaps even some feelings of relief, knowing they were participating in an activity that enhanced the memory process and made them necessary in a world that sometimes questions the necessity of its oldest members.

I learned that within the context of this nursing home writing group, "a writer" was someone who held some prestige in the writer's eyes. A writer had to "earn" the recognition of her or his peers. Some of the individuals I interviewed told me that the transition to writer took place for them when others took note of their work and praised their efforts. Also, a person was a writer if he or she participated in the writing process itself, including drafting an original piece of work, editing, and rewriting the final draft. In other words, the seriousness of the writing effort seemed to be important criteria used to judge whether or not a person was a writer. Being able to participate in the writing process independently, with little or no assistance, seemed to distinguish those who thought of themselves as "writers" from those who did not. Just as some of the residents were not able or did not desire to join the writing group for various reasons, there were residents who did not see themselves as writers due to real or self-imposed limitations.

Writing as a Vehicle for Interpreting the Social World

The power staff have to shape and create the world of the nursing home resident cannot be denied. The resident is often at the mercy of the nurse's aide, the primary caregiver. And the aide's world (at least while working) is directed by the Head of Nursing, who operates under the direction of the head Administrator, who, in turn, answers to the Board of Directors and/or owners. Nursing homes are businesses. Yet there is a constant struggle by staff persons to make the environment less institutional and more like home. Nursing home regulations (Connor, 1994) actually require administrators to explore ways in which their institution may become more homelike. The regulators' current emphasis is on quality of life, particularly in the psychosocial domain.

At Evans Nursing Home the emphasis on quality of life translated into more activities and recruitment of residents into those activities. During the week, just about every hour of the day was filled with opportunity for participation in a group activity. Dotty's piece titled *Dotty's Life in The Nursing Home,* perhaps captured the busy schedule of many residents better than any other writing I came across. Dotty's typical day began with breakfast, followed by needlework and crafts, lunch, then bingo and bowling, dinner, and after dinner, bible study. For Dotty, who loved to socialize, the nonstop activity was exactly what she wanted. To others, it may have seemed more like a rat race, or a hamster race, as portrayed in Mary's story titled *The Fenwick Fantasy.*

Not surprisingly, it was uncommon to come across a writing about life in the nursing home. For the most part, when writers chose to write about their lives at Evans Nursing Home, they wrote a piece praising a staff person or a noncritical account, like Dotty's, which simply told about life's routines, or Elizabeth's humorous story about nursing home night life, *8:00 P.M. to Midnight.* One notable exception was Paul's piece titled *Break Time.* This writing reflected Paul's extreme frustration at not being able to get assistance when he wanted it. "It seems nothing can be done around the nursing home unless people are going or coming from their break time." In his story he discussed how he had always been a conscientious worker and would never have considered taking more than two breaks a day.

The reason why the writers stayed away from writing more critical appraisals of their world were many. Paul was a man. Women of his generation were taught not to say anything unkind or to express any negative emotions. "Don't rock the boat," in other words. Also, when I asked the writers why they did not write about or voice a particular concern they had mentioned to me in an interview or informal conversation, they shook their heads and said something like, "Oh, no, I couldn't do that. I don't want to make anyone mad at me. They could get back at me and I'm helpless to do anything about it," or "What's the use?" The feeling of "What's the use?" and of impotency and vulnerability permeated the mentality of some of the writers when it came to their sense of ability to impact their world in any way. Whether these feelings were based on the truth or due to their lack of desire or energy to "get into it" with staff, I cannot say. Probably it was a little of both.

Although the writers were hesitant to write critically about aspects of a world over which they thought they had little control, they were not reluctant to speak out about issues such as racial discrimination, foul language, past abusive relationships, health problems, emergencies (like a roommate falling out of bed), relationships with family, grief and loss, pain, suffering, and joy. All of these topics and more were covered by the writers during my time with them. They reflected the writers' perceptions of their place in the world, both past and present.

In summary, I found that the writing group members experienced positive transformations in their lives including recognition as valued members of society and of their families, an increased sense of pride, and a feeling that they were making a lasting contribution. The writers' stories were often attempts to relate to self, to their colleagues, to their families, and to the world outside the walls of the nursing home. Relationships were formed or strengthened by the stories as writers shared deeply felt emotions and values and expressed opinions and thoughts on a variety of current and historical issues. The writings helped to shape the identity of the individual writers and of the group and formed a community bound by words. A nursing home writing group provides a unique opportunity for expression and for finding meaning in a world that is often bereft of purpose.

What contributions do these findings make to our understanding of the impact the writing process has on the lives of learners of all ages? One of the more fascinating aspects of this study was that it took place in an environment where there is little, if any, opportunity for expression and autonomy. Compared to most of our experiences, nursing home residents' lives are constricted and highly regulated. In this type of context the benefits writing may have on the lives of the writer— and those who are fortunate enough to read their work—become more obvious. Fortunately, most of us have much greater freedom of expression and are not experiencing decline due to very old age or illness. Therefore, it may be assumed that all and more of the benefits of writing that the nursing home residents enjoyed are available to all of us given the opportunity. As educators, helping ourselves and our students of any age to gain a deeper understanding and awareness of ourselves and of our world is an admirable goal, as is connecting with our innermost thoughts and feelings and with those closest to us. At a time when many feel isolated and without direction, writing may be used as a means to transform inner and outer worlds and as a way of connecting with one another. Writing may help us to transverse the boundaries, real and imagined, and create a community bond by words. It is by getting to know one another and seeking shared experiences that we enhance our lives and build community and a better world in which to live.

FUTURE CONSIDERATIONS

This study is only a beginning. The potential for the application of newly evolving theories on the writing process as experienced by the older, institutionalized adult, is great. My research only scratched the surface of what I perceive to be a rich and unexplored territory. Existing research studies on nursing home writing activities overlook the trans-formative processes occurring when an older individual writes and shares stories with fellow authors, staff, and family. We have a great deal to learn about the ways in which writing is used by the very old to make sense of their world, as a way of bringing deeper meaning to their experiences—both past and present—and, as a means of contributing to and speaking out on issues that are of vital importance to the writer and to society. There is no doubt that a nursing home writing group pro-vides a unique opportunity for expression and for finding meaning in a world bereft of purpose. Little is known about writers and writings in this type of setting. Therefore, further study is imperative if we are to enhance our understanding of the writing process and its impact on the lives of persons living in a nursing home.

ACKNOWLEDGMENTS

I would like to thank Dr. Gary Knowles for his guidance and support.

REFERENCES

Agar, M. (1980). *The professional stranger: An informal introduction to ethnography*. New York: Academic Press.

Agar, M.H. (1986). *Speaking of ethnography*. Beverly Hills, CA: Sage.

Atchley, R. (1989). The continuity theory of normal aging. *The Gerontologist, 29*, 183-190.

Atchley, R.C. (1991). *Social forces in aging* (6th ed.). Belmont, CA: Wadsworth.

Beach, R. (1990). The creative development of meaning: Using autobiographical experiences. In D. Bogdan & S. Straw (Eds.), *Beyond communication: Reading comprehension and criticism* (pp. 211-236). Portsmouth, NH: Boynton/Cook Publishers.

Britton, J. (1970). *Language and learning.* Coral Gables, FL: The University of Miami Press.

Britton, J. (1982). Writing to learn and learning to write. In G. Pradl (Ed.), *Prospect and retrospect: Selected essays of James Britton* (pp. 94-111). Upper Montclair, NJ: Boynton-Cook.

Britton, J., Burgess, T., Martin, N., McLeod, A., & Rosen, H. (1975). *The development of writing abilities.* Urbana, IL: Schools Council Publication.

Brody, E. (1985). The social aspects of nursing home care. In E. Schnieder (Ed.), *The teaching nursing home: A new approach to geriatric research, education, and clinical care* (pp. 34-51). New York: Raven Press.

Brooke, R. (1991). *Writing and the sense of self: Identity negotiation in writing workshops.* Urbana, IL: National Council of Teachers of English.

Connor, M. (1994, October/November). Putting the "home" back in nursing homes. *Senior Reporter,* pp. 1-2.

Courtenay, B., Stevenson, R., & Suhart, M. (1982). Functional literacy among the elderly: Where we are(n't). *Educational Gerontology, 8,* 339-352.

DeSanti, R. (1979). Cue system utilizations among older readers. *Educational Gerontology, 4,* 271-277.

Eisner, E. W. (1991). *The enlightened eye: Qualitative inquiry and the enhancement of educational practices.* New York: Macmillan.

Fisher, J. (1990). The function of literacy in a nursing home context. *Educational Gerontology, 16,* 105-116.

Friere, P. (1989). *Pedagogy of the oppressed.* New York: The Continuum Press.

Gentile, L., & McMillan, M. (1979). Reading: A means of renewal for the aged. *Educational Gerontologist, 4,* 215-222.

Giroux, H.A. (1988). *Schooling and the struggle for public life.* Minneapolis: The University of Minnesota Press.

Glaser, B.G., & Strauss, A.L. (1967). *The discovery of grounded theory: Strategies for qualitative research.* New York: Aldine DeGruyter.

Glynn, S., & Muth, K. (1979). Text-learning capabilities of older adults. *Educational Gerontology, 4,* 253-269.

Graff, H.J. (1987). *The labyrinths of literacy: Reflections on literacy past and present.* London: The Falmer Press.

Greene, M. (1988). *The dialectic of freedom.* New York: Teachers College Press.

Gubrium, J. (1975). *Living and dying in murray manor.* New York: St. Martin's Press.

Gutmann, D. (1987). *Reclaimed powers: Toward a new psychology of men and women in later life.* New York: Basic Books.

Haase, A., Robinson, R., & Beach, R. (1979). Teaching the aged reader: Issues and strategies. *Educational Gerontology, 4,* 229-237.

Hammersley, M., & Atkinson, P. (1983). *Ethnography: Principles and practices.* London: Tavistock Publications.

Johnson, C., & Grant, A. (1985). *The nursing home in American society.* Baltimore, MD: The John Hopkins University Press.

Kaakinen, J. (1992). Living with silence. *The Gerontologist, 32,* 258-264.

Kane, R., & Kane, R. (1982). *Values and long term care.* Lexington, MA: Lexington Books.

Kasworm, C., & Medina, R. (1989). Perspectives of literacy in the senior adult years. *Educational Gerontology, 15,* 65-79.

Kaufman, S. (1986). *The ageless self: Sources of meaning in late life.* Madison: The University of Wisconsin Press.

Kidder, T. (1993). *Old friends.* New York: Houghton Mifflin.

Kingston, A. (1979). Reading and the aged: A statement of the problem. *Educational Gerontology, 4,* 205-207.

Koch, K. (1973). *Rose, where did you get that red?* New York: Random House.

Koch, K. (1977). *I never told anybody: Teaching poetry writing in a nursing home.* New York: Random House.

Lovelace, T. (1979). Reading activities to enhance the lives of nursing home patients. *Educational Gerontology, 4,* 239-243.

Lumsden, D. (1979). Why Johnny's grandparents can't read. *Educational Gerontologist, 4,* 297-305.

Martin, N. (1975). *Writing across the curriculum.* London: Ward Lock.

McClusky, H. (1974). Education for aging: The scope of the field and perspective for the future. In S.M. Grobouski & W.D. Moren (Eds.), *Education for the aging* (pp. 105-137). Washington DC: Capitol Publications.

McGinley, W., & Kamberelis, J. (1991). *Personal, social, and political functions of children's reading and writing.* Paper presented at the 43rd Annual NRC Meeting, Miami, FL.

McGinley, W., & Madigan, D. (1991). *Public and private meanings: Understanding children's writing about their communities and their lives.* Unpublished manuscript.

Murray, D. (1980). Questions to produce writing topics. *English Journal, 69,* 67-73.

Myerhoff, B. (1978). *Number our days.* New York: Simon and Schuster.

Rigg, P., & Kazemek, F. (1983). Literacy and elders: What we know and what we need to know. *Educational Gerontology, 9,* 417-424.

Savishinsky, J. (1991). *The ends of times: Life and work in a nursing home.* New York: Bergin & Garvey.

Shield, R. (1988). *Uneasy endings: Daily life in an American nursing home.* Ithaca, NY: Cornell University Press.

Smith, C., & Kornblum, W. (1989). *In the field: Readings on the field research experience.* New York: Praeger.

Supiano, K., Ozminkowski, R., Campbell, R., & Lapidos, C. (1989). Effectiveness of writing groups in nursing homes. *The Journal of Applied Gerontology, 8,* 382-400.

Van Maanen, J. (1988). *Tales of the field: On writing ethnography.* Chicago: The University of Chicago Press.

Vladeck, B. (1980). *Unloving care: The nursing home tragedy.* New York: Basic Books.

Watson, D., Robinson, R., Chippendale, E., Nickolaus, F., & Jenkins, P. (1979). *Describing and improving the reading strategies of elderly readers.* Columbia: University of Missouri–Columbia Press.

Willinsky, J. (1990). *The new literacy: Redefining reading and writing in the schools.* London: Routledge & Kegan Paul.

Willinsky, J. (1991). *The triumph of literature/The fate of literacy: English in the secondary school curriculum.* New York: Teachers College, Columbia University.

Wilson, M. (1979). Enhancing the lives of the aged in a retirement center through a program of reading. *Educational Gerontology, 4,* 245-251.

Wolf, R. (1980). What is reading good for? Perspectives from senior citizens. In L. Johnson (Ed.), *Reading and the adult learner.* Newark, DE: International Reading Association.

Wolcott, H. (1990). *Writing up qualitative research.* Newbury Park, CA: Sage.

Author Index

A

Ackerman, J., 25, *39*
Agar, M. H., 219, *240*
Anderson, L., 185, *204*
Anson, C., 70*n*, 73, *96*
Aristotle, 142, *160*
Armstrong, L., 131, 133, *137*
Atchley, R. C., 210, 211, 220, *240*
Atkinson, P., 219, *242*

B

Bacon, N., 133, *137*
Bakhtin, M. M., 103, *119*
Batsleer, J., 163, *179*
Beach, R., 209, 212, 220, *241*, *242*
Berkenkotter, C., 25, *39*
Berlin, J., 175, *179*
Berube, M., 162, 163, *179*
Biggs, D. A., 2, *17*
Bleich, D., 74, 75, 75*n*, *96*
Bloom, L. Z., 22, *39*, 183, *203*

Bomer, R., 99, *119*
Borman, K. M., 127, *137*
Braine, M. D. S., 35, *39*
Brandt, D., 89, *96*, 153, 154, *160*
Brinkley, E. H., 57, 65, *67*
Britton, J., 52, *67*, 208, 209, 212, 220, *241*
Britzman, D. P., 98, 102, 103, 105, 107, 109, 110, 111, 112, 115, *119*
Brodkey, L., 122, *137*
Brody, E., 220, *241*
Brooke, R., 209, 211, 220, *241*
Brooks, J. G., 99, 115, *119*
Brooks, M. G., 99, 115, *119*
Broselow, E., 32, 35, *39*
Brown, H. D., 28, *39*
Brown, R., 21, *39*
Bruner, J., 140, 141, 154, *160*
Burgess, T., 52, *67*, 209, *241*
Burke, C., 32, *40*
Byrne, B., 23, *39*

Subject Index